ON PRACTISING THERAPY AT 1.45 A.M.

Although Professor Kahr spends most of his week facilitating traditional psychoanalytical sessions with his patients, in his spare time he has had many professional adventures outside the consulting room, broadcasting as Resident Psychotherapist for the B.B.C., lecturing about the intimacies of couple psychodynamics on the stage of the Royal Opera House, and defending "Lady Macbeth" in a murder trial at the Royal Courts of Justice in conjunction with members of the Royal Shakespeare Company.

In this compellingly written and unputdownable book, Kahr shares his wealth of adventures both inside the consulting room and in the wider cultural sphere, disseminating psychoanalytical ideas more broadly. The book suggests that the "traditionalist" and the "maverick" aspects of the practising clinician can exist side by side in a fruitful collaboration. These adventures will encourage those embarking upon their first steps in the helping professions to entertain more creative ways of working.

Professor Brett Kahr has worked in the mental health field for over forty years. He is Senior Fellow at the Tavistock Institute of Medical Psychology, in London, and Senior Clinical Research Fellow in Psychotherapy and Mental Health at the Centre for Child Mental Health. A Trustee of the Freud Museum London and of Freud Museum Publications, he has written or edited fourteen books, and he has served as series editor for more than fifty-five other titles. He is Consultant Psychotherapist at The Balint Consultancy and works full-time with individuals and couples in London.

Books by Brett Kahr

D.W. Winnicott: A Biographical Portrait (1996)

Forensic Psychotherapy and Psychopathology:
   Winnicottian Perspectives, Editor (2001)

Exhibitionism (2001)

The Legacy of Winnicott:
   Essays on Infant and Child Mental Health, Editor (2002)

Sex and the Psyche (2007)

Who's Been Sleeping in Your Head?
   The Secret World of Sexual Fantasies (2008)

Life Lessons from Freud (2013)

Tea with Winnicott (2016)

Coffee with Freud (2017)

New Horizons in Forensic Psychotherapy:
   Exploring the Work of Estela V. Welldon, Editor (2018)

How to Flourish as a Psychotherapist (2019)

Bombs in the Consulting Room:
   Surviving Psychological Shrapnel (2020)

Celebrity Mad:
   Why Otherwise Intelligent People Worship Fame (2020)

ON PRACTISING THERAPY AT 1.45 A.M.

Adventures of a Clinician

Brett Kahr

Routledge
Taylor & Francis Group

LONDON AND NEW YORK

First published 2020
by Routledge
2 Park Square, Milton Park, Abingdon, Oxon OX14 4RN

and by Routledge
52 Vanderbilt Avenue, New York, NY 10017

Routledge is an imprint of the Taylor & Francis Group, an informa business

British Library Cataloguing-in-Publication Data
A catalogue record for this book is available from the British Library

Library of Congress Cataloging-in-Publication Data
A catalog record has been requested for this book

ISBN: 978–1–78220–680-4 (pbk)
ISBN: 978–0–429-43890-5 (ebk)

Edited, designed, and typeset in Palatino
by Communication Crafts, East Grinstead

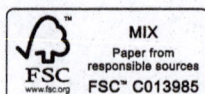

FSC
www.fsc.org

MIX
Paper from
responsible sources
FSC™ C013985

Printed in the United Kingdom
by Henry Ling Limited

For
J.V.J. and R.D.K.,
With deepest love

Children love to listen to stories about their elders.

Anonymous [Charles Lamb], "Dream-Children; A Reverie",
in *Elia: Essays Which Have Appeared Under That Signature
in the London Magazine*, 1823, p. 230

CONTENTS

ON PRACTISING THERAPY AT 1.45 A.M.

Prelude

Of mavericks and medias

La dernière chose qu'on trouve en faisant un ouvrage, est de savoir celle qu'il faut mettre la première.
[The last thing one finds out in writing a book is what to put first.]

Blaise Pascal, *Pensées de M. Pascal sur la religion, et sur quelques autres sujets, qui ont eſté trouvées aprés ſa mort parmy ſes papiers*, 1669

When people ask me what I do for a living, I reply, quite factually, that I work as a psychotherapist. And being a psychotherapist, I spend my life listening to people's most intimate secrets. Virtually every week, throughout my career, one or more of the men and women who sit in my office chair, or who recline on my consulting room couch, confess, often sheepishly:

"I've never told this to anyone before in my life . . ."

"My husband has no idea about this, but . . ."

"You're the first person to hear this . . ."

"I know that what I'm about to tell you won't leave this room . . ."

Fellow mental health professionals will recognise these remarks only too well, for over time we all become the custodians of these

1

long-held, preciously protected secrets which have often caused great anguish to our patients and clients.

The people who arrive at our offices expect complete privacy and confidentiality; indeed they demand it, and they deserve it. Without a sense of security that their secrets will remain sacrosanct, psychotherapy cannot work. My colleague Dr Susie Orbach has often stated that "Psychotherapy is not a spectator sport" (quoted in Kahr, 2017b), and I could not agree more.

Throughout my career, I have done, and continue to do, whatever I can to ensure that the identity of my patients remains unknown to any third party. Indeed, for many years I worked hard to find a private consulting room situated at the very end of a long corridor, on the top floor of an office building, hidden in a tiny mews courtyard, tucked away from the main road, and virtually invisible to any passers-by. The location of my office has helped to preserve confidentiality. Similarly, I keep a very anonymised appointments diary. Although I have never, ever lost my red leather diary or had it stolen, I have allowed for this possibility, and hence, when entering appointments, I never use the patient's real name. Instead, I have come to rely on an elaborate code. Should anyone ever steal my diary, at most, they will discover that at 7.00 a.m. on Tuesday last, I held a fifty-minute meeting with someone called X34G7. Perhaps they might imagine me to be an auto-mechanic!

It pleases me to say that most of the people with whom I associate know full well that I cannot discuss the specificities of my work with particular individuals; and to their credit, my colleagues, friends, and relatives respect the strictures of professional privacy greatly. So I never talk about my work in social or familial settings, except in the most general way, and when I do speak with colleagues about the art of psychotherapy, I refrain from offering any details that would in any way compromise my patients.

Because psychotherapy, psychiatry, psychology, counselling, and psychoanalysis must be such intensely *private* and *confidential* processes, practitioners often assume that they must be completely *secret* endeavours as well.

When I began training in the field in the late 1970s, very few mental health professionals in Great Britain had ever dared to put their heads above the parapet. Professor Sigmund Freud had vigorously resisted virtually every opportunity to collaborate with the media (Kahr, 2014, 2017b); and many of his successors subscribed to this policy. Fortunately, during the late 1930s and the 1940s, the British paediatrician and psychoanalyst Dr Donald Winnicott (1945a, 1949, 1957a, 1957b, 1987, 1993) began speaking on the wireless, delivering his now-famous talks on child psychology for the British Broadcasting Corporation; and the general public—desperate for psychological knowledge—embraced him for his frank and compassionate radio programmes about the troubling vicissitudes of family mental health. Sadly, many of Winnicott's psychoanalytical colleagues greeted him with raised eyebrows (Brendan MacCarthy, personal communication, 17 July 2002; cf. Kahr, 2015, 2018b).

Consequently, when I entered the profession in the late 1970s, I had very few role models to whom I could turn who maintained an interest in engaging with the general public. Indeed, many of my teachers explained that, in view of the necessity for psychoanalytical practitioners to preserve confidentiality, one should never engage with the media.

As a clinical practitioner, I do, of course, champion confidentiality for my clients or patients, as I have indicated, but many colleagues have relied upon the need for confidentiality as an excuse for shirking the opportunity to transmit our knowledge and understanding more widely. Nevertheless, as psychotherapists and psychologists and psychoanalysts, we *must* endeavour to find ways to enlighten the general public about the nature of our work without compromising the privacy of patients or, indeed, our own integrity in any way. Although this may not seem to be a simple or straightforward undertaking, I know that responsible public education can, indeed, be achieved. And I certainly had the good fortune to have worked with a number of pioneers in this respect.

As a very young man, I had the great privilege of meeting and, later, studying with the warm-hearted British psychiatrist Dr Anthony Storr, who directed the psychotherapy department at the Warneford Hospital in Headington, a little suburb outside central Oxford. A Jungian analyst by training, Anthony Storr occupied an unusual position in the Oxford psychiatric establishment as the sole psychotherapist on a staff comprised entirely of pharmacologically orientated and behaviourally orientated clinicians, most of whom had little patience for psychoanalytical ideas, whether Jungian or Freudian. Yet, somehow, Storr managed to have earned the great respect of all of his colleagues, in spite of his anomalous role as someone who preferred talking with patients rather than drugging them.

I shall never forget my first sighting of Anthony Storr in the common room of the Warneford Hospital, one of Oxford's premier psychiatric institutions. Then but a baby student psychologist, I had come to the hospital for an afternoon meeting with one of the senior members of staff, just in time for tea, and within moments I spotted Dr Storr, perched nearby and immersed in a conversation of his own. In his early sixties, he struck me—a mere stripling—as extremely ancient, his head crowned with wisps of wavy white hair. I could not help but overhear snippets of Dr Storr's conversation, and I thought him very wise and very engaging, and I found his vocal tones both mellifluous and calming.

The benign and benevolent Dr Storr came to have a huge impact upon me, and, in many ways, he modelled for me how one might become a contained, sober clinician by day and a public educator on mental health topics by night. Storr had a great deal of self-composure, and seemed to be not at all exhibitionistic. I learned a great deal from listening to him lecture; indeed, I kept very fit by cycling from my lodgings in the centre of Oxford up the steep hill to Headington in order attend Dr Storr's talks at the hospital, each of which proved to be quite captivating, and I rarely missed an opportunity to hear him speak, impressing me with his erudition, his urbanity, and his dignity. I particularly remember Storr's psychobiographical studies of such diverse historical characters as Sir Isaac Newton and Franz Kafka, each of which appeared in print some years later in such wide-ranging publications as the *British Medical Journal* (Storr, 1985d) and in the proceedings of a conference held at the Institute of Germanic Studies in the University of London (Storr, 1985b).

In our more private conversations, Dr Storr regaled me with wonderful tales about the early history of psychoanalysis in Great Britain, and I shall never forget his anecdote about Dr Ernest Jones, one of Freud's leading English-speaking disciples. Apparently, during the 1920s, Jones employed a valet at his Harley Street consulting room, who would greet his psychoanalytic patients at the door and take their coats. At the end of the fifty-minute session, the valet would magically reappear, coat in hand, and usher Dr Jones's patients out of the office building (Anthony Storr, personal communication, 25 February 1985). Such wonderfully vivid tales of a bygone era in psychoanalytic practice not only gratified my burgeoning historical interests but, also, fuelled them as well; and I often took careful notes after each of my meetings with Dr Storr in order to preserve some of these historical nuggets.

But Storr worked not only as a hospital clinician and as a teacher, he also held a pre-eminent position in British cultural life during the

1960s, 1970s, and 1980s as one of the leading public commentators on mental health topics, writing reviews of Freudian and Jungian books for many of the leading quality newspapers such as *The Times*, *The Sunday Times*, *The Observer*, and *The Times Literary Supplement*, as well as for magazines such as *Encounter* (e.g., Storr, 1969) and *New Society* (e.g., Storr, 1968b), or, indeed, penning the occasional chapter or "Postscript" to a popular book (e.g., Storr, 1974, 1985c). And he appeared frequently on the radio and on television discussing psychological matters, as well as making a memorable contribution to *Desert Island Discs* for B.B.C. Radio 4 in 1993. I held Storr in high esteem, and I learned a great deal from listening to his many broadcasts and from reading his many reviews, each characterised by tremendous generosity of spirit and by marvellous lucidity of expression.

On several occasions, I invited Dr Storr to deliver talks, once to a group of colleagues at a nearby psychiatric hospital where I worked, and once to an assembly of academics at an Oxford college. After one of these presentations, I arranged a supper party for Anthony Storr and a smattering of mental health professionals. Although he had long ago become the undisputed "grand old man" of Oxford psychotherapy by this point in his career, he certainly did not swan around, as many of his more grandiose co-workers did; rather, he maintained a remarkable capacity to be convivial and deeply interested in everyone else at the dinner table. He shared his knowledge liberally, and, in doing so, he inspired many people to embark upon careers in mental health. In addition to his many broadcasts, Storr's numerous books, each written in an accessible style, had a strong impact not only on mental health workers but, also, on members of the public as well, who engaged fully with his work on aggression and destruction (Storr, 1968a, 1972a, 1991), on creativity (Storr, 1972b, 1985a), on loneliness (Storr, 1988), on music (Storr, 1992), on sexual deviation (Storr, 1964), and on a welter of related topics (e.g., Storr, 1960, 1983, 1989a, 1996; cf. Jung, 1983). He also wrote the volume on Freud for the prestigious Oxford University Press series on "Past Masters", edited by the pre-eminent University of Oxford historian Professor Sir Keith Thomas (Storr, 1989b).

Fortunately, I had other good mentors who helped me to appreciate the importance of the interface between mental health and the wider public. During my mid-twenties, I spent a fellowship year in the United States of America, and, through an older colleague, I had the privileged opportunity of meeting two very special women, Mrs

Lucy Freeman and Professor Flora Rheta Schreiber—the reigning doyennes of the New York media psychology world, each well into her seventh decade.

Back in the early 1940s, Lucy Freeman had become one of the very first female reporters to work for *The New York Times*. A long-term sufferer from sinusitis and related psychosomatic symptoms, she underwent her own very favourable experience of personal psychoanalysis and ultimately wrote an extremely moving book about being a patient, *Fight Against Fears*, published in 1951, which sold over one million copies (Freeman, 1951). Through her work as *The New York Times'* first ever official mental health correspondent, and through the many books and articles that she would write over nearly half a century, Freeman did more than most practising clinicians to publicise, to demystify, and to popularise psychology and psychoanalysis in a highly responsible manner (e.g., Freeman, 1959, 1969a, 1969b, 1969c, 1970, 1971, 1972, 1973, 1978, 1979, 1980, 1983, 1984a, 1984b, 1985, 1989, 1992). Before Freeman undertook her pioneering work as an educator, few people knew the differences among psychiatrists and psychologists and psychotherapists and psychoanalysts, and virtually no one knew how to find one. During those pre-Oprah Winfrey times, most men and women regarded mental health professionals as little more than witch-doctors or charlatans. Americans called us "head-shrinkers", and Britons referred to us as "trick-cyclists" (a corruption of "psychiatrists"). Fortunately, Lucy's myriad publications helped to educate people greatly by offering scholarly, well-informed, yet highly readable, accounts of what actually happens in the consulting room, and thus she did an enormous amount to help shape a psychological culture (Kahr, 1999c, 1999d).

I first visited Lucy at her lovely apartment on Manhattan's Central Park South; and in spite of an age difference of nearly forty-five years, we became great friends, and she took me under wing, introducing me liberally to her old colleagues from the New York psychoanalytic community, virtually all of whom encouraged me warmly in my studies. Whenever I visited Lucy, she would open the door to her hallway cupboard, which contained literally hundreds of her many books, and at the end of each visit, she would ply me with spare copies, beautifully autographed. During my lifetime, I have met few people with Lucy Freeman's warmth and generosity of spirit, and I sat happily at her feet as she told me how she had not only become the first reporter to cover mental health stories for leading newspapers but, how, additionally, she had set up the very first press office on behalf of the American Psychoanalytic Association, an organisation that had previously wished to maintain a low profile in order to avoid attacks from those critics who, back in the 1930s and 1940s, regarded psychoanalysis with extreme suspicion.

Lucy also kindled my nascent interest as a psychiatric and psychoanalytic historian. She knew virtually everybody in the English-speaking mental health world, and she generously devoted long hours to regaling me with stories about many famous psychoanalysts who had known Sigmund Freud, ranging from Dr Ernest Jones, the dean of British psychoanalysis, to Professor Karl Menninger, the archdeacon of American psychiatry. I made meticulous notes of Lucy's reminiscences, and much of this unpublished material has found its way into my current writings.

Flora Rheta Schreiber, a great friend to Lucy Freeman, would never tell me her age, and, out of respect, I certainly never sought to find out. She subscribed to the quaint old-world view that a lady should keep such information a mystery. Since her death, researchers have disclosed her birthday as 24 April 1918. So I now know that I had first met Flora shortly after she had turned sixty-six years.

The bibliophilic daughter of two librarians and the sometime fiancée of Eugene O'Neill, Jr, son of the celebrated playwright, Flora Schreiber ultimately became an academic, serving as Professor of English and Speech, as well as Director of Public Relations, at the John Jay College of Criminal Justice, part of the City University of New York. After having written a number of straightforward books on such topics as children's speech (Schreiber, 1956) and on the field of law enforcement (Schreiber, 1970), Flora ultimately made literary and psychiatric history through the publication of her overnight best-selling book, *Sybil* (Schreiber, 1973), the true story of an horrifically abused woman who, in response to massive traumatisation, developed multiple personality disorder (now more commonly known as dissociative identity disorder), and who subsequently became a more integrated personality through the steadfast commitment of Dr Cornelia Wilbur, a noted psychoanalyst. Flora told me that literally dozens of publishers had turned down the typescript of her book, thinking the subject matter both unpalatable and bizarre, but the Henry Regnery Company in Chicago, Illinois, took a punt on Schreiber's work, and before long they reaped rich dividends as the book sold extraordinary numbers of copies and did more, perhaps, than any other book for many decades to alert people to the realities of grotesque forms of child abuse. *Sybil* became the subject of two television films; indeed, the actress Sally Field earned an Emmy Award for her magnificent performance as the eponymous heroine in the two-part version, broadcast in 1976, while Jessica Lange starred in the 2007 remake as the psychiatrist, Dr Cornelia Wilbur.

Many people refused to believe that "Sybil" actually suffered from multiple personality disorder, and many sceptics who knew neither "Sybil" nor Dr Wilbur, let alone Professor Schreiber, have staked their careers on reviling the book (Nathan, 2011; cf. Suraci, 2011). Indeed, I myself remember that when I first encountered the book *Sybil* as a very young teenager, it struck me as almost a work of science fiction. But after I began to study psychology and psychopathology, I quickly learned that women and men have struggled with dissociated personalities for centuries, invariably in response to massive psychological trauma; and we now have overwhelming evidence that these states of fragmentation really do exist (e.g., Nemiah, 1979; Keyes, 1981; Crabtree, 1985; Carlson, 1986; Peterson, Gooch, and Freeman, 1987; Spiegel, 1990; Goodwin and Fine, 1993; Carlson and Armstrong, 1994; Putnam, 1994; Hacking, 1995; Cohen, 1996; Sinason, 2002a, 2002b, 2002c, 2011a, 2011b, 2011c; Schäfer, Ross, and Read, 2008). In fact, in 1987 Flora trustingly showed me a trunk full of letters that she had received after the publication of *Sybil*, from women and men all over the world who had written to her explaining that they, too, had multiple personalities, and that no one had ever believed them before. Although a sceptic might dismiss these plaintive fan letters as exhibitionistic scrawlings, I read through them in some detail, and I could not fail to be moved by the plight of these many correspondents who had also suffered physical or sexual abuse, and whose stories had remained hidden and disbelieved. Flora had, in fact, asked me to work with her to edit a selection of these letters for publication, in the hope that these documents would help raise further awareness about the plight of the abused, but, alas, she soon developed cancer of the bowel and died, shortly thereafter, on 3 November 1988 (Kahr, 2002b, 2011a).

Ten years after the appearance of *Sybil*, Schreiber (1983) published another book, which stirred even greater controversy—a study of the multiple murderer Joseph Kallinger, entitled *The Shoemaker: The Anatomy of a Psychotic*. In 1974 and 1975, Joseph Kallinger, a middle-aged American cobbler, and his thirteen-year-old son Michael Kallinger, embarked on a killing spree in various locations in the eastern United States. Spurred on by persecutory auditory hallucinations, Kallinger intended to kill every single human being on the planet. In the end, he murdered three people in cold blood, and he spent the rest of his life incarcerated in a high-security psychiatric institution in Waymart, Pennsylvania.

Shortly after Kallinger's arrest, Flora Schreiber gained privileged access to this killer, and she then spent several years interviewing him in great depth about his childhood. Throughout the course of their tape-recorded conversations, many of which I listened to years later, it emerged that Kallinger had experienced grotesque physical abuse at the hands of his adoptive parents, who forced him to kneel on sandpaper until he bled; who hit him on the head with a hammer; and who thrust his hand into the flames of the cooker as punishment for various childhood misdemeanours. With the skill of a consummate psychoanalyst, Schreiber painstakingly traced every detail of Kallinger's murderous behaviour in adulthood to the tortures that he himself had experienced as a child. To date, no one else has written such a profound book on the psychology of the killer, based heavily on documentable material, which included eyewitness testimony from those who had known Kallinger and his parents years previously and could confirm, independently, that the boy really did suffer such obscene abuses.

Flora became great friends with Joe Kallinger, and the two maintained an active correspondence until her death. On one occasion, back in 1985, Flora took me with her to the high-security institution to meet with Kallinger, and I spent an afternoon with him, both horrified to encounter a man who had committed such unspeakable murders and, yet, also sympathetic, knowing that, years and years earlier, Kallinger had lived in fear for his own life.

Anthony Storr, Lucy Freeman, and Flora Schreiber—all very different sorts of people—took me under wing and provided warm encouragement of my burgeoning interest in mental health. I knew them all while in my early twenties—a deeply impressionable period in the life of a man—and each of them became a significant role model. In varying ways, these three grandparental personalities impressed upon me the importance not only of reaching out to people, but, also, of being a *maverick*. Certainly, none of them had cookie-cutter careers. Anthony Storr, the only clinician in this memorable triumvirate, championed the work of Jung and Freud and helped to popularise psychological thinking among a sceptical British public at a time when virtually every respected psychiatrist endorsed the more traditional somatic approach to mental illness. Lucy Freeman and Flora Rheta Schreiber, both journalists by training, worked on an even bigger canvas, demonstrating that the general public ached for good psychological knowledge, and as such, they reached enormous audiences, with Lucy having sold over one million books and Flora having sold multiple millions—untold figures then, and virtually unheard of nowadays in our oversaturated book market.

Of course, I had other great teachers: quiet teachers, sober teachers, teachers who never published a single paper, teachers who became nervous in front of the class, teachers with thirty or forty years of clinical experience under their belts, teachers who dedicated their working lives to the private, careful, and slow understanding and treatment of the individual patient. And of course, these teachers had the most enormous impact of all and helped me, I believe, to become a clinician.

Somehow, through these rich sets of encounters with the more inward-looking members of my profession, as well as with the more outward-facing ones, I gradually began to develop a position from which I could make a small contribution of my own to the mental health field—one that allowed me to combine the often silent work of the consulting room with the more outspoken work of broadcasting.

Although it may seem surprising, I had never consciously intended to pursue a path in the field of media psychology. When I began my training, I had every intention of becoming a full-time mental health practitioner, lecturing in a university every now and then and writing, perhaps, a few scholarly books and papers. Public education never really formed part of my plan. But, in 1984, while still in my early twenties, I accepted an invitation to appear on a radio programme about psychoanalysis, on B.B.C. Radio Oxford. Apparently, I must have acquitted myself sufficiently well, and before long I began receiving further invitations to broadcast about a variety of psychological matters. One year later, in 1985, I conducted my first television interview—for an American cable network—and also, at that time, I wrote my first article on psychoanalysis for a newspaper, *The Times Higher Education Supplement* (Kahr, 1985). Perhaps people liked the sound of my speaking voice; but, for whatever reason, I gradually received more and more offers from producers and, eventually, I developed a portfolio of work, recording or filming over two thousand radio and television interviews, culminating in my very public appointments as Resident Psychotherapist on B.B.C. Radio 2, speaking to an average of fifteen million Britons weekly, and as national Spokesperson for the British Broadcasting Corporation's mental health awareness campaign "Life 2 Live".

All the while, I maintained my clinical psychotherapeutic practice, always ensuring that I never cancelled any patients or rearranged any patients in order to record a radio interview or film a television programme. As my work with patients has always come first and always will do, I attend to media assignments only outside ordinary working hours.

The day-to-day stream of fifty-minute appointments remains the absolute foundation of my work. And as I get older, psychoanalytic practice absorbs me more and more. I keep this work confidential, and I enjoy the silent satisfaction of watching the people who have come to speak with me go on to lead lives of decreased anguish and torment and of increased satisfaction and creativity.

But in addition to my regular psychotherapeutic work with individuals and couples, I have always preserved a small amount of my time for collaborating with the media, as a radio broadcaster, as a television presenter and commentator, as a consultant to public relations companies and film companies, as the author of articles for newspapers and magazines, and as a lecturer at public cultural institutions. In this way, I satisfy my strong need to sit quietly and silently in my little consulting room, and I also manage to make what I hope might be a useful contribution to the dissemination of psychological knowledge.

These two strands—the inward and the outward—may seem completely antithetical, but, in fact, I find that each complements the other in a host of ways. I suppose that I have become, in many respects, a maverick within the British mental health community, although I cannot claim to be the only one, by any means.

Between 2005 and 2011, I had the privilege of writing a quarterly column for the venerable psychoanalytic journal *American Imago*, founded in 1939 by the Viennese émigré psychoanalyst Dr Hanns Sachs (1939, 1944), in collaboration with Professor Sigmund Freud. *American Imago: Psychoanalysis and the Human Sciences* specialises in the interface between psychoanalysis and culture at large, and its Editor at the time, Professor Peter Rudnytsky, knowing of my work both inside and outside the consulting room, kindly gave me an opportunity to author a regular column, "Letter from London", for the journal's predominantly American readership. Earlier incarnations of the chapters that follow first appeared in *American Imago* and demonstrate, I hope, something about the ways in which one can be a psychoanalytic maverick, working quietly and unobtrusively by day, helping a small number of patients, and, by night, reaching millions of people out of office hours, still speaking in a calm, contained voice, but through a microphone at the B.B.C.'s Central London headquarters in Langham Place.

I have divided these essays into four sections, each reflecting my divergent but, also, intertwining interests. In Part One, I present a selection of columns based upon my clinical work in the consulting room. In every case, I have written about areas of seeming minutiae, neglected by most other writers, covering such ostensibly insignificant matters as the handshake, the ten-minute gap between sessions, and the box of tissues. Although these topics might appear, at first, to be of little import, I find that they convey something quite fundamental about the lens of the psychotherapist, revealing how a clinician focuses on the apparently trivial, and how he or she might use these pieces of information as points of often very profound contact with patients in distress. In Part Two, I describe my work outside the office: making television programmes about psychological topics or playing the piano at the Royal Opera House and, in one case, participating as an "expert witness" in the trial of "Lady Macbeth" at the Royal Courts of Justice, to help raise money for a worthy cause. In Part Three, I offer a smattering of my long-standing passion for, and devotion to, the history of psychoanalysis, demonstrating my indebtedness to my honorary grandparents and great-grandparents in the field and helping to explore, *inter alia*, Sigmund Freud's complicated relationship to the media. And, in Part Four, I offer some glimpses into the mind and soul of the clinician by sharing two private passions, music and bibliophilia, which have, nonetheless, contributed substantially to the texture and atmosphere of my day-to-day psychological work.

I have chosen as the supra-title for this book *On Practising Therapy at 1.45 A.M.* This derives from my experiences of talking to millions of Britons about their mental health needs, at times rather early in the morning. And I have chosen as the subtitle for this collection *Adventures of a Clinician*. I have tried to write each of the chapters as an adventure—the adventure of a hopefully sober but, also, hopefully playful maverick who has endeavoured to work in mental health, both off camera and on, with a quiet voice heard sometimes only by one patient in the sanctity of the consulting room and sometimes by a rather larger number of people unsure of what a therapist looks like or sounds like, or, indeed, how one finds a therapist in the first place.

Although I have written most of the chapters in the past tense, reflecting upon various clinical and media psychological adventures,

I have, on a small number of occasions, scripted a handful of these contributions in the present tense, thus endeavouring to recreate the immediacy of the situation. As these articles appeared originally on a quarterly basis—hot off the press—writing in the present tense seemed fitting at the time and, I trust, might still do so, especially when describing such projects as the commissioning and production of two television programmes: *Britain's Sexual Fantasies* and *Making Slough Happy*.

So, I hope that you will enjoy these maverick adventures of a clinician, and I trust that, for those who may just have begun to take their first steps in the helping professions, you might feel encouraged to entertain creative ways of working and of contributing. Perhaps we may soon discover that the maverick and the traditionalist can, indeed, come to exist side by side in a fruitful partnership.

Introduction

On practising therapy at 1.45 a.m.

> Todo esto viene en medio del silencio profundo
> En que la noche envuelve la terrena ilusión.
> [All this comes in the midst of the profound silence
> In which night enwraps the earthly illusion.]
>
> Rubén Darío, "Nocturno", in *Cantos de vida y esperanza:*
> *Los cisnes y otros poemas*, 1905
> [Darío, 1905, p. 150]

In July of 2004, I became the Resident Psychotherapist for B.B.C. Radio 2, the most popular radio station in the United Kingdom, which attracts approximately 15,000,000 listeners weekly from all parts of the British Isles. Some four months earlier Lesley Douglas, the forward-thinking and visionary new Controller of Radio 2, had invited me for a breakfast meeting atop St. George's Hotel in Langham Place, near her offices at Broadcasting House in Central London, to discuss the possibility of presenting solid psychological and psychotherapeutic ideas on the radio. As we munched on delicious croissants, Lesley told me that as the new Controller she not only hoped to maintain and, indeed, to expand upon the high quality of Radio 2's current music and arts programmes, but she also wished to find a way for Radio 2 to help foster a greater sense of well-being and "citizenship" in Britain,

15

and she wondered whether a mental health professional might be able to make a contribution to the network.

I had made my first radio broadcast some twenty years earlier, in 1984, back on the *Dave Freeman* programme on B.B.C. Radio Oxford, defending psychoanalysis against heated attacks from the vituperative behavioural psychologist Professor Hans Eysenck; and in the intervening decades I had accumulated a goodly amount of media experience. I applauded Lesley Douglas on her very exciting proposal, and shortly thereafter I met her senior colleague, Dave Barber, Editor of Specialist Programmes, and his "Social Action" team, consisting of Senior Producer Mark Hill and Broadcast Assistant Nicky Davidson. Within a matter of months, we had created the infrastructure for a nationwide radio initiative, "Life 2 Live", designed to provide coverage of psychological themes and topics in the most basic language, for members of the general public. We launched on 23 July 2004, on *Jeremy Vine*, the flagship lunchtime news programme, discussing the psychology of intimate relationships, and I responded to callers who wished to speak about the causes of marital breakdown and related topics.

Lesley Douglas had planned for me not to have my own slot on Radio 2 but, rather, to visit as many of the already existent radio programmes as possible as a guest, thereby helping to disseminate a psychotherapeutic presence across the radio station. During my tenure at Radio 2, I made frequent appearances on such staple shows as *Jeremy Vine* and, also, *Johnnie Walker*, the early evening Drivetime programme, as well as the highly popular and hugely durable *Steve Wright* afternoon programme. We developed a special "Life 2 Live" section on the B.B.C. website, for which I would write regular short pieces (book reviews, fact sheets, responses to Frequently Asked Questions about the nature of therapy, and so forth), and through which I would conduct web-chats with members of the public who wished to speak to a psychotherapist more directly about particular mental health matters. The website, diligently maintained by my colleague Terri Sweeney, a woman who had extensive experience of working for B.B.C. Interactive, helped the "Life 2 Live" campaign reach an even wider audience, and we received tens of thousands of page impressions weekly. We also maintained a B.B.C. Message Board, where members of the public could write to me with their personal problems—often about quite heartbreaking difficulties and traumas—to which I would respond with referrals to mental health practitioners or mental health organisations throughout the United

Kingdom. In doing this work, we made, I trust, a contribution to raising the level of public awareness about psychotherapy and mental
health issues, especially in less well populated parts of the country
where we, as mental health professionals, had not yet made much of
an impact.

Initially, when we discussed how I should be referred to on air,
colleagues at the B.B.C. wondered whether I could be called a "life
coach". I told them that this would not suit me, as I have neither
trained as a "life coach", nor would I describe myself as one. I
explained that I would prefer to be known quite straightforwardly
as a "psychotherapist", my professional title. The Social Action team
seemed somewhat concerned that this very clinical-sounding term
(at least to their ears) might be too off-putting or indeed too scary
for some listeners, but I held my ground; and soon thereafter, each
week, the announcers would introduce me as "Radio 2 Resident Psychotherapist Brett Kahr". So, if nothing else, I succeeded in having
the word "psychotherapist" broadcast regularly on Radio 2, turning
a hitherto "taboo" title into a more user-friendly one.

After I had begun to find my sea legs, talking to the hosts of the
daytime radio shows, speaking with callers, and suchlike, Dave Barber rang me to enquire whether I would be willing to make a regular
appearance on Radio 2's late-night music programme, hosted by the
delightful and talented presenter Helen Mayhew, who had just joined
the network. Essentially, I would go on air with Helen from 1.30 a.m.
until 2.30 a.m. in the Saturday night/Sunday morning slot, to chat
with Helen about psychological matters and then to take calls from
listeners, "*Frasier*-style". Although somewhat concerned about my
ability to function therapeutically at such an unusual hour, I nevertheless accepted the challenge with alacrity, prepared to plunge in at
the deep end.

On 17 October 2004, I braced myself for my first late-night appearance, napping, uncharacteristically, during the afternoon so that I
would be sufficiently alert to engage in on-air psychotherapeutics in
the small hours of the morning. I arrived at Broadcasting House at
around midnight, greeted Helen Mayhew and the team, and settled
down to drink several cups of boiled water, which kept my throat
well lubricated, and then I prepared for the red light to appear, sig-
nalling the start of the programme: live, unedited, with no turning
back! Fortunately, due to the considerable preparation of my Senior
Producer Mark Hill, Helen and I had already made a pilot programme together, complete with real callers, so that we could begin

to acquaint ourselves with one another, and so that we could test the technology, as Helen would be working from a completely new studio and would have to operate many of the control panels herself, bringing callers on air and then signing them off again. So, in spite of the unusual nature of our task, both Helen and I felt reasonably ready.

When I had begun my job as "Resident Psychotherapist" for Radio 2, my colleagues at the B.B.C. had asked me whether I might want to know beforehand who the callers would be and what their problems would be. After thinking carefully about this matter, I explained that I wanted to be surprised. I reasoned that if I knew the nature of the calls in advance, I might find myself researching the problems or, indeed, pre-scripting my answers in ways that might not be particularly helpful. Instead, if I could respond spontaneously, exactly as I would do in the consulting room, this would give the audience a clearer and more authentic idea of how psychotherapy proceeds. So after some preliminary chat with Helen about the "Life 2 Live" initiative, the producer signalled that we had our first caller on the line—and neither Helen nor I had any idea what we might expect. I knew only that I would have approximately three, or four, or, at most, five minutes with the caller. (This may seem a ridiculously short period of time in which to touch on crucial matters, but radio producers consider five minutes an eternity—a luxury, in fact—and I felt privileged to have even this short amount of time in which I might try to say something psychotherapeutically edifying.)

Because several million people would be listening to each of my broadcasts, this raised important questions about confidentiality, as callers would be speaking about intimate matters before a large audience. Those ringing in could, of course, opt to use a pseudonym, if they so chose, but most, it seems, decided to introduce themselves by their real names. The expert broadcast assistants who screened the telephone calls in advance would, at my insistence, discuss questions of informed consent, asking the callers if they had really thought carefully about whether they wished to discuss their private concerns on national radio.

In thinking about whether to accept this post at the B.B.C., I spoke, of course, with several of my mental health colleagues, all of whom encouraged me to undertake this piece of work. My former boss at the Tavistock Clinic told me, "Brett, I know that you'll speak to the callers with compassion. By doing that in front of millions of people, you have a real opportunity to destigmatise therapy. Of course the callers will be sharing their real problems, but they are entitled to do that. They are entitled to talk about their own lives. And you'll respond respectfully. The callers won't be shamed. So go ahead. Do it!" Fortified by encouragement of this sort from senior colleagues, I persevered.

After I grappled with a crackling headphone, which had to be rapidly repaired by the sound technician, my first caller appeared on the line. In her calm and soothing voice, Helen Mayhew entreated the caller to tell me his problem: "Hello, 'James', you're on the line with our psychotherapist, Brett". "James", a middle-aged man, said "Hullo", in a deeply flattened tone of voice, and after I greeted him with a "Good morning, 'James'", I asked how I might be of help. In a teary voice, he told me that his wife, only forty years of age, had died just a few weeks previously from an undiagnosed brain tumour. Her headaches had come on rapidly, and shortly after entering hospital she had lapsed into a coma from which she never emerged. So James had no opportunity to say goodbye to his much-loved spouse, and now he had to care for their three tiny children all by himself. Quite understandably, James had already used up *three* minutes of our allotted five-minute time in telling me his story. Through the glass partition of the studio, I could see my producer looking anxious. I contorted my shoulders, clenched my teeth, and made a desperate face to the producer, trying to communicate with gestures: "Look, this is a serious trauma. We will need more time . . . please!"

I began my response by extending my deepest condolences to James in my most heartfelt voice. Any reasonable human being—clinician or otherwise—would have done exactly the same. I then asked a few pointed questions as to whether James had any support network available (family, friends, work colleagues) to help him through this absolutely ghastly, traumatic loss. Unfortunately, James seemed to have devoted most of his time to his wife and children, and therefore he had few friends and no work colleagues to whom he felt particularly close. His work mates did, of course, know of his wife's death, but James explained that they tended to avoid talking to him about his bereavement, as they found the subject too painful, too awkward. I then commented on the importance of connectedness and of the dangers of isolation, and I tried to think with James about how he might access more sources of psychosocial support. James then confessed that he and his children had not managed to shed a tear since the unexpected death of his wife.

At this point, Helen intervened, helpfully, and asked me whether James *should* be crying and whether there might be certain stages in the grief and bereavement process that listeners might wish to know about. I could have hugged Helen for asking this question at this time because earlier she and I had both discussed the fact that in three or four minutes we would not manage to "solve" anyone's problems, but we could, at least, try to transmit some basic mental health advice not only to the caller but to the millions of listeners as well. I then did my very best to provide a brief, clear, potted summary of the contributions of Dr John Bowlby about the impact of separation and loss, and the work of Dr Colin Murray Parkes about the stages of grieving. I explained to James that he might still be entrapped in the first phase of the grieving process, namely, palpable shock and numbness. As James realised that he might improve and move on to further, more manageable stages of grief, he began to cry for the first time. I praised him on national radio for his ability to begin risking tears, explaining that, ultimately, this would bring relief.

By now, I had used up *nine* minutes of highly precious, highly expensive broadcast time, nearly twice the length allocated, but we soldiered on. James spoke more about the lovely qualities of his wife and of his children. I then explained that, of course, we would not be able to talk about all the important aspects of his circumstances on this occasion, but that if he stayed on the line, one of my colleagues would speak with him at greater length and would recommend the name of a counselling agency in James's local area, far from London. I asked James whether he thought that some bereavement counselling might be of assistance, and he agreed that he would think about this as a possibility.

Helen and I both extended further condolences and warm wishes to him, and we said our goodbyes—again, all on national radio—finishing just a few minutes before the 2.00 a.m. news bulletin.

After James rang off, Helen and I had a chance to speak about James's situation, still on air, and we both praised him for his courage, having taken the risk to telephone and to talk about his almost unspeakable personal and family tragedy. Helen then suggested to listeners that if anyone at home wished to convey a message to James, they would be welcome to do so, by telephone, by text, or by e-mail. We then switched to the news bulletin, having spent fully ten minutes on James's call. My producer certainly understood that we could not have offered this man any less, and, undoubtedly, we could have provided a lot more. I sipped some of my hot water, which had now gone cold, and after the news bulletin I read out some e-mails to James from various listeners, very much of the "Well-done-James-keep-your-chin-up-mate" variety, but welcome nonetheless. Each person, in his or her own emotional vocabulary, wanted to reach out and make at least some contact with this likeable bereaved gentleman. Having struggled heretofore with loneliness, I hope that James found some of these simple, gentle expressions of kindness and camaraderie to be helpful and touching.

One of my specially trained colleagues spoke to James at greater length later that morning, and she offered numerous sources of local professional support. James seemed more calm, and we told him that he would be welcome to make further contact with us at any point in future, and that he could avail himself of our "Life 2 Live" Message Board at any time, as well as our "Life 2 Live" telephone helpline.

Helen and I then took several more callers, including a woman who had suffered sexual abuse at the hands of a close family member many decades earlier, and who had now begun to experience panic attacks, having seen her abuser again, after many, many years, at a family funeral. Needless to say, this call required more than three or four or five minutes as well.

After the programme ended, at 2.30 a.m., Helen, the producer, the sound engineer, and I had a "de-briefing" meeting. The producer told me that, in future, we would have to think twice before putting "depressed" callers on the line, as depressed people do not make for "good radio". Helen, to my relief, upbraided the producer and told him that she thought that James had made a wonderful guest, and that by daring to speak of his bereavement and by crying on national radio, he would have helped many men (and women) in comparable circumstances to know that one *can* reach out, and that talking to a psychotherapist need not be a scary experience. I could not have agreed more.

At that moment, the telephone rang. James had called back, asking whether he might speak with me directly. The producer found me a quiet cubicle off the studio, and I took the call. James and I talked privately, off-air, for another hour, as he wanted to thank me for help-ing him. He knew that he had to cry. He knew that he had to have help. And now, the grieving process could begin. I spoke with James about a referral to an organisation in his local area, far from London, and he seemed very grateful indeed.

A chauffeured B.B.C. car returned me home at approximately 4.00 a.m., but, I must confess, it took me more than two hours before I could wind down from the experience, and I did not fall asleep until nearly 6.00 a.m. In the months that followed, I appeared many more times on the *Helen Mayhew* show, and somehow I found a way to fall asleep more quickly upon my return home and to incorporate these extremely late-night and early-morning radio psychotherapy forays into my weekend timetable. Rather than regarding them as a disruption, I came to consider them a real pleasure and a real privilege—an opportunity to reach out, in some small way, to those people round the country who had never before encountered a mental health professional of any shape or form.

Of course, these little conversations—only three or four or sometimes five minutes in length—in no way represent the ordinary psychoanalytic work that I undertake during my typical clinical day, consisting of fifty-minute sessions that unfold over years and years, in which I endeavour to render deep unconscious interpretations of, and engagements with, private free-associative material. But in the absence of being able to offer intensive psychoanalysis to everyone, I regard this media psychological experiment as an important means of allowing people to experience something of the seriousness and the compassion that only the mental health professional can provide. Although I never embarked upon a full course of psychotherapy or psychoanalysis with anyone who approached me through the B.B.C., I do know that by having dipped a toe into these larger waters, I did have the opportunity to reach many millions of people whom I would not have encountered otherwise.

I really do take my hat off to the British Broadcasting Corporation for having established the "Life 2 Live" project with such seriousness and such professionalism, and I feel honoured to have taken part in this campaign. When I first began working on the project, I wondered whether a few minutes of therapy here and a few minutes of therapy there would make much difference, but having immersed myself in the process for the three years of the campaign, I came to know, from letters and e-mails and postings on our Message Board, that people really did listen and, also, derived benefit. Indeed, during my tenure as Resident Psychotherapist I referred an untold number of individuals to colleagues for psychological therapeutic work—people who, under ordinary circumstances, would have steered clear of practitioners such as ourselves.

Perhaps I had some small success in helping to destigmatise psychotherapy among my fellow Britons. Four minutes on air may seem a drop in the ocean, but when 15,000,000 people listen to those four minutes. . . .

PART I

CONSULTING ROOM ESSAYS

I had much Conversation with him and some of it very free.

John Adams, the future American President,
on speaking with a sometime army officer

Diary entry, 10 December, 1775, in John Adams, *Diary and Autobiography
of John Adams: Volume 2. Diary 1771–1781*
[Adams, 1775, p. 225]

CHAPTER ONE

The handshake

And none can touch that frowning form.

William Blake, "The Mental Traveller", c. 1803, Stanza 26, line 101

Being of Austrian–Jewish extraction, I grew up in a family in which everyone hugs and kisses when we meet. Indeed, in my private life, I would regard myself as a rather physically affectionate person. But in the consulting room, during my working day, I adopt a very different stance. Although I endeavour to be both professionally friendly and also at ease within my body during analytic sessions, I do maintain a physical distance from my patients, and I keep myself seated in my leather chair, perched behind the couch. I do so for all the obvious reasons. I regard psychotherapy and psychoanalysis as cognitive-affective relationships in which one provides healing through compassion, reliability, and understanding—not through cuddles or embraces. Furthermore, I know only too well that the vast majority of my patients, if not all of my patients, will have experienced some form of noxious physical contact—however mild—during infancy and childhood, and, consequently, many of them maintain a phobic reaction to actual touch; therefore, like most psychoanalytically inclined mental health professionals, I adopt a "hands-off" policy in order to refrain from retraumatising the men and women who come to work with me.

In fact, in more than thirty-five years of practice, I can recall only *one* instance when I had to touch a patient (other than offering a handshake at a first meeting). Some thirty years ago, while working in the mental handicap field with clients who had suffered from brain damage and who would, therefore, often manifest various forms of "challenging behaviour", I received a referral request from a psychiatric colleague to assess a woman afflicted with compulsive head-banging—a most distressing presenting symptom. This lady, who also suffered from mutism, would slam her head vigorously against a wall many times during the day, causing great distress to the nursing staff who had to work with her and who, during eight-hour shifts, became frustrated and exhausted.

In view of this woman's primary symptom, I thought it likely that she would try to bang her head in my presence, and, indeed, within minutes of arriving in my office, she began to do so. No sooner had I introduced myself—"Hello, I'm Brett Kahr . . ."—than my new patient instantly hurled herself against the far wall of my office and started to thwack her cranium against the plaster, creating a huge thud. She did this twice in rapid succession, and I desperately interpreted, "You're really showing me how distressed you are, and how you want to knock some terrible thoughts out of your head." Sadly, this remark, which I assumed to be a reasonably well-phrased interpretation, seemed to have had little impact on my new patient. This troubled woman, in fact, continued to bang. I became increasingly agitated, both by the loud noise and by the fear of the patient inflicting further brain damage. "Please stop", I cried. "I am deeply concerned that you are hurting yourself." This more directive remark did not achieve the desired effect either, and, frighteningly, the lady continued to bang her head. Eventually, in blind terror that she would bloody herself, I stood up from my seat and gently placed my hands on the patient's shoulders, and then I steered her away from the wall, subsequently guiding her into a comfortable chair. This episode remains a very stark exception to my long-standing "hands-off" policy in the consulting room.

Virtually every clinician that I know could relate comparable stories of extraordinary, *unexpected* physical contact. During the course of researching my book *D.W. Winnicott: A Biographical Portrait* (Kahr, 1996a), I had the pleasure of interviewing Dr John Padel (Kahr, interview, 4 December 1991), now deceased, a distinguished member of the Independent Group of British psychoanalysts who had participated in seminars with Dr Donald Winnicott in the 1950s, during his studentship at the Institute of Psycho-Analysis in London. Padel recalled that, on one occasion, Winnicott shared a clinical vignette about an acrobatic female patient who, in the middle of a session, managed to perform a backwards roll while still on the couch, and had ultimately landed up in Winnicott's lap! Winnicott turned to the students and asked them how *they* would have handled this unusual situation of physical contact between patient and analyst, before explaining to them how he himself had responded. Winnicott explained to the trainees that he wished to remove the patient from his lap at once, for obvious reasons, but that he also recognized, quite palpably, both the patient's wish for, and need for, contact. And so, he placed a hand on her shoulder and stood up very slowly, allowing the patient to slip gently off his body. When both parties had arrived in a standing position, Winnicott kept his hand on the patient's shoulder and paced up and down the consulting room, entreating the lady to recall the very last thought in her mind before she had catapulted herself from couch to lap.

Winnicott's admirers would no doubt praise his ingenuity in such compromising circumstances. His detractors (and we have many in London) would no doubt wonder what he might have done to stimulate such arguably eroticised, acting-out behaviour in the first place (Kahr, 2006a). Whatever the cause of such consulting room drama—and one must not forget that Winnicott often accepted highly regressed patients for treatment, many of whom had endured previously unsuccessful analyses with more "traditional" colleagues—each of us would benefit from studying such stories, as one day we, too, might find ourselves in the presence of a compulsive head-banger, or a couch-propelled acrobat, or, even, as Dr Michael Balint (1968) reported, a patient who performed a cartwheel in the midst of an analytic session.

The prospect of physical contact between patient and clinician appears in numerous other guises, not only through direct requests from the patient during regressive or potentially regressive moments (Casement, 1982, 2000), but also, quite regularly, in psychotherapeutic work with children, in particular (Holder, 2000). Of course, the question of touch and physical contact also becomes a serious issue in cases of overt, gross forms of sexual abuse between the psychoanalyst and the analysand (e.g., Walker and Young, 1986; Gabbard and Lester, 1995).

The question of physical contact emerges not only in these extraordinary, unusual instances, but it presents itself more prosaically in our daily work. Each Monday through Friday, virtually every single psychoanalytic clinician will find himself or herself confronted regularly with the most common and under-theorised aspect of our work—namely, the *handshake*.

In spite of the growing literature on the question of touch, not only in psychoanalysis (e.g., Galton, 2006; King, 2006; Langs, 2006; Orbach, 2006; Sinason, 2006), but also in psychotherapy (e.g., Smith, Clance, and Imes, 1998), in developmental psychology (e.g., Field, 2001), and in neuroscience (e.g., Sunderland, 2006), the question of the handshake still remains a highly neglected area, perhaps, in part, because of its near ubiquity, especially during the first consultation or assessment session.

Scouring the technical psychoanalytic literature, renowned for its attention to detail, one will find virtually no references at all to the handshake. Dr Edward Glover, one of the pioneers of psychoanalysis in Great Britain, referred to the handshake dilemma, quite early on, in his lectures to candidates at London's Institute of Psycho-Analysis. Glover (1928, p. 15) explained that in one's first encounter with a patient, "no sooner does the door open than we are presented with our first problem in technique. How are we to greet him? Shall we shake hands or not?" He then underscored the problematicity of the handshake, instructing his students,

> we have to remember that the significance of a handshake is very different for an hysterical, an obsessional or a depressed case. In fact it might be said that the deeper the patient's regression or the earlier the fixation, the more significant do such details of analytic behaviour become. For the hysteric a handshake may be a promise, for the obsessional a challenge, for the narcissistic type it may be an attack. On the whole it is advisable to omit the procedure. [Glover, 1928, p. 15]

Edward Glover's preoccupation with the meaning of the handshake might seem somewhat precious to many contemporary readers, but one must remember that Glover wrote at a time when not everyone regarded the handshake as a natural form of greeting. According to the American cultural historian Professor Mark Lynn Anderson, so-called "hand-shakers" (quoted in Anderson, 2011, p. 40) would often be regarded derisorily in the 1920s as superficially ingratiating.

When, during the 1950s, Glover (1955, p. 24) revised his lectures for publication in a more comprehensive textbook on technique, he relented, and perhaps softened his approach, advising colleagues, "when in doubt behave naturally". Psychoanalytic workers will often be constrained by an historical and cultural context and might, on some occasions, also help to shape that very context.

Contemporaneously, the distinguished American psychoanalyst, Professor Karl Menninger (1958, p. 40), described the general posture of abstemiousness adopted by most Freudian practitioners, noting that, "This means that one doesn't *chat* with patients, touch them (*e.g.*, shake hands) unnecessarily, ask favors of them or accept favors or gifts from them, attend small social engagements where they will be, or discuss their 'material' with numerous other colleagues."

In 1973, in the first of his many encyclopaedic books on clinical practice, the thoughtful psychoanalyst Dr Robert Langs (1973, p. 201), a well-known antagonist to physical contact between analyst and patient, noted, "There are, of course, legitimate moments for touch between patient and therapist, and these deserve mention. A handshake before and after the first meeting with the patient is quite appropriate, as it is at the time of a new year, before and after a long vacation, and at termination." Already, Langs's comment, mentioned briefly as part of a section on "Not Touching the Patient", in his very first book on technique, might well evoke numerous reactions among diverse practitioners. Although many British clinicians, in particular, shake hands at the *beginning* of a treatment, I know of very few who do so either at vacation times or at the start of the New Year, for example, although I have heard of at least two senior colleagues who have done so over the years.

Langs (1973), of course, appreciated that the handshake evokes more complex dynamics, and he commented sagely:

Occasionally, a patient will continue to offer his hand before or after sessions at the beginning of treatment. Such a practice usually reflects special needs for closeness, unconscious sexual fantasies, the need to undo possible aggressions, and uncertainty in relating to others. When this occurs early in treatment, it is best not to interpret it because of the anxiety and sense of humiliation and rejection this may engender. Usually, when the therapist does not initiate such handshakes, the patient stops this practice. If not, simply and tactfully asking the patient about it is often enough to call it into question and the patient will desist. If he persists, the therapist can eventually interpret its use in the context of the material at hand, emphasizing, since it is early in treatment, the defensive aspects of this behavior. [1973, pp. 201–202]

Langs's measured and insightful commentary would, I suspect, typify the traditional, classical psychoanalytic viewpoint on this matter.

Other writers, though few in number, have offered a somewhat more liberal approach to the handshake. Professor Horacio Etchegoyen (1986, p. 62), for example, arguably the most intricate theorist of formal clinical matters, and author of the unsurpassed textbook *Los fundamentos de la técnica psicoanalítica* [*The Fundamentals of Psychoanalytic Technique*], has no objection, in principle, to a handshake at the outset of treatment, noting that, "No soy personalmente para nada partidario de una apertura ambigua y reñida con los usos culturales" ["I am not in favour personally of an ambiguous opening in opposition to cultural usage" (Etchegoyen, 1991, p. 47)], as this might cause undue anxiety to the prospective patient. He would regard such matters as being "parte de un estilo personal y no elementos estándar de la entrevista" (Etchegoyen, 1986, p. 80) ["part of a personal style, not standard elements of the interview" (Etchegoyen, 1991, p. 64)], remarking that some psychoanalysts prefer to establish an authoritarian contract, whereas others will adopt a more democratic one.

Continental psychoanalysts do, it seems, shake hands far more frequently than British and American colleagues. According to Dr Herman Gijsbert van der Waals,

> I think every analyst in Europe, at least every analyst I know, shakes hands with his patient at the beginning and the end of the hour. It gives valuable information about the mood of the patient, his reaction to the hour, etc. In Europe it would be a technical error not to do this; patients would think it very queer. [Quoted in Menninger, 1958, p. 40]

Dr Alex Holder (2000), a Swiss colleague who had trained in Great Britain in both adult and child work, and who eventually came to practise psychoanalysis in Germany, noted, even more fully, the importance of cultural factors in the determination of the handshake:

> When I went to London from Switzerland nearly 40 years ago to embark on my psychoanalytical training, my first training analyst, with whom I shook hands at the beginning and end of each session, asked me after a few sessions to refrain from shaking hands. At first I felt hurt by this request but gradually came to accept it as a

cultural difference between my home country and England, rather than as an expression of her wish for greater distance between us. I subsequently adapted to this English habit and refrained from shaking hands with my own patients after the first meeting. [2000, p. 49]

But later, when he established himself in Germany, Holder realised that the English and American reluctance to shake hands after the initial session could prevent the psychoanalyst from learning a great deal of additional information about the patient. As Holder (2000) has observed,

> Just think of the patient who always manages the handshake in such a way that you can only get hold of his fingertips rather than the whole hand; or the patient who does not really grip your hand but presents you with a flabby hand to grasp; or the patient whose hand feels moist either at the beginning or end of a session, thus revealing something about the emotional state in which he is coming or going; or the patient who, at a certain point in the analysis, conveys a sense of wanting to hold onto your hand, of not wanting to let it go; or, conversely, the patient who seems to push you away rather than coming closer as you shake hands with him or her; or finally, the patient who rebels against the customary and suddenly refuses to shake hands at the end of a session because the fury, disappointment, or narcissistic hurt are so intense. [2000, p. 49]

Finally, Dr Nina Coltart authored an engaging essay on manners in the psychoanalytic situation, first presented to the Squiggle Foundation in London, in which she described the handshake dilemma. Her observations underscore, once again, the importance of both personal style and national style, to the extent that one can ever discriminate between these two aspects of one's character. Speaking of the management of manners, Coltart (1990) explained,

> An example of the more specialized kind is handshaking, about which there is a surprising number of different opinions, veering from one end of the spectrum where analysts never, under any circumstances, shake hands with patients, to the other end where there was Michael Balint. I introduce him here, in this rather bald statement, because he exemplified an extreme position so clearly and so consistently. He shook hands at the beginning and end of every session, a demonstration, at least in part, of how strongly one's early national culture—in his case, Hungarian—can imprint habits on to one's behaviour. In Britain, learning of this practice

usually provokes quite strong reactions, including in myself; my main objection to it is an idea that it could interfere with the flow of the process, especially in an acutely negative phase, rather as if having to reassure one's analyst at the end of every session, especially an angry, hostile one, that one still loves him. [1990, p. 141]

Professor Paul Roazen (2000), the American historian of psychoanalysis, observed that in Heidelberg, Germany, most practitioners would shake hands as a matter of course. Have we in the United Kingdom begun to make too big a deal out of something so ordinary?

In the early years of my work, I had certainly internalised the typical British psychotherapeutic practice of shaking hands at the beginning of a treatment, and also at the end of a treatment, but only *if* the patient had extended a hand *first*. As my professional life developed, and as I became increasingly more natural and comfortable in the consulting room, I began to find myself taking the initiative to offer a hand at beginnings and at terminations, and this seems to have proved very unproblematic. On a few occasions, I have refrained from doing so, especially with grossly sexually abused women, in particular, for whom even the most benign of culturally sanctioned handshakes might feel rather like a retraumatising rape. On the whole, however, I have restricted my handshaking to the very first and very last encounter.

Some years ago, however, I began to treat a brain-damaged forensic patient who came to see me via a public sector mental health clinic. This middle-aged man, disinhibited through organic handicap and through horrific neglect and molestation in early childhood, had begun to assault elderly ladies, and his probation officer had made arrangements for psychotherapeutic treatment. At our first session, I shook hands with Mr A, thus offering a typical greeting. He returned the handshake, and then I offered him a chair. Our first session then unfolded with Mr A talking, and with me listening. At the very end of this initial encounter, Mr A extended his hand to me, and I shook it. He departed. At our second session, and for each and every session thereafter, Mr A spontaneously offered his hand both at the beginning and at the end of each fifty-minute hour. In true Langsian fashion, I interpreted this gesture from every conceivable angle: a wish for closeness; a wish to transform the consulting room into a friendly place; a wish to project all the aggression into the old ladies whom he had assaulted, thereby keeping his touches with me quite safe; and a whole host of other analytically orientated observations. After months of analysis, Mr A still kept extending his hand, and I felt it would be both rude and counterproductive to refrain from shaking, especially as he worked so well and so dedicatedly during the main body of his sessions, attending punctually, free-associating diligently, and paying reliably.

After six months, Mr A told me for the first time that he suffered from a profound visual disturbance, and that he would often see double, and that, in recent weeks, he had begun to observe black bars across his field of vision. Previous ophthalmological investigations had revealed that Mr A had inherited a degenerative eye disease known as retinitis pigmentosa and, that owing to the hastening deterioration of his retinae, he would, in all likelihood, be fully blind in a matter of years. This crucial revelation of medical data offered me a further insight into Mr A's unremitting handshaking behaviour. I found myself interpreting, "Perhaps you are worried that one day you will not be able to see my face at all, and therefore the physical contact with my hand has become especially important to you as a way of taking me in." This comment seemed to have little overt impact on the patient, and it certainly did nothing to alter the recurring handshaking behaviour.

After approximately one year of treatment, I finally dispensed with my attempts to interpret the patient's handshaking, and I persevered with the other much more important aspects of the work. Mr A stayed with me in treatment for a full ten years, during which time he managed to forge a loving and intimate partnership with an intellectually disabled woman, maintain a full-time job, and, most vitally, cease all of his forensic activities and become a law-abiding citizen. Mr A developed a healthy play function, and he even began to undertake charity work for the handicapped and for those with grave medical illnesses, raising a lot of money through his efforts. He also bore his growing blindness with appropriate "depressive position" acceptance and with fortitude. He still shook my hand at the beginning and end of each and every session, and in spite of this, or perhaps, in part, *because* of this, he made very impressive strides in all aspects of his life.

Some years later, I began to work with another patient, Mrs B, a middle-aged woman with a painful history of intrafamilial sexual abuse. Like Mr A, she, too, shook my hand at the start and finish of each session. My interpretations about the possible meaning of "safe" touch with a man, or of "testing" me out, had no effect on her external behaviours, though they may have impacted on her internal world.

After about two years of regular handshaking, Mrs B began to query her own behaviour, and wondered, "Gee, it's odd, but I've just realised that I don't *have* to shake your hand. Maybe I needed to at first, but now, I think I don't." And so, from that moment on, she stopped herself from shaking hands. Mrs B remained in psychotherapy for nine years, and during that time, she made terrific progress in many arenas. In retrospect, I suppose that I might have stopped the handshaking sooner, but it may be that Mrs B benefited much more from having choreographed this process herself.

In the space of a short communication of this nature, I cannot provide as much intricate clinical material about Mr A and Mrs B as I would like, exploring the pros and cons of returning the handshake; instead, I have offered these very brief vignettes, as well as the comments from some of my historical predecessors, as a means of foregrounding the question of the handshake, not only as a topic in its own right, but also as a further contribution to the debate on naturalness and style, which may help us to think about whether psychoanalytic work should be conceptualised as a clinico-technical procedure with rules and recommendations, or whether it could be thought of, more profitably, as a safe, informed conversation about one's biography, or as some combination of both.

In 1983, I had the privilege of meeting Dr Muriel Gardiner (personal communication, 7 October 1983), one of the great heroines in the history of psychoanalysis. Reflecting on her analysis in Vienna before the Second World War, Gardiner told me that she and her analyst, Dr Ruth Mack Brunswick, would shake hands at the beginning and end of every single analytic hour, and that Professor Sigmund Freud would do so as well with his patients, albeit sometimes clutching only the patient's fingers, rather than the entire hand (Grinker, 1940). At times, Freud would even shake a patient's hands twice at the end of the hour (Wortis, 1934).

Dr Abram Kardiner (1977, p. 19), the American psychoanalyst who underwent a brief analysis with Freud from 1921 until 1922, underscored that, "To usher the patient into the office, Freud opened the door to the waiting room, with an extended hand coming and leaving." Professor Paul Roazen (1993, p. 27), the psychoanalytic historian who, during the 1960s, had interviewed many of Freud's surviving analysands, further elucidated, "That Freud shook hands before and after every analytic session was just a central European custom" (cf. Roazen, 1995). Dr Richard Sterba (1982, p. 35) confirmed that the pre-war Viennese psychoanalysts would shake hands with patients at both "the beginning and closing of each session", and that this would be regarded as "an established custom" (Sterba, 1982, p. 35). In similar vein, Mrs Lydia James, a London-based psychoanalyst, whom I met in 1996, told me that Dr Grete Bibring, the distinguished Viennese analyst from Freud's circle, would shake hands with her patients at the beginning and at the end of every single session, just as Freud had done (Kahr, interview with Lydia James, 12 October 1996).

Although the Viennese clasped hands quite regularly with their patients, they did, nonetheless, psychoanalyse the precise way in which patients would engage in such physical contact. As a young man in Vienna, Richard Sterba attended Dr Wilhelm Reich's seminar on psychoanalytic technique. He recalled that Reich paid especially close attention to all of the stylistic aspects of a patient's communications, which included not only the nature of the patient's voice and the way in which the patient entered the consulting room, but also the style of the handshake itself (Sterba, 1982). This close concentration on detail no doubt contributed to the development of Reich's (1925, 1933) seminal work on characterology.

The handshake proved so popular in Central Europe that not only did Freud and his predominantly Jewish Viennese colleagues shake hands with their analysands on a regular basis, but Dr Carl Gustav Jung, a Swiss Gentile, did so as well (e.g., Reith, 1975).

By contrast, I know of a colleague who underwent a very long training analysis in London during the 1970s and 1980s with a very senior, extremely eminent psychoanalytic clinician. At the end of the treatment, the candidate—now qualified—extended his hand for a final shake. But the training analyst refused to touch the patient's hand; instead, he merely stood in place with fists clenched by his sides, not wanting to "contaminate" the treatment with any physical contact. The candidate lurched out of the consulting room, feeling as though this one final gesture of rigidity had poisoned the entire experience of analysis and had thus left a most bitter taste. Years later, this particular training analyst eventually became the president of a highly respected professional organisation, and it will perhaps come as no surprise that he alienated a great many colleagues for his innumerable rigidities as a leader.

The handshake reflects, perhaps, something of the essence of the person. Years ago, I had the pleasure of interviewing Mr Hans Hoxter, a venerable man who, during his career, had worked as General Secretary of the Nursery School Association of Great Britain and Northern Ireland and as Chief Career Adviser of the London Borough of Newham, and who, in later years, became one of the key founders of the British Association for Counselling (now the British Association for Counselling and Psychotherapy). In his long lifetime he had met a wide variety of distinguished people, ranging from Mohandas Gandhi to Professeur Jean Piaget to Mrs Melanie Klein. But in our conversation he singled out two very memorable people—namely Dr Donald Winnicott, whom he had met in London, and Mrs Eleanor Roosevelt, whom he had met in Poughkeepsie, New York—for their very special, warm handshakes, stressing the importance of the handshake in forging a relationship (Kahr, interview with Hans Hoxter, 30 November 1995).

To be frank, I very much suspect that most psychotherapeutic encounters will neither succeed nor fail on the presence or absence of a handshake. Reliability, dependability, compassion, concern, thoughtfulness, insight, playfulness, and many other factors undoubtedly constitute the more important ingredients of psychotherapy and psychoanalysis. But it would behove us, as practitioners, to know that our neighbours in cognate fields would regard our dithering over a handshake as rather shocking. Dr Tiffany Field (2001, p. 15), the internationally distinguished developmental psychologist and Director of the Touch Research Institute at the University of Miami's Miller School of Medicine, in Miami, Florida, has written that, "As Freudian psychoanalysis (which discourages touch) is waning, doctors are becoming more willing to touch their patients. Some medical schools, such as Duke and Harvard, have even included touching as part of their medical school curriculum." In her book, *Touch*, Field has explored the multitudinous healing consequences of being touched appropriately, whether through therapeutic massage, acupuncture, or the physicianly or sacerdotal laying on of hands, all part of the historical tradition of healing. Field has even decried the psychoanalytic embargo on touch, citing the aforementioned Professor Karl Menninger (1958) as prototypically Freudian in his opposition to a simple handshake. Although Dr Field may not fully appreciate the thoughtfulness within psychoanalytic circles around the handshake, and the range of opinions about the handshake, I find it sobering to learn how senior researchers from *other* disciplines regard those of us committed to the Freudian style of thinking and to the continued search for secret meanings.

As we have indicated, different cultures have adopted a whole welter of approaches to the question of the handshake. According to a textbook of international etiquette, published in 1994, a handshake in Indonesia usually lasts for anywhere between ten to twelve seconds, whereas in the United States of America, most handshakes require no more than three to four seconds. In the Philippines, men shake hands with one another but will not touch a woman's hands in public unless she should offer to do so first; likewise, although men in Nicaragua greet each other with handshakes, women will be more likely to touch one another on the forearm or on the shoulder. In Turkey, one greets another person with two hands on first meeting, but only with one hand upon departure. And in Hong Kong a bow may be more typical than a handshake (Morrison, Conaway, and Borden, 1994). Thus, in view of the tremendous cultural variation in handshaking practices, we, as mental health professionals, will, no doubt, have to find a way to position ourselves in our own orbits of familiarity and acceptability.

During the late nineteenth century, the British composer Sir Arthur Sullivan had had a falling out with his long-time collaborator, the lyricist and librettist William Schwenck Gilbert. Desirous of reconciliation, Sullivan approached his comrade and intoned, "Let us meet and shake hands" (quoted in Baily, 1973, p. 105). Clearly, the clasping of hands can function as an act of reparation.

The handshake not only provides a means of meeting, but it also furnishes a great deal of useful psychological data. A little-remembered British novelist, Rayner Heppenstall (1939, p. 3), whose wife Margaret Heppenstall had once worked as secretary to Dr Donald Winnicott, observed in his novel *The Blaze of Noon*, that, "The handshake and a few words of conversation are enough. I rarely fail to receive the total impact of a woman on meeting her." Heppenstall's simple comment bristles with profundity. A handshake, followed by conversation, provides the crucial *entrée* that we require in order to undertake psychotherapeutic work.

Although mental health professionals devote much time to careful thought and reflection about every aspect of our patients' lives, perhaps—just *perhaps*—psychoanalytic practitioners often fetishise thinking and, also, fetishise tradition. And sometimes, just maybe, we dispense with what might be quite natural and ordinary and that, therefore, we "think" just a bit too much.

CHAPTER TWO

Tissues

Being Set at meat Scratch not neither Spit Cough or blow your
Nose except there's a Neceſsity for it.

George Washington, *Rules of Civility and Decent Behaviour
in Company and Conversation*, c. 1745

Every year, I spend a comparatively large amount of money on
tissues. No doubt many householders purchase a few boxes of
tissues from time to time, but I do so perhaps more regularly
than most.

I suspect that the young woman who operates the cash register
at Boots, the chemist on Hampstead High Street, must find me a bit
dotty. Each month, I come into the shop, and, instead of stocking up
on shampoo, nail clippers, shaving foam, or aspirin tablets, as all the
other customers do, I buy six or eight extremely large "Man-Size"
boxes of Kleenex at a time. Although the saleswoman does seem to
arch her eyebrow in curiosity, she has never asked me why I might
need quite so many tissues. Perhaps she has comforted herself with
the thought that I must have a particularly nasty, lingering head-cold
and might therefore need to blow my nose many, many times each day.

My fellow comrades who work in the mental health field may
have their own versions of this story, although I suspect that I have

more need of tissues than the average workaday psychotherapist. I use these "Man-Size" Kleenex for two distinct functions. First, as one might expect, I place a box of tissues on the bottom shelf of the book case in my consulting room, within easy reach of the patient's leather chair, so that in the event of a sudden stream of weeping, those who feel so inclined can help themselves and thus stem the tide of tears and mucus. But I also use the tissues for another purpose.

Although I do work with patients who sit upright in the chair, and although I do see couples and families who, likewise, adopt a vertical posture, I suspect that at least 65% of my patients use the analytic couch and, hence, will lie down. This arrangement suits both me and my patient simultaneously. The couch provides me with the opportunity to listen very acutely, unencumbered by the need to make eye contact; and the patient, similarly, can engage in the highly special experience of regressing in the service of the ego and embarking upon a magic-carpet ride of rich and intricate free association.

Of course, when patients choose to lie down, they invariably rest their heads on a pillow, placed strategically at the upper end of the couch. This raises a very important question of both technique and hygiene—namely, when patients utilise the pillow, do we provide them with some sort of coverlet, and if so, what variety should we offer? My beloved old training analyst used to have a selection of fabric squares that matched the upholstery on the couch. He claimed to have a different square for each patient and would change the squares moments before the arrival of each new analysand. In similar fashion, one of my former clinical supervisors—a playful Winnicottian—used to have a large and colourful collection of terry cloth towels—one for each patient. Another supervisor—a fervent Kleinian—used no covering at all. Each patient would rest his or her head on exactly the same battered leather pillow for decades on end.

I must confess that I warmed to none of these arrangements, and, instead, I have opted to cover my couch-pillow with two large tissues, which can be placed on the pillow shortly before the arrival of the patient and disposed of immediately after the end of the session. Perhaps other colleagues employ a similar system. Certainly, I find that this satisfies my need for cleanliness; and although all of my patients seem to have very freshly washed hair, some do have marked obsessional tendencies and would balk at having to rest their own heads on a cushion used by other people.

Whatever the most felicitous arrangement might be, I have become quite happily accustomed to this one, spreading out two large tissues for each patient prior to the start of the analytic session. Thus, I use tissues in a two-fold manner: for drying tears, and for resting the head.

As the years have unfolded, I have come to realise that the tissues function not only in practical ways, keeping the consulting room protected from dandruff and from lachrymal floods, but, additionally, the tissues serve, quite unwittingly, as a Rorschach test.

Every patient relates to the tissues in a different way. Some will reach for large handfuls of tissues, using half a box in each session, while others will not even notice that I have tissues available and will go for years without shedding a single tear. At first, I did not attribute a great deal of meaning to "tissue behaviour" in the consulting room, but, over time, I have come to realise that not only might one's relationship to tissues represent some aspect of the patient's intrapsychic life, but that any *changes* in the use or non-use of tissues over time might serve as a helpful marker of therapeutic development. I shall illustrate my thoughts on tissues with reference to seven very brief clinical vignettes.

Vignette 1:   Miss C's compulsive spitting

Having spent many years working in the field of "mental handicap", now known as "learning disabilities" or "learning difficulties" or "intellectual disabilities", I have had the privilege of providing psychotherapy for many men and women with a range of organic impairments and challenging behaviour. Miss C, a sixty-year-old schizophrenic woman, had suffered from perinatal anoxia and from a host of other symptoms. She arrived at my office at the behest of the social workers in her care home because she had become increasingly violent to staff, throwing kitchen utensils at them, including forks and knives, whenever she could. Miss C also spat compulsively, and she would bedew the consulting room floor with copious amounts of spittle during the early years of our treatment.

A lengthy and involved analysis ensued, generously supported by the care staff who escorted Miss C to and from my consulting room with supreme reliability and who waited patiently outside my office door as auxiliary "containers", as Miss C had a penchant for running out of my consulting room at regular intervals and would attempt to burst into the offices of other colleagues in my suite. Fortunately, through sustained psychotherapeutic work over eight years, Miss C became infinitely more calm, her auditory hallucinations disappeared, and she stopped attacking staff members in her residential home.

Her compulsive spitting, however, proved a more difficult symptom to shift, and it continued unabated throughout the first three years of our psychotherapeutic work. I became quite despairing, convinced that Miss C would never stop spitting. Slowly and painstakingly, we traced the spitting symptom to a childhood sexual trauma that had involved enforced fellatio. Together, we discovered that Miss C still fantasised about the semen that had become lodged in her throat; and in an effort to expel the traumatic memory of this unpalatable substance from her body, she would spit at regular intervals, hoping magically to undo the sexual assault.

Once we had begun to understand the origin of the symptom in this fashion, the behavioural spitting began to decrease in its intensity, and, after several months, Miss C would spit less frequently in sessions. On one very momentous day, during the eighth year of psychotherapeutic work, Miss C surprised me. For the very first time, she noticed the box of Kleenex perched on the bottom shelf of my bookcase, near the patient's chair. Previously, she had never clocked the tissues and certainly had never used them. But on this occasion she reached into the box and produced a lone tissue. She then stared at it very scientifically, examining it all over. Eventually, she expectorated into the tissue. And from that moment on, she would no longer spit on the floor of my office, as she had done for the previous seven years. Indubitably, her appropriate use of a tissue as a container for the imaginary toxic liquids in her mouth represented a genuine marker of progress that something *could* actually be contained and need no longer be expressed as a violent and intrusive assault.

Vignette 2:   Miss D's inability to leave an impression

Miss D suffered from anorexia nervosa. Fortunately, she had always managed to maintain a reasonable body weight, thus avoiding the need for institutional treatment. But she had always looked extremely thin, and she had always found food to be a nuisance and could not enjoy meals as a source of comfort. Miss D spoke quietly, and she wore very unassuming, colourless clothes. Sadly, she had no friends, and she complained repeatedly that whenever she walked down the street, no one would notice her. I always thought that Miss D struggled not only with a *nutritional* anorexia, but also with a *psychic* anorexia, restricting her life experiences and her capacity for zest and joy, exactly as she had done with her food.

A schizoid personality by anyone's standards, Miss D found people extremely frightening, and she would hide herself away in her tiny one-bedroom flat as much as possible. She did manage to work in an office, undertaking fairly pedestrian, non-creative tasks, and she did succeed in attending all of her psychoanalytic sessions; but afterwards, she would retreat home and would often sit in a darkened flat, not even allowing herself to watch television or to listen to music for company.

The waif-like Miss D underwent a four-times-weekly analysis with me for many, many years. During the first six years of our work, Miss D would always recline on the couch, but, unlike many of my other analysands, she would barely ever move a muscle. She remained stiff and corpse-like, whispering her words to me, moving her mouth but otherwise not stirring at all. I noticed that when she sat up at the end of the session, she had left virtually no dent at all on the two tissues spread out over the couch-pillow—a stark contrast to all the other patients, who would crumple, tear, or disturb the delicate arrangement of Kleenex.

At first, Miss D found my interpretations and other verbal interventions completely unwelcome, and she ridiculed practically everything that I said to her with great contempt. I found her impenetrable, and she treated my words phobically, exactly as she treated food and companionship. Eventually, however, as both of us persevered unwaveringly in the pursuit of therapeutic gain, Miss D began to soften, and, gradually, she started to develop a greater trust and appreciation of my long-suffering attempt to reach her.

One day, during our seventh year of psychoanalysis, Miss D arose from the couch, grabbed the large coat that hid her skeletal body, and shuffled out of my office, just as she always did. However, on this particular occasion I noticed that, for the very first time in more than one thousand sessions, Miss D had actually left a proper head-print on the tissues. It seems that, during this session, she had really allowed the pillow to carry the full weight of her head and, further, that she had shifted her position a few times during the course of the session, so that when she departed from the room, she had left the tissues in a slight state of disarray. For the very first time, it looked as though someone had actually been there.

Although research psychologists and directors of managed care companies might not be at all impressed that it had taken me seven years of traditional psychoanalytic work for Miss D to crumple a tissue, I experienced this session as a breakthrough and as a harbinger of the more profound intrapsychic changes that began to occur thereafter. Eventually, during her eighth, ninth, and tenth years of analysis, this very troubled woman found a boyfriend and had her first sexual experience—a disappointing one, it must be said, but a sexual experience nonetheless. More significantly, she began to eat enthusiastically and she eventually developed very pleasing female bodily curves, in which she took pride. Her voice became louder and richer, and she began to socialise—albeit somewhat clumsily—and, after a while, she would join her fellow workmates at the pub on an increasingly regular basis.

Miss D's capacity to dent the tissues beneath her head proved to be not only a very useful projective test of her ability to make an impression on the world, but it also helped me to keep hope alive in what had always felt like rather a weighty and colourless analysis, in spite of my many attempts to represent alertness and aliveness. Her relationship to the tissues continued to deepen, and, eventually, she developed the ability to fidget and to tear at the tissues on the couch, helping me to remember that she did have the capacity to become more awake.

Vignette 3:   Mr E's consulting room myopia

Although I found the fifty-five-year-old Mr E quite bubbly and entertaining, I could not help noticing that he suffered from extreme grandiosity and other features characteristic of a narcissistic personality configuration. An academic who had published virtually nothing, Mr E would regale me with "new" theories, which, he claimed, would set his field of specialisation ablaze, if only he could manage to put pen to paper. Mr E spoke so rapidly that I often found it difficult to create a space in which I could intervene, and I sometimes had the countertransferential fantasy that if I popped out of the consulting room for a cup of coffee in mid-session, the patient might not even realise.

Mr E seemed to notice nothing about either me or my office. Some patients might comment if I had recently had my hair cut, or if I had purchased a new pair of spectacles; others might stare at my bookcase and ruminate about some of the titles, which would trigger off a chain of associations. But Mr E remained oblivious to his surroundings, as though trapped inside a self-contained, narcissistic bubble. During the third year of twice-weekly psychoanalytic psychotherapy with Mr E, the buzzer to my office rang in the middle of one of Mr E's session. Evidently, someone had pressed the wrong bell mistakenly, thus disturbing the onslaught of Mr E's invariably self-obsessed musings. The buzzer startled him, and he wondered whether my next patient had arrived early, and whether I would have to answer the door. I replied very factually that we still had twenty-five minutes left to our session, and that someone must have rung the bell in error. To my surprise, Mr E looked around the room, until his eyes landed on the entryphone buzzer system attached to the wall, inches away from the office door. Mr E exclaimed, "I never noticed that entryphone before. Did you just have that installed?" I explained that this entryphone had been in exactly the same position for the entire duration of Mr E's psychotherapy.

Together, we began to wonder why Mr E had not noticed the very visible entryphone before. This exchange prompted some much-needed insight, as Mr E began to admit that he often does not "clock" other people and that sometimes his self-absorption lands him in "hot water" at work.

Later that week, Mr E returned for his next session. He lay on the couch, as usual, and he rested his head on the two tissues spread out on the pillow, as usual. Mr E then started to finger the tissues beneath his head and inquired, "When did you start putting tissues on the couch?" I told him frankly that I have always placed two tissues on the pillow, from the very start of his analysis with me, in fact. For the first time, Mr E paused to collect his breath, and then he announced, "I can't believe these tissues have been here all along. How could I not have noticed them before?" Naturally, I connected his sudden awareness of the tissues with his sudden awareness of the entryphone in the previous session. Gradually, Mr E began to become more cognisant of everything in the room, and everything about me. Consequently, the analysis became much richer and fuller, and through the plodding process of working-through, Mr E became increasingly less narcissistic.

Vignette 4:   Mrs F's phlegm

Unlike Miss C, who "remembered" early episodes of sexual abuse only after many years of psychotherapy, Mrs F, by contrast, knew all about her sexually traumatic past only too well. An older woman, Mrs F had survived the London Blitz during World War II because her parents had evacuated her to a farm in the North of England. Although safe from the threat of falling bombs, Mrs F and her sister both endured sexual abuse at the hands of the farmer who had offered to care for these young girls. Mrs F had vivid memories of performing fellatio on the farmer and of rushing to the bathroom afterwards in order to expectorate the semen from her mouth.

From the very outset of psychotherapy, Mrs F would cry as she told me about her early abuse, and she would also develop globus hystericus symptomatology in sessions and would start to choke. Thereafter, she would reach for the box of tissues and produce a staggering amount of phlegm, which she would then discharge into the mass of Kleenex. This anxiety attack recurred frequently during the first year of once-weekly psychotherapy—a process that Mrs F seems to have found cleansing, both physically and psychologically.

As we worked on this aspect of her history over the next two years, Mrs F finally found a way to make some peace with the internal mental representation of the persecutory farmer, and she no longer remained so tormented by the lifelong memories of the fellatio trauma. Eventually, Mrs F stopped coughing up the semen-phlegm in sessions, and ultimately she had no further use for the tissues. Whereas Miss C, the compulsive spitter, demonstrated progress by reaching for the tissues for the first time, Mrs F, by contrast, offered evidence of progress by *refraining* from using the tissues.

Vignette 5:   Mr G's fear of the Christmas break

Mr G had suffered an enormous amount of deprivation during his early childhood. He had lost all four of his grandparents before the age of five, and his elder sister had died from a severe bronchitis during Mr G's seventh year. At the age of ten, Mr G's parents sent him to an old-fashioned English boarding school, which he experienced as deeply scarring. The academic terms seemed to go on endlessly, and Mr G craved a return to his family home. At the age of eleven, Mr G packed up his trunk and waited for the family chauffeur to collect him from school and bring him back home for the Christmas holiday. Shortly after his return, he learned, shockingly, that on that very morning his father had broken his neck during a horse-riding incident and had died en route to hospital. Christmas-time would, thereafter, always be a very painful period for Mr G.

In middle age, Mr G embarked on five-times-weekly psychoanaly-sis, and he settled in rather quickly—although, as one might expect, he always feared that I would die "in harness". As our first Christmas break approached, Mr G began to have panic attacks, imagining that I would be killed in a plane crash while jetting off to the Caribbean. He lived in an understandably fearful state, and it certainly would not have occurred to him that I might choose to spend a quiet Christmas, safely at home in London.

On the Friday session before the three-week Christmas break, Mr G stood up and reached for his coat. He then said goodbye to me and wished me a pleasant Christmas rest. He turned to exit the consult-ing room, but then he walked back towards the couch and quickly plucked the tissues from atop the pillow and crammed them into his pocket. He nodded at me, and I nodded at him, and then he left.

Evidently, the tissues represented a much-needed transitional object or linking object for Mr G. In his regressed, abandoned, infan-tile state, he required concrete objects from the pillow–breast (Winni-cott, 1955) to keep with him as a token of my physical presence; and the milky white tissues no doubt served this role very adequately indeed.

Vignette 6:   Mr H's love of static objects

Some of my patients use the couch during their sessions and lie down for classical psychoanalytic work. Others, by contrast, will opt to sit upright on a chair. In the few minutes before a new "couch patient" arrives, I place the tissues on the cushion at the top of the analytic divan. Once in a rare while, a couch patient will ring up at the last moment to cancel his or her session; and, rather than removing the cushion tissues, I leave them in place, ready to be used by the next couch patient when he or she arrives later in the day. In consequence, a "chair patient" may, from time to time, enter the room and observe tissues spread out on the pillow at the head of the couch.

Mr H struggled with social relationships, preferring the company of computers, timepieces, and train timetables. One day, Mr H arrived for his session, and he noticed, instantly, that I had covered the cush-ion on the couch with tissues—something that he had never seen before in my consulting room. Some patients might have responded to the tissues as evidence that a rival patient might just have left the office, or might be coming later; other patients may have wondered what it might be like to recline on the couch. But for Mr H, preoccupied with the world of non-human objects, the tissues became items of extreme fascination, and, to my surprise, Mr H could not stop talking about them.

I then reminded Mr H that, previously, he had taken a great deal of interest in my light bulbs, having become very absorbed by the fact that one of the bulbs had stopped working and that I had not yet replaced it. I commented, collectively, on Mr H's growing fascination with the tissues and his previous fascination with my light bulb as a real indication of his excitement about physical objects in preference to people. Mr H became downcast as he recognised that his excitement about the object world protected him from the more challenging task of engaging with the human world. Thereafter, he began to relate to me more as a person than as a piece of furniture.

Vignette 7:   Mr I's and Mrs I's struggle with the tissue box

Mr I and Mrs I, a husband and wife of long standing, attended for their very first session of couple psychotherapy. Mrs I complained bitterly that she found Mr I to be very withholding in every single respect—emotionally, financially, and practically. She fumed, "He holds everything back. He keeps everything to himself!" At one point during the consultation, Mrs I started to cry and then ferreted through her handbag, searching for tissues, but could not find any. She looked around my office to see whether I had any tissues, and within seconds, believing that I had none to offer, Mrs I started to scream at me for being so withholding as well. In a calm voice, I indicated that I did, indeed, have a box of tissues available, just six inches away from her chair, and that she would be very welcome to use them.

This interchange proved most helpful, because it provided us with an immediate and powerful demonstration of the way in which Mrs I would make false accusations as a means of ridding herself of powerful and unpleasant emotions. As I came to know Mr I, the husband, better in the sessions, I found him warm and attentive to his wife—not withholding at all—but for some months to come Mrs I still had a need to portray him as a stingy, tight-lipped, tight-fisted man not unlike her own father. The story of the tissue box became a revealing and recurrent anchor point in our work and a constant reminder of the way in which Mrs I would attack first and ask questions later.

* * *

One could, of course, make reference to numerous other cases concerning the ways in which patients discuss tissues, or use tissues, or, even fail to do so, thus providing us with privileged glimpses into the mind, much as a dream or a slip of the tongue might do. Mr J, for instance, began his session by asking me for permission to take one of the tissues from the box. It then emerged that his boss had just informed him that he would soon be despatched on a crucial business trip for five weeks to a foreign country. This displeased Mr J, as he did not wish to interrupt his sessions. I interpreted that, by having asked to use a tissue, perhaps he really meant to ask whether he could have my permission to stay in London, to remain in treatment, and to really use his psychotherapy. Within moments, tears of relief began to trickle down Mr J's cheeks. And although neither he nor I could avert the business trip, I believe that he did feel a sense of immediate understanding and that the tissue provided a point of entry for what seemed to be an important moment of psychological understanding.

Another patient, Mrs K, would cry extensively and would crumple up tissues and then drop them on the floor in front of her. At the end of the session she would rise from her chair, put on her coat, and then exit the consulting room, but she would leave the used tissues on the floor for me to clear up. After this ritual had occurred on several successive weeks, I debated how best to intervene. Gradually, I managed to formulate an interpretation linking her early experience of being sent to boarding school—which pained her greatly—to her treatment of the tissues. Once, when recounting a tale of having had to say goodbye to her neglectful parents, she burst into tears and reached for a tissue. I reminded her that, over the last few meetings, she had left her tissues on the floor, unattended, and that perhaps she wished to provide me with a concrete experience of how, in childhood, she had felt like a used, abandoned, wet tissue, having to wait by herself in the rain on the platform of the local station, en route to her school far away. Once we began to discuss these sorts of experiences in greater detail, Mrs K remembered to pick up her tissues and would then no longer scatter them mindlessly on the floor.

In preparation for writing this essay, I asked several of my colleagues about tissues. Very few had anything particularly edifying to report. But one woman informed me that she keeps several boxes of tissues in her office—one by the patient's chair, one by the couch, and another on the table beside her own chair. She told me that she regards analysts who hide their tissues as sadistic. Another colleague opined that the tissues must be kept discreetly out of view, so that the patient will not be bombarded by tissues, in case he or she should feel that all tears must be wiped up immediately. And still another colleague, an elderly male psychoanalyst, informed me that he offers no tissues at all. He brusquely explained that in this day and age, patients who might require tissues could very well bring their own. After all, he announced, if he provided tissues, then his analysands might also expect tea and coffee.

Yet another colleague told me that one ought to dispense with any tissues because, in point of fact, the *psychoanalyst* should function as the tissue, mopping up the patient's projections.

As with so many matters of technique, our senior instructors never teach us about tissues in "shrink school"; consequently, each of us must find his or her own way of furnishing our consulting rooms, and of understanding how our analysands either use or do not use these furnishings as communications and as expressions of their unconscious structures and their internal worlds. Personally, I have found the tissue to be a remarkably little studied aspect of our work, yet one that provides us with a veritable Rorschach test of the patient's intrapsychic state. Of greatest importance, the use of the tissue serves as a key marker of progress within the course of a long and sometimes "stuck" treatment experience. Thus, a closer scrutiny of the tissue behaviours of our analysands may yield interesting returns for the practitioner and, ultimately, for the course of the psychotherapeutic treatment itself.

CHAPTER THREE

The ten-minute gap

What is this life if, full of care,
We have no time to stand and stare.
No time to stand beneath the boughs
And stare as long as sheep or cows.

William Henry Davies, "Leisure", in *Songs of Joy and Others*, 1911
[Davies, 1911, p. 15]

Every morning, I unlock the door to my consulting room at approximately 6.35 a.m., sometimes even earlier. I do so for several reasons. First of all, I need to ensure that I arrive well before my first patient, whose session begins at 7.00 a.m. Additionally, I must switch on the lights, turn on the heating on winter days, and place large tissues over the pillow on the couch, so that each patient will have a hygienic coverlet on which to rest the head. I also scan through my appointment diary, refresh myself about the previous day's work, and prepare myself for the day ahead.

After years of practice, my patients tend to arrive with utter precision, and the bell will ring promptly at 7.00 a.m. I undertake my work with the patient in question for the requisite fifty-minute hour, and then, at 7.50 a.m., precisely, I shift in my seat behind the couch and uncross my legs, thus indicating in a subtle yet clear manner that the session must now end. The patient sits up from the couch, retrieves coat, umbrella, and briefcase, and heads for the door. I now have a *ten-minute gap* before my 8.00 a.m. analysand arrives.

Our professional psychological literature consists of a myriad of books and articles that detail what happens *during* the course of a fifty-minute hour, but these many publications contain virtually nothing at all about what happens *between* these fifty-minute hours, during that much-practised, much-needed, but little theorised, ten-minute gap. At various points in my day, across my working week, and throughout my clinical career, I have utilised the ten-minute gaps in different ways and for different purposes; and I hope that colleagues will permit me to reflect about this seemingly trivial but, I would suggest, quite vital transitional space in which one bids good-bye to patient "A" before greeting patient "B".

I do appreciate, of course, that not all of us space our appointments on the hour, or that all of us work in fifty-minute chunks; in fact, some may see clients or analysands for as few as forty-five minutes or, indeed, for as many as sixty minutes. Those who practise in the Lacanian vein might rely upon the so-called "shortened session" or the "variable session", and I have met at least one Lacanian psychoanalyst who will, from time to time, stop sessions after only twenty minutes! But in Great Britain, at least, fifty minutes remains the gold standard for session length among most of my colleagues within the psychotherapeutic milieu.

However, not all of us allow ourselves a ten-minute gap. I know many people who schedule patients with a mere five-minute breather at 7.00 a.m., 7.55 a.m., 8.50 a.m., 9.45 a.m., and so on, throughout the day. Indeed, Dr David Forsyth, the pioneering British psychoanalyst, indulged in just such a practice. As he explained

> Even allowing for unexpectedly vacant hours the physician would soon become tired by the close succession of a number of cases and the continuous attention required of him hour after hour, to say nothing of the cramped feeling after sitting so long at work. To obviate this he might allow himself half-an-hour or more of free time now and again, but a better plan is to leave five minutes free every hour—*i.e.*, each patient begins five minutes after the hour, the "hour" really being fifty-five minutes. [Forsyth, 1922, p. 30]

Analysed in Vienna by Professor Sigmund Freud, Forsyth may have adhered to the fifty-five-minute hour in emulation of the father of psychoanalysis, who, likewise, permitted himself only a five-minute gap each hour across his long working day (Jones, 1955).

Others do not even allow themselves so much as five minutes and take absolutely no break whatsoever between patients, operating something more akin to a conveyor belt system. As one of my colleagues explained, "I don't really need a break. I would rather bunch patients up without a break. This way, I get to see more patients, and go home earlier." Indeed, if one works with, for instance, eight patients per day and honours the ten-minute gap, this will keep one in the office for, at minimum, a good seven hours and fifty minutes. But by shaving away the gap to *five* minutes, eight patients would therefore consume only seven-and-a-quarter hours of time. And by eliminating the break completely, treating eight patients without any pauses would necessitate a mere six hours and forty minutes in the consulting room. Thus, preserving one's ten-minute break adds, automatically, one hour and twenty minutes *extra* per day—enough time in which one could treat at least one more patient, or start one hour later, or go home one hour earlier. Keeping the ten-minute gap adds not only an additional eighty minutes to the working day, but another four hundred minutes to the ordinary working week, and more than eighteen thousand minutes—in other words, three hundred hours— to the clinical year (based on an average year of forty two weeks).

I now realise that I spend approximately twelve-and-a-half days *more* per year in my consulting room than Dr X, who has no use for the break whatsoever. Should I, therefore, shorten my gap to five minutes or, indeed, eliminate it completely? Or should I, in fact, lengthen the gap to twenty minutes, as in the case of the colleague reported in Mrs Pauline Hodson's marvellous book *The Business of Therapy: How to Succeed in Private Practice*? This particular clinician noted that she "felt a seismic change for the better when she decided to have a 20-minute break between sessions" (Hodson, 2012, p. 78).

Personally, I shall continue to preserve my ten-minute gap because, quite frankly, it suits me very well indeed. When I worked in private practice, years ago, on a very part-time basis, I had less of a need for gaps. If, for example, I wished to see two patients in the late afternoon or early evening after completing my teaching and clinic duties, I did not find this at all physically taxing. Indeed, compared to my other jobs, I experienced my private practice as rather quiet and relaxing by contrast, affording me the luxury of focusing on only one person at a time, unlike a teaching context in which one has to fend off hordes of hungry students. But now that I work full-time in private practice, the break has become even more essential.

What happens in the ten-minute gap? After years of fine-tuning, I have now developed the use of these ten precious minutes into something of an art form. As soon as the first patient leaves the room, I first remove the tissues from the pillow, discard the used ones, and then replace them with fresh ones for the next patient. This generally consumes about thirty seconds. Just before I substitute new tissues for old, I do scrutinise the state of those used tissues very carefully. As my practice has unfolded over the years, I have come to realise that I can often learn a great deal about a patient by examining the state of the tissues and, also, the coverlet on the couch after the patient has departed. As I have already indicated, those who leave no imprint on the tissue whatsoever will, in fact, be recreating the quiet, withdrawn, mousey attitude that characterises their daily interactions in the outside world. Those who squirm aggressively, ripping the tissues in the process, will be conveying something about their obstreperousness, or their grandiose need to consume space, as well as their need to make an impact. As I indicated in the previous chapter, I always know that I have begun to make a difference as a clinician when I can detect a change in the state of the tissues.

After absorbing myself in the psychodynamics of tissues, I then dial my answering service to check for any telephone messages on my land-line, and then do so, likewise, with my mobile telephone. Depending upon the number of messages that I may have received between patients, this can take up to two or three minutes. I will return only urgent calls or demonstrably short calls during the ten-minute break. Otherwise, I would have to be rushed, and one risks being rude to one's caller by prefacing one's remarks in manic manner: "I'm just between patients, so I shall have to be quick." Calls that will, I suspect, require more uninterrupted time must wait until the end of the working day.

Having dealt with the tissues and the telephone, I now have a luxurious choice as to how I shall spend the remaining five minutes. I tend to place bodily needs above all others at this point, and as I age, I find I have more frequent need for a sip of tea or coffee or water, or for a bite of an apple, or, indeed, for a comfort break. Occasionally, I will call my spouse, just to "check in", or I might glance at my incoming post. I do not keep either a computer or a laptop in my consulting room, because the presence of a visible piece of machinery might be too provocative for certain patients and would, in all likelihood, be too distracting for me. I do not deal with e-mails and other professional correspondence until the working day has ended. If someone needs to reach me more urgently, he or she can always telephone.

Sometimes, I use the last five minutes of the gap to jot down some pertinent notes for my private clinical files, or, if I need to record the details of a particularly resonant dream or fantasy, I will do so while the material remains quite fresh in my mind. Alternatively, I might use the five minutes to peruse my bookshelves, check a bibliographic reference, or flip through the pages of a journal. I discovered long ago that it makes little sense to attempt to read two pages of a textbook or an article in a five-minute window, as one would barely absorb more than a small portion of the work; instead, I might set my sights on scanning a brief book review in an academic journal, which can be read successfully in only a mere matter of minutes. And if I should feel at all stiff from a long spell of sitting, I might stretch my arms and legs. Professor Joan Raphael-Leff (2002), a psychoanalytic colleague in London, has written a wonderful chapter full of practical stretching exercise suggestions for the busy clinician, which I recommend heartily.

After my private practice grew in size and I found myself managing a full complement of patients, I suddenly realised that I need not use the five-minute or ten-minute gap for any particular purpose. I joyfully discovered one day that I could, in fact, simply sit in my chair and relax, allowing my mind to go blank for a few moments, as a crucial means of creating mental space before the arrival of the next patient. Alternatively, I might review my notes about the incoming patient in order to refresh my memory about where we had left off in the last session.

On billing day—the first of the month—I use the ten-minute gap to place each patient's bill into an envelope, which I then put on the window ledge near my chair, so that I can easily hand this to the patient at the end of the session. I always bill patients on the first day of each calendar month for their previous month's sessions.

No doubt there may be other very good uses of the ten-minute gap. Professor Sigmund Freud would often emerge from his consulting room between sessions and make a brief appearance in the family quarters of his Viennese apartment. Freud's inter-session behaviour reminded his niece Mrs Judith Bernays Heller of the little man who pops out of cuckoo clocks (Roazen, 1993).

Other psychoanalysts and psychotherapists have used the gap in their own special ways. I recently discovered a marvellous passage about the ten-minute gap in Miss Dorothy Gardner's elegant biography of the pioneering British developmental psychologist and psychoanalyst Dr Susan Isaacs. Gardner (1969, p. 131) recalled, "She certainly packed a great deal into her life and was an adept at not wasting the odd ten minutes. I have known her use such an interval for adding a paragraph or two to a book or article. She could also relax equally quickly and, if needed, could use the ten minutes for a refreshing nap." Dr Donald Winnicott, too, used his ten-minute gap in creative fashion. While researching the biography of Dr Winnicott, I had the opportunity to interview his long-standing secretary, Mrs Joyce Coles, on many occasions. She told me that Winnicott would use the time between sessions for two purposes: either he would pop down the corridor from his consulting room to Mrs Coles's office in order to dictate notes about the most recent patient session (Kahr, interview, 18 December 1994), or, indeed, he would bound upstairs to his drawing room and play some chords with gusto on his John Broadwood piano (Winnicott, 1978; Kahr, interview with Joyce Coles, 15 January 1995; Kahr, 1996a). Perhaps if I had a secretary or, indeed, a piano in my consulting room, I would do likewise.

In thinking about the ten-minute gap, one must appreciate that one will not always have a full ten minutes at one's disposal. For instance, although most patients leave their sessions in a reasonably integrated manner, some find themselves in a temporary regressive state of mind or will be more permanently enmired in a deep psychic encumbrance. Such individuals often take a great deal of time to leave the consulting room. I shall never forget a female patient whom I saw many, many years ago—a survivor of a series of actual physical tortures during childhood in a country overseas. This deeply traumatised woman would stand up at the end of her session and would take at least five or six minutes to put on her shoes, her coat, her gloves, and so forth, securing each button in the most painfully slow-motion manner that one could imagine, thus revealing a great deal about her depression, her fear of leaving, and, some might argue, her aggression in consuming a greater amount of my time than we had contracted. Those who overstay their welcome in such a way will often evoke a certain amount of countertransferential annoyance or hatred, which one must tolerate. Hopefully, as treatment progresses, each patient will manage to adhere more successfully to the fifty-minute hour and not stretch it to fifty-five minutes. Still others come early, even though I do impose a carefully articulated boundary, having initially requested that all of my patients endeavour to ring the bell of my office door exactly on time. I would estimate that approximately ninety percent of patients do so with great precision and reliability.

The ten-minute gap constitutes a crucial but, often, neglected component of the psychotherapeutic and psychoanalytic situation—one that will be known to every single practitioner of the mental health arts—but it remains an aspect of our work about which we rarely speak or write. In summary, the ten-minute gap can be utilised in a number of ways. It provides each of us with an opportunity for setting up the room for the next patient, for taking notes, for reading, for eating, drinking, or peeing, for making telephone calls, and for attending to a variety of other practical tasks. Additionally, and perhaps more importantly, the ten-minute gap offers a space in which one can contemplate and reflect upon one's work. And it allows us to discharge potent affects by sighing or huffing after a particularly vexing patient has left the room. Finally, by reading literature, or by chatting on the telephone, the ten-minute gap permits each of us to enjoy a small moment of contact with the outside world.

In terms of the clinician's state of mind, we can approach the ten-minute interval in at least three different ways. By rushing around the room, with a telephone in one hand, a tea kettle in the other, and a box of tissues gripped between our teeth, we move into a manic mode, avoiding the anxiety of clinical work by endeavouring to perform too many practical tasks. Or, we can become depressive, aware of the slow, painstaking, uncertain nature of our labours, and of the potential for loneliness when working psychologically in a quiet room with very ill individuals. But as a third possibility, we might also try to find a way of using the space creatively, by allowing the ten-minute gap, rather like the dream, to help us to consolidate experience, to evacuate projections, to prepare for the arrival of the new analysand, and to enjoy a moment of transitional reverie. Over the years, I have known all three of these ten-minute gap states of mind.

Might ten minutes between sessions be too much time? Might ten minutes be not quite enough time? Does it really matter how we use the time?

Every practitioner will have rather a different theory about this special and unusual space that separates our working day into segments, and it would be useful to hear views from other colleagues. Some may regard the ten minutes as a bit of "throwaway" time that could be used more efficiently. I strongly endorse the view that the ten-minute gap serves essential psychological as well as pragmatic functions and that, above all, it allows for the creation of a *psychic welcome mat*, so that one can transmit a message to the next analysand, both consciously and unconsciously, that his or her hour has arrived and that each of us as a clinician will be ready to offer a temporary home for the next fifty minutes.

One can, of course, become rather obsessional about such time-keeping matters. Who can forget Leo Tolstoy's description of the maddening Prince Nikolái Andreevich Bolkónski in the 1865 master-work *Voyna i mir* [*War and Peace*]? Tolstoy described the prince thus: "As the prime condition of successful activity is order, order in his household was exacted to the utmost. He always appeared at meals in precisely the same circumstances, and not only at the same hour but at the same minute." Certainly, Freud shared this characteristic (Roazen, 1993; Freud-Marlé, 2006).

But good time-keeping need not be a tyranny or even an irritation. Years ago, I attended clinical supervision with a very senior psycho-analyst, who taught me an enormous amount about our profession. My clinical work improved greatly under his tutelage, as did my confidence in general. My supervision session commenced precisely at 2.25 p.m. and ended, therefore, at *3.15 p.m.* But I always regretted that my supervisor's very next session, with a rather fragile-looking patient, began at *exactly 3.15 p.m.* The supervisor would, therefore, keep lecturing me on my session notes until *3.14 p.m.* and then whisk me out the door while beckoning the patient in at the same time. I doubt that this method of exiting and entering helped the poor patient. It certainly made me feel rather guilty, as though I had become an intruder into that person's psychoanalytic hour, leaving the room as I did in a sometimes confident, collegial manner, having just learned a great deal more about my own patient through a very helpful supervision. I wish that as a young man I had had the courage to tell my supervisor that he might want to consider instituting the ten-minute gap. After all, the days of assembly-line private practices should, by now, be long over (Greenson, 1974).

The gaps between sessions evaporate quickly. But they do offer an opportunity for rest and repose, for stretching, for a sip of water, for a call of nature, or what have you. As the existentialist psychoanalyst Professor Rollo May (1975, p. 131) explained, "All of the gaps are automatically filled by our imagination." The mind continues to work, and the ten-minute gap permits us to breathe.

Our patients deserve to consult with a clinician who has had, at the very least, a token symbolic five-minute or ten-minute rest in-between appointments. The mental health practitioner needs this and deserves this as well!

CHAPTER FOUR

On painting the consulting room

They looked blankly at the object before them, but through it, as it were, and into the grief beyond. In moments of pain, have you not looked at some indifferent object so?

William Makepeace Thackeray, "Autour de mon chapeau", 1863

S ome years ago, I arranged for my consulting room to be redecorated. The administrator of the office building in which I work notified me that, during the upcoming summer holiday, some painters and decorators would be undertaking repairs, replastering and repainting the hallways, and she wondered whether I might wish to avail myself of the opportunity to have them spruce up my office as well. As I had not updated the décor of my consulting room in quite a while, I responded with enthusiasm and arranged for new paint on the walls, fresh carpet on the floors, as well as more modern chairs and pictures. The work began on 1 August, at the start of the analytic summer holiday, and finished in plenty of time before my return to work on 1 September.

In spite of the cosmetic changes, I did, however, keep my stalwart analytic couch. In fact, I have used the same couch for approximately thirty-five years. It has served me well, supporting patients both concretely and psychologically. I know that my analysands have become quite attached to this particular couch, as have I, and thus, I saw no reason to purchase a new one.

The workmen undertook the refurbishment in a most straightforward manner, and the new chairs arrived in goodly time. Before long, the room looked much more zestful, and, in spite of the lingering smell of new paint and new carpets (which would soon fade), I returned to work with an extra spring in my step, enjoying my revivified surroundings, which I surveyed from my comfortable new leather chair.

I suspected that patients would, in time, notice the various changes, but I had no preconceptions about how each particular person would respond. Early on Monday morning, Ms L entered the room and lay on the couch. She immediately clocked the transformation and chirped straight away, "You've got new carpets. That fits my mood perfectly. I found a new boyfriend over the summer. He's older than I am, but he's lovely. I feel that the new carpets are symbolic of what I hope will be a new chapter for me." In retrospect, this response seemed to be a perfect representation of Ms L, and of her approach to object relations. A reasonably healthy, high-functioning patient, Ms L would often adopt a cheery, if not bubbly, attitude, sometimes to her detriment, but often to her benefit. Certainly, I would not describe her as manic or even as hypomanic. Ms L's instant association to new carpets as harbingers of new relationships struck me as not only characteristic, but also as delightfully admirable.

Mr M arrived one hour later, and, with a dramatic flourish, he collapsed into the chair across the room, as he had never used the couch. Mr M had endured a difficult summer break and had to fend off creditors to whom he owed a great deal of money. He allowed his head to flop back against the top of the chair, and then he stared at the ceiling. "Ah, the crack up there is gone", he sighed. This observation instantly unleashed a chain of associations about the cracks in his life, and about his anxieties that *he* might crack up from all of his many work pressures and marital upheavals. I wondered what he thought about the fact that we had had a long summer break and that, upon returning from this break, he had discovered that I had repaired *my* crack in the ceiling, whereas he still had many cracks remaining, and that, perhaps, he felt cross with me for having left him during the month of August without a psychological plasterer or painter. He chuckled affectionately at this fairly simple transference interpretation and told me that he could have used a session or two with me over the break, but that he felt pleased to be back nevertheless, so that we could resume our work. Mr M then quipped, "I really need some spackle for the inside of my head."

Mr N, a five-times-weekly psychoanalytic patient, returned from his summer break and lay on the couch in a state of utter hopelessness. He had missed both me and his sessions over the four-week recess, and although he could acknowledge that I might have had need of an opportunity to re-charge my internal batteries, he resented me for having done so, especially as I had left him all alone. Throughout the next fifty minutes, he made absolutely no reference at all to the freshly painted, newly carpeted room, but, as he grabbed his coat and headed towards the exit, he stared at one of the recently acquired pictures on my wall—actually a beautiful framed photograph of a street scene—and muttered, "That picture looks as black as I feel." Interestingly, most people who have seen this picture respond to it with a smile, but Mr N felt internally wretched, and hence he viewed this photograph, projectively, through his own particular lens.

One by one, my patients resumed their regular session times: intensive psychoanalytic patients found their way back to the couch, and once-weekly or twice-weekly psychotherapy patients returned to their chair, as did marital couples. Gradually, each patient found some means of acknowledging the external changes in the consulting room, providing me with recognisable glimpses of his or her internal world.

Mr O and Mrs O, an elderly married couple, with whom I had worked for some time, made absolutely no direct, conscious reference to the bright walls and the pristine carpet, or to the new chairs and pictures. But they must have absorbed the atmosphere because, within a short period of time, Mrs O began to bemoan the state of her marital home, which she described as run-down, shabby, and neglected. She lamented, "God, I just don't understand why it takes us so long to tidy up. We haven't cleaned out our dining room in ten years." This comment, arguably shaped by the new surroundings, permitted me to explore the long-standing inhibitions that had prevented them from functioning as a creative couple who might become sufficiently lively and might, thus, clean up the house together, both practically as well as metaphorically.

Mr P and Mrs P, another marital pair, noticed the changes instantly. A very wealthy couple, obsessed with material possessions at the expense of internal riches, they joked, "You'd better not raise your fee to pay for these new chairs." I commented about how quickly

Mr P and Mrs P related to me and to one another in terms of finances and furnishings, and that perhaps this felt more comfortable than acknowledging that we had had a break and that we had not seen each other for several weeks. This observation unleashed a useful conversation about how the external world becomes privileged over the internal world, and about how neither of them had ever managed to acknowledge the absence or presence of the other.

Mr Q, a young, unmarried man who worked in the advertising business, clocked, quite accurately, the fresh coat of paint in the hallway *outside* the consulting room, but seemed not to notice any new paint *inside* the consulting room itself. In fact, he went so far as to admonish me, "The hallway out there looks so much better. You should get your room painted too." I debated whether to remain silent or whether to affirm that I had, in fact, repainted the office. In the end, I opted for the latter solution and wondered aloud why Mr Q had noticed the new paint in the dimly lit outside hallway, but not the new paint in the reasonably well-lit consulting room, which he knows extremely well. This comment permitted us to explore how, as a salesman in advertising, Mr Q has to relate to people superficially. Eventually, he himself admitted, "I only know the outside of people, never the inside." This thoughtful observation opened up a rich canvas of conversations in future sessions.

Mr R, a traditionally "macho" sports enthusiast, had come to see me at the insistence of his wife, who claimed that Mr R had managed to bypass the entire feminist movement; indeed, she complained that she had married an "emotional Neanderthal" who would never inquire about her feelings, about her inner world, or about her dreams and aspirations, and that her husband would never even notice what she wore. As Mr R told me many times, he would return home nightly from his exhausting office job and plonk himself on the sofa, drinking beer and watching television, causing his wife to become apoplectic with rage. By the time I had repainted the consulting room, Mr R had already spent four years with me in psychotherapy, and he had become much more emotionally sophisticated in consequence. After the summer break, Mr R returned for his sessions, and within moments he remarked, "You've painted the door to your office. It looks nice. But I have to tell you, I'm not crazy about the colour." I smiled quietly as Mr R lay on the couch. He had noticed that I had repainted the door to the consulting room, but he seemed to be consciously unaware that I had also repainted the four walls, had hung new pictures, and had installed new carpet and chairs. In many respects, his rather restricted observation about the door to the office made me realise that although his sensitivities had improved, he still had much more to notice about the "feminine" matters of home and hearth. I also felt pleased that he could offer an opinion about the colour of the door. Previously, he would not have engaged with colours or fabrics or textures at all.

Mr S, a hugely narcissistic patient who attended five times weekly, made no reference to the changes in the room whatsoever. He seemed not to have any inkling that I had redecorated the consulting room. Indeed, Mr S's silence proved rather striking in comparison to the other patients, virtually all of whom had made at least *some* acknowledgement of the new décor. After one week of sessions, I heard absolutely nothing in Mr S's material that might have made me suspect that he had become aware of the paint and the carpets—not even covertly. I struggled as to whether I might say something to Mr S, or whether I should allow him the right not to notice. After six consecutive sessions, Mr S had still not uttered a peep about the changes in the consulting room, but he did complain bitterly about a business colleague who had withdrawn from an important deal, accusing Mr S of being "completely self-centred". Mr S found his colleague's accusation rather laughable, claiming, as most severe narcissists do, that he has no narcissistic features whatsoever. I then made a quiet comment that perhaps there may be times when the rest of the world disappears from his view, and I then remarked on his failure to notice the changes in the consulting room as a case in point. Mr S sat bolt upright on the couch and looked around the room, utterly horrified that he could have avoided so much data about the "outside world" for so long. In the end, this proved to be a most useful interchange.

Ms T noticed the painted walls instantly, and she complimented me on the refurbishment, telling me how the new colours struck her as rather warm and welcoming. Two weeks later, however, Ms T reported a dream in which I had evicted her from analysis and had forbidden her to return. As I encouraged the patient to articulate her free associations to the dream, Ms T told me that she thought at once about the new paint in my office. She confessed, "When I first saw the paint-job, I got really happy, because the room looked so good. But then, as I began to think about it more, I thought that you must have had workmen here over the summer, invading this room. And that sickens me." As a woman who had survived several different types of sexual abuse in childhood and in adulthood, the presence of strange men in the cosy consulting room made her feel rather unsafe, and at one point she became slightly paranoid and thought that I might have invited the workmen into the office specially, in order to test her in some way. Eventually, we worked through these anxieties, and although Ms T found the conversation somewhat painful, this incident did afford us an opportunity to explore her fears of penetration and invasion.

Throughout the week, each patient made other conscious or unconscious observations. Mr U did not seem to notice the repainted consulting room, but he did wonder whether I had had a haircut over the summer or whether I had lost weight, as he thought that I looked slightly different. Another analysand, Mrs V, commented upon the newly refreshed consulting room, which delighted her, and she praised me for *my* ability to change and not to remain stagnant. Still another patient, Ms W, told me that the new colours on my wall reminded her of her childhood nursery, which she had hated. And Mr X—a black man—associated that the walls of my office now seemed to be darker and, therefore, more "user-friendly" to a man of colour.

As a final example, I must mention Mr Y, a mentally very chaotic and disorganised person, who always paid his psychotherapy bills erratically and who often forgot to bring his chequebook for months at time. Mr Y suffered a very profound reversal in his business affairs in the wake of Great Britain's economic recession of 2008, and as a consequence he started to pay my bills much later than usual. It took Mr Y nearly *four years* to notice that I had painted the office, and I found myself really struck and surprised when he entered the consulting room in 2012 and announced, "Gosh, you've got new chairs." I did explain that I had had these chairs for quite some time, but that perhaps he had finally begun to notice certain external realities. In the next session, he settled his outstanding bill.

Painting the consulting room hardly qualifies as a landmark moment in the psychotherapies and psychoanalyses of the patients with whom I have worked. In many respects, this episode deserves no more comment than a routine summer break, an unplanned absence due to winter flu, or a cancellation of a session for personal reasons—the sorts of events that constitute the ordinary bread and butter of psychoanalytic work. But I would also regard such inevitable events, including redecoration, as both impingements into the fabric of psychoanalytic regularity and opportunities for examination of the impact of these unavoidable intrusions of everyday life.

Having now had the chance to reflect on the repainting my office, I can report with good cheer that this experience has damaged no one. Everyone survived the new coat of paint. But the redecorating process, and the reaction of my patients, helped to underscore the very powerful impact of unconscious mental processes and the very deeply entrenched nature of character structure. In other words, because each patient responded to the paint in his or her own particular idiopathic style, no two patients had exactly the same reaction to the new walls and to the new chairs. Some became distressed, some became calmed, and some reacted with indifference at first and then more strongly later on. This experience—a controlled experiment of sorts—allowed me to appreciate better the way in which a full-time mental health clinician must always be on the alert, never assuming that any two patients will respond to the same seemingly simple event in the very same manner. Each clinician must, therefore, always maintain a huge sensitivity to the complex vicissitudes of the constantly shifting transferences that may be evoked.

My consulting room, like those of most modern mental health professionals, might best be described as relatively neutral. Yes, of course, I do have books and papers, a telephone with answering machine, a kettle for tea tucked away discreetly on a window ledge, and so forth; but unlike Sigmund Freud, I do not use the office to house a very large collection of antiquities. One wonders whether Freud's patients became engaged by his hobby or whether they became distracted each time he "repainted" his room with a new importation of an ancient artefact.

Clinicians have spent so much time concentrating on the *internal* furniture in the minds of our patients that we have written very little about the actual *external* physical atmosphere that each practitioner creates. This seems to me a fruitful area for ongoing thinking and reflection. Indeed, some years ago, on a visit to London, my American colleague, Professor Peter Rudnytsky, came to my office, and he expressed surprise that my chair and the couch actually abut one another quite closely, remarking that many American colleagues, by contrast, leave a much larger gap between the analyst's chair and the patient's couch. He also expressed surprise that I have a completely flat couch with one pillow, whereas many American psychoanalysts have an arched couch with a raised headrest. Although these details might seem trivial, it may be that the very precise arrangement of chair and couch will make an enormous difference as to the amount of regression that our patients will experience. I urge colleagues to share further observations and thoughts about the external furnishings of their offices, and about how these might impact upon our patients' internal furnishings.

CHAPTER FIVE

The bookshelf

Come and take choyſe of all my Library.

"Titus", in William Shakespeare, *The Most Lamentable Romaine Tragedie
of Titus Andronicus: As it was Plaide by the Right Honourable the Earle of
Darbie, Earle of* Pembrooke, *and Earle of* Suſſex *their Seruants*,
c. 1588–1593, Act IV, scene i, line 34

Recently, I visited the new home of two dear old friends. Both lawyers, they had just moved from a large house on the outskirts of London into a reasonably small flat in the centre of town. In order to accommodate their more modest spatial circumstances, my friends had done a "cull" of their personal library. Apparently, they had no choice. As I glanced at their reduced library, I wondered aloud how they had decided which books would be executed and which would survive. As the husband looked somewhat bereft, the wife explained, "We made a ruthless decision. If neither of us had opened a certain book during the last ten years, then we sent it to the charity shop. Plain and simple." I quaked inside. How could one possibly discard a precious volume in such a cavalier fashion? After all, if one had not talked to a certain cherished old friend for more than ten years, one might still be happy to resume contact. Surely?

My friends merely chortled at my hypersensitivity about their discarded books. In fact, over many years, I have had to arrive at the painful conclusion that not everyone suffers from advanced bibliophilia, as I do.

Ever since early childhood, I have always enjoyed my books. As the son of parents who collected antiquarian tomes, I grew up savouring leather-bound volumes as great aesthetic thrills. But I have not only enjoyed the books that I have read at home, I have also relished my trips to the library, those great temples devoted to the care and protection of these remarkable objects.

The American author, Emily Dickinson, had long ago found just the right words to describe what those of us with a bibliophilic disposition often experience when we enter one of those magnificent storehouses. In her poem, "In a Library", penned sometime in the nineteenth century, Miss Dickinson opined:

> A precious, mouldering pleasure 't is
> To meet an antique book,
> In just the dress his century wore;
> A privilege, I think.

Other great writers have extolled the pleasures of the library in more fulsome words, among them the mid-twentieth-century American, Betty Smith, who, in her novel *Joy in the Morning*, described so beautifully the delight experienced by "Annie Brown", a teenage newlywed, whose husband, "Carl Brown", a struggling law student attending a Midwestern college in the 1920s, allows her to borrow his precious library card. As Smith (1963) described,

> Now it was time to go to the library. She prepared for it the way a girl prepares for a party. She bathed and dusted herself with talcum powder; put on fresh makeup. She changed into her other slip, brassière, and pair of step-ins. She brushed her hair, annoyed with the defective brush and aware that no matter how she arranged her long hair, she'd look out of place among the bob-haired coeds. [1963, p. 51]

Smith explained further that

> Annie climbed the wide steps and entered the library with the exultant reverence an art lover has entering the Louvre for the first time. She believed what Carl had told her—that there were more than a million books in that library. [p. 51]

Indeed,

> She went from room to room, floor to floor, stack to stack, reveling in books, books, books. She loved books. She loved them with her senses and her intellect. The way they smelled and looked; the way they felt in her hands; the way the pages seemed to murmur as she turned them. Everything there is in the world, she thought, is in books. [p. 52]

Ultimately,

> It was like old times to Annie to come upon *David Copperfield* in the "D" rack. She smiled at the book and said, "Hello, David", then looked around embarrassed, hoping no one had heard her. [p. 52]

When one savours the poetry of Emily Dickinson and the prose of Betty Smith, one realises, with great relief, that one has friends of similarly bibliophilic persuasions.

Fortunately, I have always appreciated that books—blissful refuges though they may be—rather pale in comparison to interpersonal exchanges. As the seventeenth-century French aphorist, François, the Duc de la Rochefoucauld, observed in his *Réflexions ou sentences et maximes morales* [*Reflections or Sentences and Moral Maxims*] written between 1665 and 1678, "Il est plus nécessaire d'étudier les hommes que les livres" ["It is more important to study people than books"]. And with that end in mind, I have long harboured a fascination with the ways in which patients relate to the books in my office.

As I practise from an ordinary-sized consulting room, I have very limited space in which to store my books at work. In fact, I keep most of my library at home. In spite of the recommendation of my Freudian forebears that one should provide patients with a neutrally furnished consulting room (i.e., "Spartan"), I have always had two large standing bookshelves in my office, each positioned on the far wall, across from my chair, and across the room from the analytic couch. Most of my patients treat these bookshelves as old furniture; indeed, I have had these same wooden containers for years, and they have not changed. They have simply become part of the fabric of the office. But, from time to time, some of my patients will engage with these two lone bookshelves in a more animated fashion.

When Mr Z first saw the books on my shelves, he felt quite overwhelmed, and he gawped, "My God, I've never seen so many books in my life." I had to resist the urge to reply, "Really? But this is *nothing*. These two bookshelves are just the tiniest overspill of my proper library." Of course, I restrained myself from speaking. Indeed, I soon came to realise that Mr Z had grown up in the most impoverished of homes—impoverished financially, and impoverished emotionally. His parents kept absolutely no books at their council flat other than the Bible; moreover, they never read to Mr Z during his childhood, and, certainly, they never took him to a library. No one else would be at all overwhelmed by my two bookshelves, but Mr Z found them quite shocking. This simple response to a simple stimulus taught me a very great deal about this particular patient's home environment—much more, in fact, than I had learned from a more straightforward recitation of his early memories and impressions.

Mrs AA, a woman who grew up in France, had many anxieties that I might not be able to understand her. She had a thick French accent, and quite a number of British people had found her to be off-putting. As a French speaker myself, I had no great difficulty deciphering her accent or her cadences, and I treated her in an ordinary fashion. But for various intrapsychic reasons, Mrs AA still felt rather alien. One day, she experienced an urge to study the volumes on my shelf more closely, and she noticed that I had a French book, *La Psychanalyse de l'enfant* [*The Psychoanalysis of the Child*], written, unsurprisingly, by a French psychoanalyst (Smirnoff, 1966). At this moment, she became instantly more relaxed and relieved to think that I might now have a better chance of understanding her, and, consequently, our work proceeded quite well from that point.

Mr BB had certainly clocked the books on my shelves, but early on in our work he also noticed that I kept an additional pile of books underneath a table positioned in the far corner of the room. One day, Mr BB chastised me for storing books on the floor, in spite of the fact that I had arranged them relatively neatly. He scolded me, "Really, if they can't fit on the shelf space, then you ought to put them somewhere else. I would never leave books on the floor." At this point, I did not know that Mr BB had suffered for many years from a very covert hand-washing compulsion and from a very severe form of obsessive-compulsive disorder, which caused him great shame and which he took huge troubles to hide. Naturally, a pile of books beneath my table would have irritated him; and yet, but for those particular volumes, I might not have learned about the patient's hidden obsessive behaviour for quite some time.

Mr CC came to see me four times weekly. He suffered from a moderately severe form of alcoholism, which had improved steadily over the course of three years of psychoanalytic work. Sometimes, at the outset of treatment, he arrived for sessions slightly inebriated or hung over. One day, Mr CC looked at the bookshelf for the first time from his position on the couch. Previously, he had never made any mention of the books. Mr CC noticed that he could, to his surprise, actually see the titles on the spines of quite a few of the books from where he lay. He scanned the shelves and then murmured, "*Psychonephrology*? You've got a book on psychonephrology. Wow, that's a funny title for a book. What does it mean?" I decided that I would reply in a direct fashion, and I explained that this book contained material on the psychological aspects of patients with kidney disease (Levy, Mattern, and Freedman, 1983). "Kidney disease?", he blurted. "I may not have kidney disease, but I've probably got *liver* disease from all my drinking. Well, I hope I *don't* have liver disease, but I *might*. Anyway, at least I can see the book on kidney disease, so that means my eyesight is still pretty good. Funny, . . . before today, I didn't even know that one could get special diseases of the kidneys." The unusual book title had provided us with a guidepost that underscored that Mr CC, previously drunk or semi-comatose, had now begun to perceive reality in a more sober, more acute fashion. His eyes just happened to alight on the book about psychonephrology, which gave us an indication of his fears of having damaged his internal organs through drinking—an idea that he could not have dared to entertain three years earlier, when he consumed alcohol unthinkingly, unceasingly, and self-destructively.

Ms DD, a paranoid patient, had noticed that, between her Tuesday session and her Wednesday session, I had, in fact, removed one of the books from the shelf, because I needed to consult the volume in question. This made her quite terrified, and she reported that her whole world had begun to crumble. I endeavoured not to torment myself for having dared to use one of the books in my office; but this interaction did help to make me increasingly aware of the deep fragility of this lady and of her profound craving for constancy in the psychoanalytic setting.

Another patient, Mrs EE, had recently cheated on her husband, and she felt absolutely racked with guilt for having embarked upon an extramarital affair. Distracted, and ashamed to look me in the eye, Mrs EE stared at my bookshelf instead, and her eyes locked on a particular title. She croaked, "*Sexual Fidelity*. God, I wish I could have had some sexual fidelity; then I wouldn't be in this mess." I decided, in this instance, that I would not tell Mrs EE that she had committed a most relevant parapraxis, for she had cunningly misperceived and misread the title of Professor Lisa Diamond's (2008) book *Sexual Fluidity: Understanding Women's Love and Desire*, substituting sexual *fluidity* with sexual *fidelity*!

Mr FF, a young first-time father-to-be, had grown up in a fairly non-academic family, and he had displayed no interest in my books at all until the day before his older, middle-aged wife had to attend an appointment with her obstetrician for an amniocentesis test. Out of all the books on my shelf, he had spotted a volume by the French psychoanalyst Madame Maud Mannoni (1973) on *The Retarded Child and the Mother: A Psychoanalytic Study* (in its English translation), a book that had appeared originally in French (Mannoni, 1964). He spoke the title out loud and, of course, in doing so, gave us a great opportunity to explore his fears and his fantasies of fathering a defective child. To my surprise, Mr FF had not only managed to verbalise his anxieties of having damaged the foetus after engaging in sexual intercourse with his pregnant wife on several occasions, but, he also succeeded in accessing the more unconscious wish that his wife might miscarry, or might give birth to a brain-damaged child who could then be put up for adoption, as Mr FF had very, very mixed feelings about becoming a parent in the first place.

These book-related encounters have provided me with very useful clues about the inner states of my patients and about their fears and wishes, as well as the split-off aspects of their psychological worlds, and much more besides. In most cases, I suspect that we might have discovered the same material through other means, but the bookshelves helped to underscore certain components in a very clear, very timely, and very helpful manner.

Not all of my book-related encounters with patients unfolded in such a straightforward fashion. On one occasion, a patient actually attempted to destroy one of my books.

Nearly thirty years ago, I worked for a specialist government-funded project that provided psychoanalytically orientated psychotherapy for child and adolescent sex offenders. The majority of these patients became depressed after they had received a diagnosis, and felt great shame about their sexual crimes; but Master GG, by contrast, a nineteen-year-old child rapist, found it very difficult to admit that he suffered from uncontrolled rage or that he might need to have psychotherapy. I undertook a lengthy, intricate, and complex period of ultimately quite useful work with Master GG, which I cannot possibly summarise in this context (cf. Kahr, 2004, 2020). But I *can* report that, on one occasion, shortly before the first Christmas break,

Master GG became increasingly rude to me in the session, no doubt, I thought, in anticipation of the upcoming separation.

With an eerie grin on his face, Master GG leapt up from his chair, and he proceeded to pluck a book from my shelf and ran his fingers over the dust jacket in a tantalising way. As it happened, Master GG had chosen one of my favourite books, the correspondence of the American psychoanalyst Dr Karl Menninger (1988), and I became nervous. This aggressive forensic patient taunted me, pretending to rip the cover. I made some sort of interpretation about his fear that I had ripped him out of my calendar and out of my mind by having arranged to take a Christmas break, and that now, he wished to do the same to me by threatening to damage the book. Apparently, Master GG did not particularly relish my interpretation, and he then attacked the dust jacket, creating an actual tear some three inches long. In all my many years of clinical practice, none of my patients had ever destroyed any of my property, either before or since. Eventually, Master GG became so enraged that he toppled one of the bookshelves entirely, and the contents came crashing to the floor.

I felt rather shaken by this violent incident in the consulting room, and I wondered then, and now, whether I might have contained the violence more effectively or whether this highly aggressive rapist had to find some way to enact his murderousness in my presence. In any case, I had to pick up the pieces, quite literally, of both the bookshelf and of the treatment. Eventually, we survived this singular aggressive episode, and Master GG made some positive strides; and to the best of our knowledge, he did not re-offend in future.

I shall conclude this brief tour of the way in which analysands will use the bookshelves in the consulting room and, also, the books contained therein, by referring to my work with Mrs HH, a woman who first arrived at my office in a deeply decompensated state, suffering from many crippling symptoms. Extraordinarily, Mrs HH, who used the couch, would glance at my books only once or twice a year. After the first *tranche* of analysis, her eyes fell upon a volume about schizophrenia (Andreasen, 1994), as she worried that she might be diagnosed as psychotic in some way. After one further year of very sustained and dedicated work on both my part and on hers, Mrs HH began to show some signs of psychical growth; and, one day towards the end of her second year, she glanced at the bookshelves once again, and she soon found herself very preoccupied with Dr Otto Fenichel's (1945) classic tome *The Psychoanalytic Theory of Neurosis*. I had reminded her that, one year previously, she had focused on a book about schizophrenia, and that now, one year hence, she found herself staring at a text on neurosis. She smiled—a rare occurrence—and she muttered, "Perhaps I am getting just a little bit better. But only a little bit." By the end of her third year, Mrs HH noticed a new book, which I had only recently purchased, namely, Dr Norman Doidge's (2007) *The Brain That Changes Itself: Stories of Personal Triumph from the Frontiers of Brain Science*. She could not have seen the subtitle, but she could certainly read the supratitle from her position on the couch, and she told me that she had at last begun to believe that her brain could change.

I gradually came to realise that Mrs HH would use the bookshelves as a remarkably helpful guide to her progress, and mine, throughout the course of our slow, painstaking psychological work. I will not pretend that Mrs HH chose one key book per year with clockwork regularity, but she would, thereafter, from time to time, glance over her shoulder at the spines of my books and choose a title that would catch her special attention. Having progressed from schizophrenia, on to neurosis, and then on to brains which can change, it delighted me that, after six years of work, Mrs HH finally noticed a very slim volume that had sat quietly and patiently on the shelf all along: Professor Reuben Fine's (1985) excellent and much overlooked text, *The Meaning of Love in Human Experience*. We both smiled.

Of course, the vigilant clinician must attend not only to the ways in which patients use the books on our shelves, but also how our analysands relate to every single object in the consulting room. Ms II, a very attractive young woman who dated endless numbers of men, could not, alas, ever forge a long-term romance. Thankfully, as our work progressed, she became increasingly able to tolerate intimacy in all its vicissitudes. One day, after approximately two years, she glanced over at the far corner of the room and remarked on the presence of a blue chair, identical to the one in which she had sat for each of her sessions. I do indeed keep two very similar chairs available in the room for couple psychotherapy, but when working with an individual such as Ms II, that second blue chair remains perched against the far wall. On this occasion, Ms II asked whether I had only just purchased a second chair. I replied by explaining that this "extra" chair had sat there all along, and I wondered whether the fact that she now came to notice it for the first time represented an increasing readiness to become part of a "twosome" rather than a "onesome".

Ms II giggled. In the very next session, she spoke with enthusiasm about having recently met a delightful young man. Nine months later, this gentleman proposed marriage, and Ms II accepted the offer. At last, she had become ready to form a partnership. It pleases me to relate that, ten years hence, the young couple remain happily married, and they have now purchased not one, but two additional chairs for their new children.

As I have indicated in several of the essays in this collection, the physical setting deserves our most serious and most detailed consideration. The way in which our patients engage with boxes of tissues, with painted walls, and with bookshelves, *inter alia*, provides us with immensely rich and intricate information about the deep unconscious preoccupations and structures that form the very basis of the human mind.

CHAPTER SIX

Baseball caps, overcoats, orange suits, and neckties:
on patients and their clothing

Extraordinary apparrell of the body, declareth well the apparrell
of the minde.

Thomas Wright, *The Passions of the Minde*, 1601
[Wright, 1601, p. 219]

I should like to begin with a cautionary tale.

Some years ago, a very frightened and suspicious—arguably
paranoid—gentleman came to see me for a consultation. Mr JJ told
me immediately that he had already tried to engage with a psychoanalyst once before, but that he found my colleague to be reprehen-
sible. I inquired delicately as to the nature of his discontent, and he
responded, "Well, she kept analysing my baseball cap."

Apparently, the patient had come to his first consultation with a
highly regarded colleague, wearing his headgear throughout, and
the psychoanalyst in question had made a number of remarks about
this. The patient recalled, "Within seconds of meeting me, she made
some really clumsy comments. She told me that by wearing my hat
in the session, I didn't want her to know what might be going on in
my head. Can you believe the arrogance? Anyway, I found this very
intrusive, and so I left her. I'm not going to have my clothes psychoanalysed."

The patient had told me the name of the colleague who had, purportedly, psychoanalysed his baseball cap. I know this woman to be a decent and thoughtful person who would not, I suspect, make gratuitous interpretations to a patient, and certainly not in the very first moments of the first consultation. But, nevertheless, Mr JJ felt intruded upon, and consequently he bolted.

This vignette raises a number of questions about how we, as clinicians, might make comments about patients' clothing, or, whether we should refrain from doing so. I suppose that one could host a very interesting seminar on the baseball cap incident alone. Should one mention the fact that the patient has covered his head up indoors during a first consultation, especially with a paranoid patient? Should one interpret the patient's fear of having his mind penetrated? Should one, perhaps, note the creativity in a paranoid patient coming to the session with some protective headgear? Or should one say nothing, merely clock the hat privately and be reminded of the patient's fear of the process, and thus proceed diplomatically?

Failure to remove one's cap might well be indicative of the dread of penetration. Alternatively, it might represent an act of contempt or superiority. As a matter of historical interest, when, in 1806, Prinz Klemens von Metternich, the great Austrian statesman, first encountered the French Empéreur, Napoléon Bonaparte, he recorded,

> I found him standing in the middle of one of the reception rooms with the Minister for Foreign Affairs and six other members of his court. He was wearing his hat. This latter circumstance, improper in every respect since the audience was not a public one, struck me as uncalled for pretentiousness indicating the parvenu. I even felt like putting my own hat on. [Quoted in Milne, 1975, pp. 37–38]

It surprises me how little attention psychotherapeutic workers have paid to the ways in which our patients dress. It seems that if we do notice the patients' clothing, we prefer to be very reticent writing about this topic. This reluctance to theorise about clothing makes great sense, in view of the potential sensitivities surrounding this issue. I must confess that I rarely make comments about patients' clothing, as I have a strong awareness of the way in which such verbal observations might be construed as intrusive, seductive, or unnecessary. So I would always proceed very cautiously. But, at the same time, one can become too phobic about mentioning clothing, particularly when it may provide a source of much important information.

Mr KK and Mrs KK, an attractive young couple, came to see me for ongoing marital psychotherapy. I found this couple to be reasonably healthy, highly motivated, greatly intelligent, and deeply committed to improving their relationship. I enjoyed working with them very much, and I had the impression that we could talk about difficult aspects of their histories and of their family lives in a reasonably straightforward way. Over the last five years of marriage, Mrs KK had given birth to three healthy children. Thus, I knew that this couple did have a sex life. Indeed, Mr and Mrs KK told me that, in spite of their rows, they still enjoyed sex with one another and that their physical relationship did not seem to be one of the contentious areas of their marriage. I suppose I took Mr and Mrs KK at their word in this regard.

On one occasion, Mrs KK came to the session on an ordinary British spring day, dressed in a heavy overcoat, buttoned up all the way, which she wore throughout the entire analytic hour. I certainly noticed the coat immediately, but I made no direct comment about this, and I could not find any references in the material that might illuminate why Mrs KK did not take off her coat at the outset of the session. The next week, Mrs KK returned, and once again she wore the coat throughout the session, whereas Mr KK, by contrast, had removed his. After three weeks of this coat-wearing behaviour, I made a quiet observation, wondering whether Mrs KK felt all right, as her reluctance to remove her coat in such mild weather had rather perplexed me.

And then the floodgates opened. Much to my surprise, Mrs KK burst into tears, and she explained that she often struggled with feelings of self-loathing towards her own body. I wondered what Mrs KK—a beautiful woman by anyone's standards—had in mind. She told me, quite bravely, that she hated the look and feel of her genitals, which, after the birth of her third child, now no longer seemed the same. She also confessed to me that she regarded her genitals as loose and messy, and that she feared that her husband did not enjoy sexual intercourse as much as he used to do before she had become a mother. Mr KK tried to reassure her, but she refused to believe him.

We had a set of useful conversations about this topic over the next few weeks, but still Mrs KK would not remove her coat. I made a "couple interpretation" to Mr and Mrs KK, wondering whether Mrs KK's buttoned-up coat reflected not only Mrs KK's recently articulated bodily shame and anxieties, but also whether Mrs KK had become the spokesperson on behalf of other "buttoned-up" aspects within the marriage.

Mrs KK looked at her husband knowingly, and she goaded him, "Go on, *tell* him." Mr KK turned crimson, and he averted his glance. "Go on, *tell* him, it's *really* important", Mrs KK urged. And then the truth emerged. Apparently, Mr KK had contracted an infection, which had caused a raft of rashes and eruptions on his penis, and which resulted in great embarrassment, especially as all attempts to treat the dermatological symptoms by ordinary medical means had failed.

Both members of the couple had now admitted to me that they harboured secret feelings of shame and loathing about their sexual organs, which had become so pronounced that, since the birth of their third baby, they had not enjoyed any sexual relationship at all. No doubt, this sort of information would eventually have emerged in the course of a long-standing, ongoing psychoanalytic marital psychotherapy; but I had the strong impression that Mrs KK's use of the prominent overcoat served as a lightning rod, which encapsulated both sets of genital anxieties. In retrospect, each member of the couple agreed that although it felt uncomfortable to discuss vaginal tearing and genital infections, this conversation had to happen at some point, and eventually both husband and wife experienced a huge sense of relief that, through verbalisation, the secretive aspects and also the shaming aspects of the situation became much less toxic.

Another patient, Ms LL, a young woman who suffered from extreme anxiety and from a host of psychosomatic symptoms, arrived for a first assessment session. She came from a very provincial family who lived deep in the country, away from any major cities. She claimed that she knew nothing about Freud or about psychology, and that she consulted me only because her family doctor had absolutely insisted that she must do so. As she spoke, beads of perspiration formed on her brow, and I could see her discomfort all too palpably.

As this first interview progressed, Ms LL talked to me about her many symptoms. As I listened, I found myself very preoccupied by her unexpected choice of costume. Ms LL had arrived wearing a bright orange blouse, a rich orange skirt, and shiny orange shoes, as well as a large orange beaded necklace with matching orange earrings. She did strike me as very stylish and very well groomed, but I must confess that I had never seen a woman so fully festooned in shades of orange before. At any rate, I did no more than notice her colour choice, and I kept silent.

As the interview unfolded, I offered a few trial interpretations, attempting to make some sense of Ms LL's material. But each time I spoke, she looked at me with a baffled expression; and on one occasion she told me that she found one of my ordinary interpretative remarks to be rather bizarre. "I don't understand what you're saying", she muttered, "I just don't understand you, and I'm not sure that therapy is really for me." I tried very hard to make sense of her and to find a form of words that would engage her and make her feel understood, but it seems that I failed to do so.

As the session neared its end, I wondered aloud whether it might be useful for Ms LL to come back for a second consultation, so that we could have more time to think about her situation and about whether psychoanalytic work might be of value to her. She looked downcast and told me that she did not want to come back, as she had found the meeting to be not quite what she had expected. As Ms LL began to collect her handbag and prepared to leave, I suddenly found myself inspired by her orange clothing and, on rather a gamble, I addressed her: "I do appreciate that you have never met anyone like me before and that you have found this to be a confusing experience. And, of course, you are well within your rights not to come back. But before you go, I must just say that I have found myself wondering about all of the orange clothes that you have worn to our meeting." Ms LL now looked at me with even more incredulity and bewilderment. But I persevered. "Well", I said, "I am very struck by your orange blouse and skirt and by your orange shoes. And I am suddenly reminded that *orange* is the official colour of international *rescue*, and that perhaps you do really want to find a way to be rescued from all of these very painful and crippling symptoms with which you have been struggling for so many years."

I held my breath in anticipation of an angry response. But to my pleasant surprise, Ms LL put down her handbag, and she told me that she *would* like to arrange a time for a second consultation. She did indeed return, and shortly thereafter she became a most engaged, committed, and rewarding psychoanalytic patient with whom I ultimately had the privilege of working for more than twenty years!

I shall conclude with a few more examples of sartorial interpretations.

Mr MM and Mrs MM, a very depressed couple, had come to see me at the recommendation of a psychologist who thought that they would benefit from ongoing marital psychoanalytic work; and after a period of assessment, I began to offer weekly sessions, not in my private office, but, rather, at a specialist marital clinic. Neither member of the couple reported any gross traumatic experiences such as a bereavement or an extramarital affair that might have prompted the referral; instead, they told me that they had gradually grown apart, and that, although they still love each other greatly, they had "run out of things to say" and would often pass the evenings in silence. Both Mr and Mrs MM struck me as anaemic and colourless in appearance, with downcast, grey eyes and with an evident lack of libido. They had not had sexual relations for many years.

Working with this couple often proved quite taxing, owing to the weightiness of their depressions; and during the early months of treatment I sometimes found myself fending off drowsiness. Time would tick by at a very turgid pace, and the sixty-minute sessions (the standard length of Tavistock-style couple psychoanalytic psychotherapy) would seem infinitely longer. I often had private images of myself swimming through molasses.

I spent a great deal of time interpreting the different qualities of the silence in the sessions, hoping that through a careful differentiation I might be able to make some sense of their shared internal world. But often my interpretations would elicit no discernible response. As silence filled the room, I had ample opportunity to look at Mr and Mrs MM and to observe their physical appearance. Mrs MM dressed in clean but neutral clothes and rarely wore any bright colours. Mr MM arrived in threadbare grey suits. He also seemed to wear the same necktie every single week: a very unusual necktie adorned with a large picture of a butterfly—the sort that one might have worn to a fancy-dress party during the 1970s! Although I enjoy people who sport bright and playful clothing, Mr MM's tie struck me as rather awkward. The oddity of the tie became compounded by the fact that he seemed to wear this item at each and every meeting.

During one particularly dead session, I decided that I would dare to ask Mr MM about his tie. In doing so, I secretly hoped that we might investigate an important, hitherto overlooked clue to some aspect of his internal world. With a certain amount of tentativity, I commented that I had noticed that Mr MM had worn the same tie for the last several weeks, and I wondered whether this had any particular meaning.

To my delight, Mr MM became quite animated that I had expressed an interest in his tie. With pride, he beamed, "I've not only worn it *just* for the last few weeks. I've worn it *every* single week since I've been coming here. Without exception." He smiled broadly at his wife, who then turned to her husband and beamed, "Go on, Lamb Chop, tell him about it. Tell him about your tie." I braced myself, thinking that I had at last uncovered the key to their unconscious minds.

Mr MM, in spite of his initial enthusiasm, tucked his head into his chin and mumbled, "There's nothing to tell. I just like it, that's all." Mrs MM, by contrast, grasped the opportunity to provide more information, and she told me, "You know, he really loves that tie. He has others, but he always wears just one tie until it becomes completely worn down." As one might surmise, I seized upon this reference to worn-down ties, and I made an interpretation about the way in which the lively butterfly aspects of themselves had become worn down, rather like the tie. Mrs MM replied, "Yes, that's correct. We do feel worn down."

I then offered the following observation: "Perhaps I might share a thought with you both, if I may. I wonder whether, in part, the tie might be emblematic of the very dead, stuck part of each of you, and of your marriage, in fact, the part that is reluctant to change or try anything new—the part that feels depressed. But judging from the great colour and the bright butterfly pattern on Mr MM's tie, perhaps it also conveys some sense of *hope* that something bright, and something non-depressed, might still emerge."

Both husband and wife smiled, relieved, perhaps, that I had noticed the stagnant tie, worn week after week, which nonetheless contained a dash of something colourful and hopeful, if a bit gauche. Mrs MM responded to my comment with particular relish, noting, "He doesn't like change. That's why he wears the tie again and again. He really doesn't like change." Then, turning to her husband, Mrs MM asked, "Lamb Chop, do you think it has anything to do with the fact that you had to move house about twenty times when you were little?" In a soft voice, Mr MM replied, "Yes, I think that's right. I don't like change."

The couple then managed to construct a joint conversation in which they told me all about the many house moves that Mr MM had to endure in boyhood as his father had worked in the diplomatic corps and had changed postings very regularly indeed. Mrs MM then told me that she and her family had moved quite frequently during her childhood as well.

I wondered with this couple whether Mr MM's loyalty towards his necktie represented some unconscious attempt to find something constant and consistent in their lives and whether, by wearing the same tie, both members of the couple could derive satisfaction about something upon which one could rely. The couple responded enthusiastically to this simple observation.

In the very next session, Mr and Mrs MM returned, and, to my amazement, the husband wore a *new* tie of muddy brown wool. And in the very next session after that, Mr MM boasted a shiny, purple silken tie. In the wake of six previous months of what can only be described as *sartorial stagnation*, Mr and Mrs MM had at last introduced something new, something different, into the landscape of our weekly psychotherapeutic sessions. I shall refrain from attributing grand significance to this new gesture, which Mr MM found to be a source of both pride and pleasure, except to note its occurrence. Nevertheless, as a practising psychotherapist, I have come to recognise that these first "baby steps" may well represent the beginnings of a developmental maturation upon which one might elaborate in weeks and months to come.

Mr MM explained that he had begun to wear some new ties, in part, because he felt rather anxious that I might "call" him on the tie, and that I would berate him for his lack of creativity. But then the patient elaborated that he also wore the new ties for his own benefit, and that he could see for the first time that people might find him socially awkward and "weird", always wearing the very same costume.

Three years have elapsed since my first sartorial interpretation to this couple, and they have gone on quite a journey in marital psychotherapy, working very hard to underpin the foundations of their relationship. It pleases me to report that this couple has made excellent progress, and that, with each passing session, they have become more enlivened, more creative, and much less stagnant.

Quite another patient, Mr NN, born in a French-speaking country, entered analysis in part because of difficulties in committing himself to a female partner. A charming, seductive, and well-dressed Don Juan, Mr NN bedded many women during the early months of our work, discarding each sexual conquest in rapid succession. During our fourth year of psychoanalytic work, Mr NN fell in love with a woman called Charmian. After having slept with her on two or three occasions, Mr NN surprised himself that he wished to see Charmian ongoingly; in fact, he dared to wonder whether he might even be able to fall in love with her and make her his wife. But after approximately fifteen dates with Charmian, Mr NN became increasingly stressed. He wanted to commit himself to her—yet, at the same time, the prospect of so much sustained intimacy raised his levels of anxiety greatly; and thereafter he came to his sessions completely torn as to whether he should marry Charmian at once or whether he should "dump" her.

On one occasion, Mr NN arrived at my consulting room on a cold winter's day, and he told me that he could kick himself because he had left his very expensive silk scarf in a taxicab earlier that morning. Mr NN treasured this fancy scarf—a gift from his mother—and he kept berating himself for his stupidity. He knew that the loss of the scarf must have a special psychological meaning, because he prided himself on his obsessional attention to his wardrobe and would not, under ordinary circumstances, be so clumsy as to lose such an important item. In fact, he claimed that he had never lost anything before—clothing or otherwise!

Mr NN had lived in Great Britain for over twenty years, and he spoke English perfectly. And he talked to me in English during sessions, except on rare occasions when he could not find exactly the right turn of phrase, at which point he would pepper his free associations with some French words. Although I never told Mr NN that I speak French well, I suppose he must have known that I do from the way in which I would pronounce the names of his various French family members and friends; therefore, I took it as part of our work that we might think about his unconscious behaviours and thoughts in both English *and* French.

As Mr NN continued to lament the loss of his scarf, I suddenly realised that the second syllable of *écharpe*—the French word for scarf—sounds exactly like the first syllable of Charmian's name. I interpreted that, in recent days, Mr NN had become painfully preoccupied as to whether he should keep Charmian round his neck, or throw her away; and that as he could not solve this conflict, he unconsciously elected to discard his *écharpe* instead of his *Charmian*. Mr NN laughed heartily, and he realised that my interpretation made great sense. To my surprise, he continued to date Charmian for over a year before ending their love affair abruptly, and this had proved to be the longest relationship that he had ever had with a woman to date.

Lastly, Mr OO, a twenty-one-year-old university student, came to see me for psychotherapy, in part, because he felt directionless, and he claimed that—unlike his mates, who had applied to law school and medical school or who would soon start working for large corporations—he had no such interests and no clear plans for the rest of his life. In our first consultation, I struggled to make contact, as

Mr OO spoke in short, telegraphic phrases, and he found it difficult to elaborate on anything. Indeed, he presented himself in a restricted, inhibited manner.

Like many young men his age, Mr OO wore scruffy clothes consisting of ripped jeans and a T-shirt. This seemed ordinary enough in itself and, perhaps, called for little comment; however, I could not help but notice the inscription on Mr OO's yellow T-shirt, written in large blood-red letters: "THE ANGRY PATRICIANS". Throughout my conversation with Mr OO, I kept finding myself distracted by these words, wondering what "The Angry Patricians" might mean. I said nothing, but I continued in my strained efforts to engage Mr OO in conversation.

Eventually, Mr OO mentioned that he had recently broken up with his girlfriend and that, shortly thereafter, this young lady had begun to sleep with Mr OO's so-called "best friend". Naturally, my patient felt lacerated and humiliated, and he evoked a great deal of sympathy. Strikingly, he kept describing his philandering ex-girlfriend as "she", and he did not mention her first name at any point. Eventually, I commented that, in spite of his many complaints about the ex-girlfriend, he had not referred to her more directly, and I thought that, perhaps, this might be difficult for him.

"Pat", he replied. "Her name is Pat."

At this point, I commented that, of course, "Pat" might be the diminutive of someone called "Patricia", and that I could not help but notice his very bold T-shirt, which bore the inscription "The Angry Patricians". I wondered whether his anger at "Pat"/"Patricia" might be too enormous to put into words and whether he might, unconsciously, have relied upon the T-shirt to convey the rage that he harboured towards the woman who had betrayed him.

"Oh, no", Mr OO rebutted, "'The Angry Patricians' is the name of a rock band that I really like. Nothing to do with Pat." I asked him to tell me about "The Angry Patricians", and I soon learned that this band plays very loud heavy metal music, and I wondered again whether the T-shirt represented not only his anger towards "Patricia" but, also, something about her angry, "heavy metal" attack on Mr OO. Eventually, the patient came to realise that psychotherapists talk in an unusual way, and that we do not always approach material in a concrete manner but, rather, in a symbolic fashion; and he soon began to think about his situation more laterally.

As the first consultation drew to a close, Mr OO revealed his deep fury towards Patricia for having made him feel so castrated.

He eventually told me that not only did Patricia begin to have a very public relationship with Mr OO's "best friend" (now *ex*-best friend), but one of his other mates told him that Patricia and the "best friend" had already started sleeping together before she had broken up with Mr OO. He felt so ashamed that he could not show his face on campus for days, fearful of being mocked and teased. The T-shirt provided me with a very helpful point of entry to elicit more details of Mr OO's recent experiences and to gauge the blood-red murderousness that he harboured and that contributed to his difficulties in thinking and in finding a sense of direction. Mr OO did, eventually, engage in twice-weekly psychotherapy, and, as we spoke more and more about his angry feelings, he experienced an increasingly deep catharsis that helped to create more space in his mind to think about other matters.

Roughly one year into our work, Mr OO had managed to get a job—his first employment—and although he succeeded in arriving at work on time and in fulfilling his various tasks, he also found it stressful and often frightening. Days after his twenty-second birthday, Mr OO told me that he had spent the evening celebrating with friends at a very fancy restaurant, and that they had all had a very good time. He took the trouble to tell me, however, that before he left home to join his companions, he got into quite a "state", not knowing what shirt to wear. He could not decide whether to put on a fancy, button-down shirt with a starched collar, or whether he should wear a more comfortable T-shirt. In the end, he opted for the latter choice. He smiled and switched the subject and began to talk about other matters.

I found myself very intrigued by the fact that Mr OO, a fairly traditional, "blokey", heterosexual man, bothered to tell me about his wardrobe dilemma, and I expressed my curiosity about this. "Oh, I don't know why I told you about my shirts. It's not really important", he mumbled. I reminded Mr OO that, in our very first meeting roughly one year previously, we had spent quite a lot of time thinking about the meaning of his T-shirt and its inscription, "The Angry Patricians". He giggled uncomfortably and exclaimed, "Well this T-shirt has no writing on it. It's just a plain T-shirt." I replied that, perhaps, in spite of the lack of a logo, he might have remembered that we did have a long conversation about clothing as a means of conveying something that seems hard to talk about and that perhaps on this occasion, he wished me to know something else that he could not readily put into words. Mr OO shrugged, "Well, I don't think so."

At this point, I offered an hypothesis, and I suggested that the struggle between wearing a formal starched shirt with buttons, rather like the ones that I wear, and an informal T-shirt, with or without inscription, might represent his conflict between being an adolescent versus being a grown-up. A teenager without direction might feel more comfortable wearing a T-shirt, whereas an adult *might* prefer to celebrate his birthday in a more formal shirt. Perhaps Mr OO wanted me to know something about the conflict between the part of him that goes to work every day, and the part of him that still feels like being looked after by his parents and, perhaps, by me. Slowly, Mr OO nodded his head, and we thus embarked upon a fruitful conversation about the joys of being twenty-two instead of twenty-one, and of the pleasures of leaving the painful, directionless university years behind him. But he also confessed to renewed fears about being older, and about having to decide what he might like to do with his life.

I suggested that we could take our time contemplating these really crucial questions, which, like his relationship with "Patricia", might be difficult to think about. I also commented that because we had already spent some time "psychoanalysing" his blood-red T-shirt with the banner "The Angry Patricians", he might, in all likelihood, have hoped that I would offer some thoughts about the unconscious meaning of his current wardrobe dilemma. Mr OO smiled broadly as he realised that he used references to his clothing as a means of conveying something about more complicated topics.

Throughout the history of our profession, clinicians have often commented about the unconscious meaning of clothes. The pioneering British psychoanalyst Professor John Carl Flügel (1929) not only wrote a forward-thinking paper on clothing for *The International Journal of Psycho-Analysis*, but he also produced an important book on the subject, the richly detailed tome entitled *The Psychology of Clothes* (Flügel, 1930a; cf. Flügel, 1930b). At roughly the same time, in 1931, Dr Carl Gustav Jung, the founder of analytical psychology, told a group of North American disciples who had come to Zürich, Switzerland, to study with him: "You American women wear too fancy hats. That is because you are afraid there is nothing inside your heads. You should go and buy a plain hat on the Bahnhof Strasse; and show some respect for what is *inside* your heads" (quoted in Gildea, 1980, p. 126). Although Jung may have had quite an important insight,

I dare say that most contemporary practitioners would wield our observations more delicately—more diplomatically.

Mr PP arrived for an early-morning session and began, immediately, to tell me that the previous evening he had watched the film *The Boy in the Striped Pyjamas* on television—a harrowing tale about a youngster incarcerated in a Nazi extermination camp during the Second World War. As Mr PP spoke, I could not help but wonder whether he realised that he had worn both a striped suit *and* a striped shirt to his session. When he paused, I commented upon his choice of clothing. His jaw dropped in astonishment, and he claimed that he had no conscious awareness of having chosen these items of clothing when he dressed. A man of great psychological intelligence, Mr PP quickly realised that he had worn an outfit full of stripes in sympathetic identification with the protagonist of the film. This interchange provided us with a very rich and highly resonant opportunity to discuss the ways in which Mr PP often feels like a man imprisoned by his life and by his history. Furthermore, we also examined how he will often experience himself not only as the imprisoned Jew, but also as the Nazi who forces himself to don a concentration camp uniform, in symbolic ways, thus entrapping himself in an unhappy-making marriage and an unhappy-making profession. No doubt Mr PP and I might well have explored these subjects irrespective of his clothing, but his costume provided us with an immediate point of *entrée* into this crucial aspect of his inner world.

In this brief communication, I have endeavoured to highlight an area of work that will be familiar to every single practising psychotherapist and psychoanalyst—the clothed body of the patient. As clinicians, we always walk a tightrope between focusing too intensely on material or avoiding the material altogether, aware of the dangers of being either too intrusive or too negligent stylistically. Over the years I have found that a gentle, tentative observation about an item of clothing, conveyed in a benign tone of voice and with a deep sense of curiosity, can, in fact, yield great dividends for the enrichment of the psychological work.

CHAPTER SEVEN

On patients who remove their clothing in sessions

Stripping stark naked is not unfrequent amongst the insane.

Dr George Fielding Blandford, *Insanity and Its Treatment: Lectures on the Treatment, Medical and Legal, of Insane Patients*, 1871
[Blandford, 1871, p. 160]

A solid psychotherapy training teaches us a goodly amount about psychoanalytic theory and basic psychopathology; but, sadly, no training, however thorough, can instruct us how to handle those extraordinary, peculiar moments of clinical practice, the sorts of episodes that strike without warning. For instance, what does one do when the hind legs of the analytic couch break in the middle of the session, and the unsuspecting patient comes crashing onto the floor? This had happened to one of my colleagues, a senior Freudian psychoanalyst. Or, worse still, how does one manage when the patient starts to leave the consulting room, turns the door knob, only to hear a thud from the other side of the door, the knob having loosened and fallen off, leaving both the patient and the psychotherapist locked together in the consulting room for over an hour? To compound the problem, the psychotherapist in question had to wait until her own mother had returned home and could release the entrapped pair from this complicated arrangement. This had actually happened to another one of my colleagues, an integrative psychotherapist.

Still another colleague arrived late for her first session with a new patient, whom she found waiting, with tolerance, on her doorstep. In a frantic attempt to open the door, the psychotherapist broke her key in the lock and had to telephone for a locksmith on her mobile phone. Rather than sending the patient away, the psychotherapist entreated him to wait for nearly an hour, until the locksmith arrived. Needless to say, this treatment lasted only three or four sessions in total; for, in spite of the otherwise high degree of skill and compassion of this psychotherapist, the patient never recovered from that early experience of professional ineptitude.

And what does one do when showering in the gym after a workout (an experience that most chair-bound psychotherapists may not enjoy very often), and one's same-sex patient walks into the communal showers? This happened to another one of my colleagues, a Jungian analyst, who has since emigrated overseas—though not, I believe, as a direct result of this shower episode.

Of course, all of these uncomfortable interactions pale into insignificance when compared to the plight of the German-born psychoanalyst, Dr Ernst Simmel, who had to escape through the window of his home in mid-session, accompanied by his analysand Dr Martin Grotjahn (1987), in order to avoid arrest by the Nazis (cf. Danto, 2005).

The aforementioned incidents—whether collapsing couches, faulty door knobs, broken keys, communal showers, or menacing Nazis— all have to be managed on the spot with quick-witted responses, in spite of the fact that none of our lecturers or supervisors had ever taught us how to cope with these challenging moments in "shrink school". Fortunately, none of our mentors would ever have expected us to be *so* well prepared that we would know exactly how to handle *every* unusual incident; rather, most of us would agree with the London-based Kleinian psychoanalyst Mrs Jane Temperley (1984), who noted that, as long as one possesses an analytic setting in one's mind, one will be able to confront most complex clinical interactions with thoughtfulness, poise, compassion, and wisdom.

Like most colleagues, I, too, have had my fair share of unanticipated interruptions or oddities during my years of private clinical practice: a doorbell ringing in the middle of a session with a depressed and regressed patient; a window cleaner suddenly appearing on an outdoor scaffold, glancing into the consulting room; a neighbour's cat leaping through the open window on a hot summer's day; and many more besides. In my institutional setting, at a mental health clinic, I have had to deal with a multitude of such infractions: an altercation with the clinic handyman who interrupted a session, insisting that he must paint my consulting room there and then, in spite of the fact that I had a patient already seated on the chair inside, and in spite of the fact that I had placed a very large "DO NOT DISTURB" sign on the door; an endless litany of fire drills that began to blare in mid-session; and, perhaps most frightening of all, the experience of escorting a hospitalised schizophrenic patient to my office for a psychotherapy session, only to find that, during the three minutes in which I had vacated my room in order to collect my patient from the ward, an even more troubled schizophrenic patient had crept into the office, brandishing a carving knife. The knife-wielder would not vacate my room, and yet I still had a session to conduct; so, naturally, I reported the situation to the nursing staff and then, through sheer necessity, went with my psychotherapy patient in search of another room.

The occasional death threat from a psychotic patient could not be described as pleasant, nor could the violent outburst from a pae-dophile who knocked a whole row of textbooks off of my shelf; but in the course of many years of psychotherapeutic practice, I regard these as manageable and, mercifully, infrequent episodes. In retro-spect, these happenings seem eminently survivable, indeed, they might even be amusing at times; yet in the "white heat" (quoted by Susanna Isaacs Elmhirst, personal communication, 25 January 1996) of the moment—to borrow a term used privately by both Dr Wilfred Bion and Dr Donald Winnicott—many of these vignettes caused both me and my patients a considerable amount of consternation.

Winnicott, of course, knew a great deal about "white heat", hav-ing had to manage several extraordinary encounters during his pro-fessional lifetime. You may remember that his first training patient in child analysis, whom he had treated in the 1930s, bit him on the buttocks, flooded his consulting room, and, on one occasion, stole out of the clinic building and managed to release the brake on Win-nicott's automobile, which then proceeded to roll down the road. Writing about this case some years later in his hallmark paper on "The Antisocial Tendency", Winnicott (1956) reported that he had to terminate the treatment and that this child had to be sent, eventually, to an approved school.

I must confess that although I never learned about such incidents during my clinical training or in supervision sessions, I do talk about these sorts of vignettes all the time with my own students.

Sometimes, as an educational exercise, I describe the unavoidable infraction of boundaries that might occur in daily clinical practice, usually beyond the clinician's control, and I ask my trainees to free-associate, imagining how they might handle such unusual occurrences and what the consequences might be for both the patient and the psychotherapist. I find that this sort of creative brain-storming actually reduces student anxiety, because, through our discussions of these unusual situations, we have begun the process of preparing trainees for the unexpected; and over the years, my students have impressed me with their thoughtfulness and sagacity.

One of the most singularly worrying interchanges with which I have had to struggle concerns a deeply tragic middle-aged woman with whom I worked many years ago. Trebly cursed, suffering from perinatal brain damage, as well as from schizophrenia and elective mutism, Ms QQ lived a very bleak and persecuted existence, cared for around the clock by a team of psychiatric nurses. Having worked extensively with severely handicapped individuals and having previously provided psychotherapy for psychotic patients, this referral came my way. I have published a lengthy account of my work with Ms QQ (Kahr, 2017a), but in this context I wish only to report that on one occasion, roughly three months into the treatment, Ms QQ walked into my consulting room for her usual weekly session of psychotherapy, with a kindly care worker sitting outside in the waiting room as her escort. Although mid-winter, Ms QQ wore a loose, diaphanous caftan, which struck me as rather inappropriate garb for the chilly London weather. Within seconds of entering the consulting room, Ms QQ grasped at what I soon discovered to be the Velcro clasp of her garment, and, with a single tug, the caftan fell to the floor. Ms QQ stood there with an impassive face, completely naked, wearing no underclothes whatsoever.

I cannot provide a sufficiently coherent account of my internal thought processes, or of my countertransferential responses, or of my treatment strategy, because nothing of this nature had ever happened to me before. I suppose that Ms QQ may well have wanted me to experience some sense of shock. Of course, having worked in long-stay psychogeriatric institutions and on acute psychiatric wards, I had seen many distressed patients running around at one time or another without clothing, but always on the open wards, with fleets of medical house officers and mental health nurses in hot pursuit. Under those conditions, therefore, the nudity did not seem quite so threatening. Certainly, I had never observed an ongoing *psychotherapy* patient in such a state of undress. In retrospect, I do remember a fleeting thought quickly crossing my mind: "Good grief, what if Ms QQ's care worker should walk into the room right now? Might she think that I had acted in a sexually inappropriate way?" Only later did I appreciate that my countertransferential reaction of feeling like an "abuser" may have represented a communication that, at some point in Ms QQ's history, somebody might have harmed her in a sexual manner.

I knew that I could not allow Ms QQ to languish in this nude state, and yet I also needed to explore the meaning of her behaviour with her. But, I realised, the analysis of the material would have to wait until she donned her caftan once again.

Somehow, drawing from some hidden clinical inspiration, I lowered my eyes, so that I would not look upon Ms QQ directly; but nor did I swivel my head in the opposite direction, as that might have given Ms QQ the impression that I found her body revolting. I simply tilted my head down and positioned my eyes to the right, so that I could see only glimmers of Ms QQ with my peripheral vision. I then found myself intoning in a soft voice, "You are really trying very hard to show me that your body has never been your own, and that there have been times when anybody could have access to your body." I waited with bated breath for some kind of response from the mutistic Ms QQ, but she simply remained in this naked position. I then continued, "It is very important that we should try to understand this, but, first, it would be very helpful if you could put your clothes back on."

To my great relief, Ms QQ reached down and picked up her clothing as I sat silently, wondering how on earth the staff at her institution could have sent her out to see her psychotherapist on a blustery winter's day with only one thin piece of material draped around her, and with no undergarments! After a few anxious seconds, Ms QQ redressed the situation by re-dressing. Fully clothed, she stared at me plaintively, without uttering a single word, as if to say, "Look at my dreadful plight. Please help me if you can." I glanced towards Ms QQ, trying to convey with my eyes and facial expression that I understood something about the quality of her distress.

As the weeks and months of sessions unfolded, Ms QQ gave ample signs of having experienced early sexual assaults: she would often break the pointy tips off of crayons and throw them across the room; she would draw pictures of phallic structures and then scribble all over them with fury; and, most particularly, she would spit on the tip of her finger and then ram it into virtually every bodily orifice at a feverish pace. Once, she kept assaulting her ear with a rigid finger in such a murderous manner that she actually drew blood, and I had to exhort her to stop at once.

In such a short communication, I cannot do justice to the nature of my work with Ms QQ, but I can report that she did remain with me for approximately eight years, by which time she had developed the courage to speak, and all of her sexually "inappropriate" acting-out and her "challenging behaviour" (which had included frequent assaults on fellow patients) had ceased entirely. She left my office in a much calmer state of mind and, also, as someone who could induce a pleasant smile upon first greeting, rather than a look of horror or pity.

It may be of interest to know that the progenitor of our profession, Dr Sigmund Freud, also grappled with nude patients, though perhaps not in such a dramatic manner. On 26 November 1886, the thirty-year-old neurologist presented a paper on hysterical hemianaesthesia (i.e., a neurotic condition in which the patient believes himself or herself to be paralysed on one side of the body) to his medical colleagues in the Kaiserliche und Königliche Gesellschaft der Ärzte [Imperial and Royal Society of Medicine] in Vienna, Austria. In these olden times, physicians would regularly host case conferences and would present patients with unusual symptomatology in front of their medical colleagues. Often, the patients would be required to undress and then submit to an examination. On this occasion, Freud (1886a, 1886b) displayed a patient called "August P.", a twenty-nine-year-old engraver who suffered from an hysterical paralysis of much of the left side of his body. With a cool head and a clear conscience, Freud (1886a, p. 1636) found the process of watching August P. strip most instructive, noting, "Zunächst werden die Herren, welche beobachtet haben, wie sich der Kranke mit beiden Händen auskleidete, wie er mit den Fingern der linken Hand sein linkes Nasenloch verschloss, nicht den Eindruck einer schweren Bewegungsstörung bekommen haben" ["At first, those of you who noticed how the patient undressed himself with both hands and how he closed his left nostril with the fingers of his left hand, will not have formed an impression of any serious disturbance of movement" (Freud, 1886c, p. 29)].

Sigmund Freud did not have a monopoly on the naked patient. Historians of psychiatry have since unearthed numerous additional cases of patients stripping in lunatic asylums, without having to undergo a physical examination. Dr Thomas Graham (1967, p. 48), an historian, recorded that, during medieval times, patients suffering from delirium in the Islamic world would often be permitted to roam around "denuded". And Professor Ann Goldberg (1999), author of a study of the medical records of the nineteenth-century mad-house in Eberbach, in Germany, uncovered many instances of female inmates who would remove their clothing, often as expressions of anger and rebellion. A patient called "Elisabeth S." would raise her skirts constantly and use profane language; another inmate called "Katharina J." would actually pull her skirt up over her head, laughing mockingly at her physician. As Goldberg (1999) has noted,

> Clothes were symbolic of the person; they stated who one was and where one belonged within a familial and societal hierarchy. In the asylum, where the patient had been severed from his or her home and past identity, and where identity itself was called into question and reworked by the institutional regime, clothing took on enormous symbolic significance. [1999, p. 113]

I also discovered an horrific case of a thirty-two-year-old hysterical woman called "A.L.", treated by the eminent nineteenth-century German psychiatrist, Professor Paul Emil Flechsig, who endorsed clitoridectomy as a form of psychiatric treatment. After undergoing this sadistic genital surgery, "A.L." became extremely agitated, screaming incessantly; and so, as punishment, Flechsig (1884a) stripped this unfortunate woman of her clothing and placed her in isolation (cf. Flechsig, 1884b)!

Thus, stripping may have many contexts and many meanings. But, in thinking further about Ms QQ and the extraordinary moment of her stripping, we must recognise that it occurred neither as part of a medical examination (as in the case of "August P."), nor in the case of a rebellion against hospital life (as in the cases of "Elisabeth S." and "Katharina J."), nor, even, as a form of punishment (as in the case of "A.L."). Ms QQ's undressing took place in the midst of psychotherapy, a safe and quiet arena in which patients have an opportunity to convey information about their biographies, and it represented, perhaps, a strong unconscious communication about her early sense of bodily endangerment.

I recently read a most moving article by an Italian colleague, Dr Patrizia Arfelli (2002), published in the psychoanalytic journal *American Imago: Psychoanalysis and the Human Sciences*, in which the author described her own struggle with a female adolescent patient who also removed her clothes in session. Arfelli's essay, "Affective Response and the Analyst's Freedom in Work with Traumatized Adolescents", chronicles the story of a suicidal fourteen-year-old called "Irina", whom she had treated at the child neuropsychiatry division of a children's hospital. As the daughter of a prostitute who would parade naked throughout the house, Irina, not surprisingly, took to undressing in her psychotherapy sessions with Dr Arfelli out of a desperate attempt to identify with some maternal figure.

As Arfelli (2002, p. 451) wrote, "Irina is almost seventeen when all of a sudden, during a session, she stands up, she undresses in front of me and, completely naked, goes and sits on the window-sill, and remains there, exposed, silent, motionless." With exceptional compassion, Arfelli has recounted the tender and thoughtful way in which she responded to Irina's enactment, and I recommend that one read her article in full.

It remains a considered point of technique as to whether one should avert one's gaze, as I did, or stare at the patient directly, as Arfelli did, thus giving the patient a clear communication that one has seen her pain in full. Perhaps either approach can be justified. Perhaps the dynamic between a male psychotherapist and a female patient might require more tender consideration. As with all the aforementioned "unusual interchanges", there can be no single correct answer; we can, instead, hope only that each clinician will mobilise his or her best thinking and feeling processes in order to respond to the patient in the most psychologically sensitive and efficacious manner.

In reading Arfelli's essay, I experienced great relief to know that at least one other psychoanalytic colleague has had to struggle with the temporarily naked patient. It may be the case that if more colleagues reported similar experiences with abused patients, we would eventually be able to ascertain whether nudity in sessions might come to be understood as prototypically pathognomonic of sexual abuse. In gathering this data, let us aspire to become infinitely more sensitive to the plight of other such patients—and much sooner, as well.

After having written this essay, I had a timely encounter with a new psychoanalytic patient, Mr RR, a young man in his late twenties who, while attending an English public school as a youngster some years previously, had suffered greatly after the choirmaster had sodomised him. Mr RR came to see me five times weekly, always in the early morning, before proceeding to his smart office, where all the men wore suits and ties. From the very outset of our work, it always struck me as rather odd that Mr RR would enter my consulting room, remove his overcoat and hat and gloves (in winter months), and then lie on the couch, keeping his suit jacket on his body. Other business-men who have consulted me over the years would invariably remove both their overcoat *and* their suit jacket, particularly so that they did not crease the latter. But Mr RR, by contrast, kept his jacket firmly buttoned, even when reclining.

It took me some time to realise that, in view of having had pain-ful experiences of anal rape as a young boy, it might be particularly important for Mr RR to keep his bottom covered by his jacket. Even-tually, I shared this observation with Mr RR, who seemed not at all surprised. "Of course", he said, "I never take off my jacket, even on hot days at the office. From here on in, only a proctologist will ever get to see my ass uncovered . . . and only if I should develop cancer of the rectum."

I shall not dwell upon the various ways in which Mr RR's analy-sis unfolded. Obviously, he experienced a great deal of fear at lying down five times weekly on the couch of an older man; and yet, he also craved a corrective experience, eventually learning to trust that I would be a benign choirmaster who would treat his body and his mind with respect, unlike the abusive choirmaster of yore who had scarred him profoundly. Whereas Ms QQ removed her clothing in order to communicate an experience of abuse, Mr RR did so by keep-ing his clothing on his body. Whether one removes one's clothes in session or whether one keeps oneself fully dressed, mental health professionals can benefit greatly from a close examination of the links between sartorial behaviour and early sexual trauma.

PART II

MEDIA ESSAYS

Ein angesehener Mann, von der Presse und den Reichen
unterstützt, könnte Wunder tun, um körperliche Leiden zu
lindern.
[A respected man, supported by the press and the rich, could do
wonders in alleviating physical ills.]

Sigmund Freud, Letter to Eduard Silberstein, 9 September, 1875
[Freud, 1875a, p. 144; Freud, 1875b, p. 127]

CHAPTER EIGHT

How to make a forty-seven-minute television programme in only three years

From breakfast on through all the day
At home among my friends I stay;
But every night I go abroad
Afar into the Land of Nod.

Robert Louis Stevenson, "The Land of Nod",
in *A Child's Garden of Verses*, 1885

In the spring of 2002, I enjoyed a very pleasant lunch with my friend and colleague Oliver Rathbone, at that time the Managing Director of Karnac Books, the leading psychoanalytic publishing house in Great Britain. Oliver had just released my edited book, *The Legacy of Winnicott: Essays on Infant and Child Mental Health* (Kahr, 2002a)—my third title for Karnac Books—and he wished to discuss plans for my next project. As we sipped our soup in a restaurant near the Aldwych in Central London, Oliver asked me what I had in mind for the future. To be frank, I cannot now remember exactly what idea I had suggested—possibly a selection of the very charming letters from Sir Frederick Winnicott, former Mayor of Plymouth, to his son, the psychoanalyst Dr Donald Winnicott, which I had located in the Archives of the British Psychoanalytical Society, and which now reside in the Archives and Manuscripts collection at the Wellcome

Library in London. Oliver looked bemused and, with utter tact, managed to convey through subtle movements of his eyebrows that such a volume would be of little interest to anyone other than myself and that its publication, however historically worthy, would earn very little money for the coffers of Karnac Books.

Desperately, I began to search for another topic, ranging from an introductory guide to the writings of Melanie Klein, to a book on the management of a private psychotherapy practice. I knew that at some point I wanted to produce a big text on schizophrenia, based on my clinical work, but I knew that I had not yet digested the material sufficiently to begin writing. I then offered a few more ideas. Again, Oliver tolerated my suggestions with a benign smile.

Seizing the moment, he leaned over the table in conspiratorial fashion and intoned: "Brett, I know what your next book should be." I sat with bated breath, delighted that Oliver had a clearer insight into the development of my writing career than I did. With a cheeky grin on his face, he announced, "You must write a book on the psychoanalysis of sexual fantasies!" Choking on my risotto, I became extremely disconcerted and told Oliver that I could not think of a more unpalatable or unnecessary subject for my next book. I had no special knowledge of the field of sexual fantasies, I had not studied the literature with any degree of seriousness, and besides, the American author Nancy Friday (1973, 1975, 1980, 1991) had already cornered the market on this field with a quartet of extremely well written and highly popular compendia of male and female sexual fantasies, all still in print and penned from a psychoanalytic vantage point as well. What more could one say? I quickly dashed Oliver's hopes of commissioning a bestseller on sexual fantasy, and, in spite of his excellent lunchtime companionship, I returned to my office in North London somewhat despondent at my publisher's lack of commercial interest in the wartime letters of Donald Winnicott's father.

Unbeknownst to Oliver, he had, however, planted an idea in my mind, which, to my consternation, began to take root. As I reimmersed myself in my consulting room, I suddenly became increasingly aware of the role of sexual fantasies in the lives of my patients. One male analysand began to report masturbatory fantasies about a female colleague in his office; another male patient sheepishly confessed to thinking about a sadomasochistic scenario with an ex-girlfriend while having sex with his wife; and a few of the couples whom I see for marital psychotherapy painted very compelling portraits of their divergent fantasies, which caused a veritable sexual anaesthesia in the bedroom. Sexual fantasies seemed to abound, and I quickly realised that I had not thought about the subject in a considered or systematic fashion until now. Intrigued, I returned to Nancy Friday's books, which my undergraduate tutor in psychopathology had first recommended to me in 1980. I have such great admiration for Nancy Friday that, in spite of her lack of any formal clinical credentials, I would locate her in the pantheon of pioneering sexologists such as Sigmund Freud, Havelock Ellis, Magnus Hirschfeld, and Alfred Kinsey, among others; indeed, Friday's books had caused a revolution in the 1970s, especially among women, by helping people recognise that females enjoy vibrant masturbatory and coital fantasies, and that they could be every bit as sexualised as their male counterparts.

As I immersed myself, once again, in Friday's books, I began to appreciate even more fully their historical importance, having helped to inaugurate a public discourse around the subject of fantasy. But I realised that, although I had read her writings appreciatively as a green undergraduate, I had idealised her psychological analysis. Upon rereading her texts, I did find them admirably frank and highly revealing about the content of individual fantasies but, also, rather skimpy on their deeper unconscious meanings and on the role of fantasies in the lives of those who contributed to her books. And though I admired the tremendous compassion and non-judgemental nature that Friday displayed towards her correspondents, espousing a "whatever-turns-you-on-as-long-as-no-one-gets-hurt" attitude, I wondered whether many of her research subjects would have benefited from psychotherapy or could have been helped to achieve a different set of less persecutory and less violent sexual fantasies.

Gradually, I began to scour the literature on the subject, which, I discovered, to my great surprise, to be quite sparse. I soon came to realise that although we as psychoanalytic investigators claim to be obsessed with sexuality, we actually know much more about actual sexual *behaviour* than we do about sexual *fantasy*. It became increasingly clear that the field of sexual fantasies posed many rich questions, for instance: (1) What might be the difference between masturbatory fantasies and coital fantasies? (2) Should people ever share their fantasies in the context of an intimate partnership? (3) Should couples ever enact their sexual fantasies? (4) To what extent might fantasies be autonomous creations of our minds, and to what extent do they derive, more fatalistically, from early child-rearing experiences or from subsequent trauma? (5) Do fantasies cause us harm in our daily lives? (6) Can the content of our fantasies be altered as a result of life experiences or as a consequence of intensive psychotherapeutic treatment? It seems that neither psychoanalysis nor sexology could offer a clear or well-researched answer to any of these aforementioned concerns.

I realised that the field of sexual fantasy—that most private part of our conscious mind, what Winnicott (1963, p. 187) might have dubbed the "incommunicado"—has received little or no emphasis in our training programmes as mental health professionals. It soon became evident that a study on sexual fantasy could be of some interest and, I hoped, of some value as well; and by mid-summer of 2002, I had told Oliver Rathbone, perhaps rather rashly, that I would start work on a fresh, modern, psychoanalytically orientated book-length investigation of the psychology of sexual fantasy.

My ongoing academic and clinical study of this topic took an unexpected turn in the last days of 2002, when I attended a dinner party at the home of Dan Chambers, one of the whiz kids of British media, who had worked, previously, at Channel Four Television, and who had become, subsequently, the Director of Programmes at Channel Five Television. All the guests (many of whom produced films) enjoyed a most convivial supper, and midway through our pudding, Dan—son of the child psychiatrist Dr Florence Chambers—asked me whether I had chosen a subject for my next book. Until now, I had kept my plans very much private, unsure that I would be able to acquire enough relevant clinical material about sexual fantasies and quite uncertain about the structure or methodology for the book. But, disinhibited by jet lag, having recently returned from a trip to Manhattan earlier that morning, I blurted out, "The psychology of sexual fantasies". Within a matter of seconds, six television producers leapt for their wallets or purses, and each produced a business card, tripping over one another as they frantically enquired, "Who's making the television programme?" The charming Georgina Chignell, seated on my right, then a member of the Development Team at Tiger Aspect Productions, a venerable London-based independent television company renowned for its comedy programmes but, also, for its history and science documentaries, won the commission, and within a matter of days had hauled me into her offices in Soho Square in Central London to meet with Paul Sommers, the Head of Factual programmes at Tiger.

Paul Sommers listened with analytic attentiveness as Georgina Chignell and I talked about the subject of sexual fantasies. A distinguished television producer with a sterling track record, Sommers has a reputation for being facially inscrutable—he would make an excellent poker player or, indeed, an old-school "blank screen" psychoanalyst—and during our meeting I had no idea whether he found the material of interest at all. Several weeks passed by before I heard another word about the possibility of making a television documentary about sexual fantasies, but, eventually, Georgina called me in to meet Dunja Noack, a German-born historian who had worked at Tiger Aspect Productions for several years as the Head of Factual Development—a crucial role as the person who turns germinal ideas into viable television programmes. Dunja told me that Paul Sommers had, indeed, approved the project and had authorised us begin to work together to transform a body of psychological observations into a hopefully compelling programme. In stolen time, I began to meet with Dunja for lunch or for tea, or during breaks between sessions with patients, and in the course of our conversations I would expound on the psychoanalytic understanding of sexual fantasy, explaining, in particular, Professor Robert Stoller's (1975, 1979a, 1979b, 1985) groundbreaking work on the importance of the sexual fantasy as a means of eroticising traumatic experiences. A clever academic in her own right, Dunja understood the theory straightaway, and she and I then began to outline what a documentary about sexual fantasies might look like.

We spent ages pondering whether I might have enough data for a three-part series—or, indeed, even for a landmark six-part series—on sexual fantasy; but the thought of committing myself to such a gargantuan project at this stage simply terrified me, and I plumped instead for a one-hour film (in television terms, forty-seven minutes, with a discretionary forty-eighth minute, as required, with twelve or thirteen minutes of advertisements to pay for the production costs). This seemed an altogether more manageable proposition, especially in view of my full-time work in private clinical practice.

As we explored the feasibility of making a documentary about sexual fantasies, it became palpably clear to me that I could not in any way use material from my psychoanalytic work, as that would constitute an unthinkable breach of confidentiality; and a simple review of the skimpy literature would not have given us enough meat for the programme. It would be absolutely essential for me to undertake some *new*, primary research on the topic, and I told Dunja Noack that we would need to have a substantial development period so that I could obtain fresh data. In my experience, most television producers want to keep the commissions rolling in, so that they can generate revenues with lightning speed; fortunately, Dunja appreciated the potential value of undertaking original research, and thus I outlined my wish list. I told her that, in an ideal world, I would want to conduct approximately one hundred clinical psychodiagnostic interviews with randomly selected members of the public (aged eighteen years and above), each of five hours' duration, in order to obtain a detailed life history, as well as a sexual history, with a view to establishing any correspondences between early biographical experiences and subsequent adult sexual fantasy content. I would also want to undertake a more extensive national survey of 50,000 British men and women who could respond to a multi-item questionnaire, providing more details of their sexual fantasies. Dunja gulped at the prospect of authorising a very large piece of research, but she quickly appreciated the potential merit of obtaining such primary data, especially when I told her that, in my clinical experience, many individuals suffer great embarrassment and shame about their sexual fantasies, and that a proper study could help to shed light on such a private, yet pervasive, source of human misery.

As Head of Factual Development at Tiger Aspect Productions, Dunja had made it her task to meet all the relevant Commissioning Editors for science programmes at the major broadcasters both in Great Britain and abroad. For those unfamiliar with the vicissitudes of television commissioning, I should clarify that only a small percentage of programmes will be made in-house by the channels themselves, and many of the programmes will be solicited, instead, from independent production companies such as Tiger; thus, anyone wishing to produce a television programme must first court an "indie", which will then romance one of the commissioning editors at a major broadcaster, in the hope of receiving the requisite funding. In due time, Dunja ferried me to Covent Garden to meet the delightful Justine Kershaw, commissioner for science at Channel Five Television, a close colleague of Dan Chambers, at whose late-night supper party this television idea first took shape. Justine had already heard quite a lot about the sexual fantasy project from Dan, and she swiftly provided us with development money so that I could undertake ten preliminary clinical interviews as "pilot data", to see whether we could generate enough interesting and useful stories. Shortly thereafter, we developed a relationship with the political pollsters YouGov, with whom I had worked on a previous project, and they promptly arranged for ten men and women, randomly chosen from their database, to meet with me for lengthy, confidential clinical interviews, as part of a pilot project.

Dunja arranged the timetable with military precision, and in the early months of 2004, nearly two years after my initial lunch with Oliver Rathbone, I began to interview complete strangers about the details of their sexual fantasies, sacrificing many Saturdays and Sundays in the process. The psychodiagnostic assessment interviews lasted for five hours, and the conversations proceeded with such intensity of concentration that most participants did not even stand up to stretch their legs or pop to the lavatory for a comfort break! The frankness of the interviewees, none of whom had ever before spoken about their sexual fantasies to another living soul, amazed me. They wished, nevertheless, to talk to a psychotherapist, partly to aid research, partly for confessional purposes, and partly as a means of trying to understand more about their often baffling and bewildering fantasy lives. As the interviews unfolded, I became increasingly impressed at the courage of these women and men to speak with such candour and with such seriousness. Needless to say, the data has proven to be both riveting and shocking in many instances, and these interviews ultimately came to form the backbone of the books that followed—namely, *Sex and the Psyche* (Kahr, 2007, 2008b) and *Who's Been Sleeping in Your Head?: The Secret World of Sexual Fantasies* (Kahr, 2008a).

By mid-2004, we had sent a development report to Justine Kershaw at Five, and after a few further meetings, including one key discussion with the eternally gracious and convivial Dan Chambers himself, Five agreed to fund a special one-hour television documentary, entitled *Britain's Sexual Fantasies*, with yours truly as the presenter. With the encouragement of two research-minded colleagues, Dr Avi Shmueli, a fellow marital psychotherapist at the Tavistock Marital Studies Institute in London (and now a psychoanalyst in private practice), and Professor Ann Kurth, a sexual health epidemiologist at the University of Washington in Seattle (and now Dean of the Yale School of Nursing, at Yale University in New Haven, Connecticut and, also, one of the world's leading researchers on the prevention of H.I.V. infection in Africa), I devised a lengthy questionnaire, which we sent to some 15,000 men and women on the YouGov database of randomly selected individuals, representative of each cell of the British adult population. Combining these new findings with some earlier pilot data, I eventually came to possess an archive of over 20,000 British sexual fantasies, which I then supplemented with nearly 4,000 American sexual fantasies.

After months and months of data analysis, we finally went into production in January of 2005 and began to make the film. This required much scripting and re-scripting, supplemented by further interviews with men and women up and down the country who would agree to speak on camera about the role of fantasies in their lives. Dunja Noack became the Executive Producer, and, in time, she hired a Production Manager, a team of researchers, a publicist, and many other personnel, and the hard work began in earnest. Justine Kershaw from Five went on maternity leave, replaced by Peter Grimsdale, a kindly and incisive television stalwart with whom I had worked some years previously on a Channel Four Television project. He came to supervise the programme with benignity and concern, creating the right sort of facilitating environment in which our little project could begin to flourish.

The final piece of the jigsaw fell happily into place after Dunja and I interviewed a brace of potential Producer-Directors. None of the many people with whom we had spoken initially had quite fit the bill, but eventually we met the enthusiastic Fred Casella, a sharp and witty alumnus of the University of Oxford and a former employee of the science department of the British Broadcasting Corporation. He engaged his favourite lighting cameraman and his best sound editor, and by February of 2005 we began the formal shooting.

In chapter 9, I shall endeavour to describe something of the process of filming. In the meanwhile, I hope that I have sketched out the often unexpected, fortuitous twists and turns by which an innocent lunch in the spring of 2002 became transmogrified into a national television programme, ultimately broadcast on 5 September 2005, before an audience of some one million Britons. When Oliver Rathbone and I sat down for soup in the bistro near the London School of Economics and Political Science, neither of us ever imagined that the proposed book idea on sexual fantasies would eventually develop in such a fashion. The process could in no way be described as glamorous. It consisted, rather, of much waiting, much uncertainty, and many long weekends of physically exhausting interviewing and data analysis, crammed into windows of opportunity amid the regular, uncancellable sessions of my full-time clinical practice. And yet, this project became the most extraordinary of journeys, which taught me so much about the hidden contours and caverns of our minds. I remain quite humbled by what I have learned and by what I hope to have shared, not only in the television documentary, but also in the books that followed.

But sometimes, late at night, I do wonder why it had taken me three years to make a forty-seven-minute film.

CHAPTER NINE

Filming sexual fantasies

Go, foolish heart,
Go, dreams of lovers plighted.

"The Lady Ella", in William Schwenck Gilbert,
Patience; or, Bunthorne's Bride, 1881, Act I

I am standing in the centre of London's Millennium Bridge, on a
blisteringly cold Tuesday morning in April, with St. Paul's Cathe-
dral looming behind me and a veritable flotilla of noisy tugboats
tooting below. Overhead, a bevy of jets continues to whoosh by, whip-
ping up the wind; and with no overcoat to protect me, I have begun
to freeze. Hundreds of mid-morning commuters rush past in both
directions, wondering why I remain so absolutely still in the centre
of the bridge, sporting merely a thin cashmere jacket, with makeup
smeared all over my face. I have now stood here, virtually motionless,
for approximately two hours, and I seem to have very little sensation
remaining in any of my extremities.

With a group of colleagues from the television company Tiger
Aspect Productions, I have finally begun filming a one-hour science
documentary, *Britain's Sexual Fantasies*, for the terrestrial broadcaster
Channel Five, based on my research project on the psychology of
sexual fantasies. With the assistance of the pollsters YouGov, I have

now assembled a database of more than 20,000 British adult sexual fantasies, probably the largest collection of such material in the world.

I have microphone wires concealed beneath my shirt, and a battery-operated microphone pack in my back trouser pocket. The lovely Irish makeup artist pats some foundation on my brow and smears a daub of Carmex gloss on my lips; then, doubling as a technical assistant, she removes herself some fifty paces and places her ears to the walkie-talkie so that she can receive instructions from Fred Casella, the Producer-Director of the programme, perched perhaps forty feet away, at the foot of the bridge, with an executive producer, a cameraman, a sound engineer, a production coordinator, and a "runner" (the ambitious, eager young "gofer" who fetches our tea and coffee) poised nearby. Fred speaks to the Irish makeup artist through the walkie-talkie, and he calls out "Action". She then relays Fred's instructions to me, because I cannot hear him through the London noise; and then, like a well-trained puppet, I begin to speak my carefully scripted line: "But what *exactly* does it tell us about *ourselves* if we have a masturbatory fantasy about someone *other* than our regular sexual partner?" Unfortunately, another tugboat has just motored past beneath the Millennium Bridge, and Simon Dyer, our perfectionist soundman, has indicated to Fred that we must re-shoot the entire sequence yet again.

Undaunted, I contain my mounting frustration, reminding myself that I have had a lot of personal psychoanalysis over the years; and so I resume my position, ready for another "take", only to be told through the walkie-talkie that we must now wait until the next two approaching airplanes whiz by. At last we seem to have relative quiet, and I begin to speak my line once again: "But what *exactly* does it tell us about *ourselves* if we have a masturbatory fantasy about someone *other* than our regular sexual partner?" I have delivered my words with, I trust, full vocal resonance, breathing from my diaphragm. I feel relieved and, also, eager to move to the next sequence; but, sadly, Fred comes running up the length of the bridge to join me, wrapped in his puffa jacket and looking very warm: "Sorry, Brett, we shall have to do this line yet again. You were absolutely brilliant, absolutely brilliant, but there was a young hooligan jumping up and down behind you, purposely ruining the shot." Having spent years working psychotherapeutically with young delinquents, I feel compassionate. But I am very cold, and Fred has absolutely insisted that I should not wear my comfortable floor-length overcoat in this sequence "for aesthetic reasons". Noticing that icicles have begun to form on my eyelashes, Fred takes pity on my frozen state, and he starts to pound my back and shoulders in a vigorous manner, in the hope of restoring my blood circulation. Unfortunately, in doing so, he dislodges the microphone wire taped carefully to my pectoral region, and now Simon, the sound engineer, dashes towards me, looking mortified, and eager to rectify the situation.

After another top-up of powder from the eternally patient makeup artist, and further fiddlings with the microphone, we all brace ourselves for yet another "take".

When I had told various psychotherapeutic colleagues that Channel Five Television had commissioned me to make a documentary, many of them responded with unmitigated envy: "God, how glamorous. I wish I were doing that. How much are they paying you?" How we idealise one another! As I brace myself to recite my line for the umpteenth time, I have now learned that making a film involves no glamour at all. I had to wake up at 4.30 a.m. this morning, and, in all likelihood, we will not finish filming until near-on midnight; and I must confess that I would rather be seated in the comfy brown leather chair in my centrally heated Hampstead consulting room. After all, on my ordinary clinical days I do not begin work until 7.00 a.m.

Finally, the tugboats and the airplanes and the obstreperous commuters decide to take pity on my near-glacial circulatory condition, and they all manage to remain quiet for fifteen seconds, just long enough for me to speak my carefully chosen words. After I do so, Fred cries with ecstasy through the walkie-talkie, "Excellent, everyone into the van!", and we head now for the Piazza in Covent Garden where we will film the next shot. Some kindly soul has produced my greatcoat and drapes it over my shoulders, and the young runner asks me whether I would like anything to drink. "Hot water, please", I murmur feebly, and off she dashes to the local Starbucks coffee house in search of my medicine.

I feel rather sheepish complaining in any way; after all, I have just completed a large-scale research project, fully funded by the broadcasters, which will form the basis of not only a popular psychology book for Allen Lane, the hardback imprint of Penguin Books, but, also, I hope, a spate of academic and clinical journal articles. I have had the opportunity to work with a carefully selected team of creative and vivacious television professionals; and, most of all, millions of Britons will be able to watch this film, which, I trust, will help to alleviate the widespread shame and guilt that people experience in relation to their private masturbatory and coital sexual fantasies.

All in all, I feel pleased—but certainly, no one should *ever* envy the television presenter.

After my morning of filming in Southwark, not far from the newly restored Globe Theatre of Shakespearean fame, we journey into the heart of London in a convoy of vans. The production coordinator, the makeup artist, and the runner have all bundled into one vehicle, and I take a seat in the camera van with Fred, the Producer-Director, with Will, our clever cameraman who won a British Academy of Film and Television Arts award (the British version of the Oscars), and with Simon, the sound engineer. Within a matter of seconds, the conversation turns to women—women on the streets, women on billboards, women anywhere—no doubt an attempt to fend off the homosexual anxiety created by the thought of four men enclosed in such a tiny space! Too tired to speak, I merely listen, astounded that men in the media really do talk about women in this sort of objectifying manner. I have never been in a van with three male psychoanalysts, but I can swear to you that should that ever come to pass, well-analysed clinicians would, I hope, refer to women in a rather different tone.

Following an interminably long period of scouting out locations and setting up camera angles, I then embark upon four or five hours of walking through various streets of Covent Garden: the Piazza, Neal Street, and many others besides. This time, the cameraman stands nearby, no longer positioned at the end of a bridge; and I begin to master the fine art of walking and talking simultaneously, in preparation for a series of close travelling shots. Fred barks out various challenging directorial instructions: "Now, Brett, start here at this traffic cone, then walk forward about twenty paces, and as you pass by the green-painted door on the left, turn your head sharply to the right, then look over your shoulder and walk out of the shot, while you are saying your lines." I smile to myself internally, realising that I have understood very little of what Fred has just requested; but, fortunately, after a little practice run, I discover that I have absorbed more of the directions than I had thought, and Fred pats me on the head, flattering me and calling me an "old pro"—so far, so good.

For this scene I must recite an historically orientated line: "In the nineteenth century, psychiatrists believed that anybody who had a sexual fantasy must be either a degenerate or a pervert; indeed, Sigmund Freud believed that if you fantasise, then you must be very sexually unfulfilled." Apparently, the combination of a film crew clogging up a narrow Covent Garden street, with a middle-aged, bespectacled presenter talking about perversion and degeneration, had proved too irresistible for a group of teenage boys, who took every opportunity to insert themselves into the shot, pull their trousers down, and "moon" us. With impeccable charm, Fred tried to reason with them, and eventually they acceded and tired of interrupting our filming. Needless to say, we had to re-shoot this sequence six or seven more times.

Although no one in the streets recognises me, crowds of onlookers keep gathering round to watch the filming process nevertheless. Goodness only knows what people find so intriguing: perhaps, at some unconscious level, the sight of the eye of the camera, trained so exclusively at one particular man, activates a yearning to be stared at attentively by the preoedipal mother. Whatever the explanation, complete strangers have become deeply absorbed by our outdoor shooting, and as I begin to walk through the streets of London, the swelling crowd follows in my footsteps, maintaining only a slightly respectful distance from the cameras. Japanese tourists keep stopping us for a photograph, and of course, numerous people constantly ask us, "What are you filming?"

Will and Simon, an inveterate double-act who have worked together before, knew only too well that if we told the truth, we would be lost in conversation for hours; so, without missing a beat, whenever anyone inquired what channel we worked for, the camera and sound supremos would reply in unison, "We're from the Christian Channel." Generally, this proved to be a sufficiently sober response, and people would then walk away quite quickly, unimpressed by the ostensible sexlessness of the Christian Channel. If we had told them the actual title of our programme—*Britain's Sexual Fantasies*—we would have had to endure unending interrogation.

By 7.00 p.m., we wend our way towards Oxford Street, as Fred has insisted on filming one of my lines set against a huge crowd. Unfortunately, the large red buses and the omnipresent street sweepers on Oxford Street make much more noise than the airplanes or tugboats at the Millennium Bridge, and it takes us one hour or more in freezing conditions for me to pontificate about the meaning of heterosexual people who have homosexual fantasies, and vice versa. As I walk down Oxford Street, with the camera practically stuck up against my face for a tight close-up, Fred keeps shouting, "Running up . . . speed . . . and action!", whereupon I expound, "Our survey has indicated that many self-identified heterosexual people have homosexual fantasies, and many gay men and lesbians have heterosexual fantasies." Because of the noises from the streets, we have to shoot and re-shoot and re-shoot this little sequence many times, with Fred constantly shouting, "Louder, Brett, louder!" At this point, I not only find myself frozen, but my otherwise sturdy voice has become ragged from an entire day of exterior filming. Furthermore, I feel rather silly talking about heterosexual and homosexual fantasies on Oxford Street at the top of my lungs. The crowds continue to walk by, fascinated and perplexed by my rantings. I know that, but for the very visible presence of the camera and the sound boom, the men and women passing by might have thought that I had escaped from a nearby psychiatric institution!

Because the noise problem has proved so relentless, we have had to film this one small sequence literally fifty or sixty times. Some documentary makers might regard this as excessive, but the intrepid and highly professional Fred Casella prides himself on his absolute perfectionism, and I trust him implicitly, having chosen him out of a large number of potential short-listed candidates for the job of Producer-Director.

As my tired feet begin to bleed in my tight, newly purchased leather shoes—a result of having to stand the entire day—the well-known popular actor Ross Kemp, a former star of the British soap opera *EastEnders*, suddenly ambles past me on my left-hand side as I have begun to speak my little line for the forty-third time. Infinitely more experienced before a camera than I will ever be, the generous Mr Kemp flashes a deeply supportive and sympathetic smile as he walks up Oxford Street, as if to say, "Good on you, mate, I know how exhausting filming can be!" This one simple gesture of kindness helps to fortify me for the remaining scenes in the gardens of Soho Square.

At nearly 10.00 p.m., we finish shooting the final sequence of the day, on the potential dangerousness of certain sexual fantasies and about the role of early sexual abuse in the genesis of adult sexual fantasies. Fred takes mercy on me, and he allows me to film this last segment seated comfortably on a park bench. Needless to say, a fire from a nearby building causes further delays, but, thankfully, no one perishes, and the crowd cheers the valiant fire brigade, who, rightfully, have begun to attract more attention than our tiny television crew.

After reciting the final line, "If you have been at all disturbed by anything that you have heard in this programme, then you might want to consider contacting a registered mental health professional", Fred then announces, "Well done, guys . . . that's a wrap." Fred's words bring me unparalleled joy, and I collapse on the park bench with great relief. My very maternal Executive Producer, Dunja Noack, then trundles me into a waiting taxicab to take me back home. After an hour in a near-boiling bath, my body temperature has returned to normal, and I sleep soundly, braced for yet another day in front of the camera.

Shortly after recuperating from the exhausting process of filming, the production team then sets about editing the footage, ensuring that they have pieced the different segments together in a coherent fashion and that they have managed to adjust the colour and sound quality to the right levels. Of course, I have no expertise whatsoever in these technical areas, but I did pop into the editing suite from time to time to watch the show develop. I also had to return for some additional indoor filming, some further close-ups, and for the reading of the voice-over narration that would accompany some of the frames of footage.

Eventually, the film appeared on Great Britain's television network, Five, late in the evening, on 5 September 2005. Regrettably, I could not watch the live transmission of the film with family and friends, as I had had to travel out of London to Birmingham in my role as Resident Psychotherapist on B.B.C. Radio 2 in order to go on air at midnight. Consequently, I caught only the first few minutes of the programme in my Birmingham hotel room before proceeding to the B.B.C. recording studio for my broadcast. Having already watched the film several times during the editing process, I had rather tired of seeing my face and hearing my voice by this point, and in many ways, I felt pleased that I did not have to sit through it all again! Fortunately, a number of kind people rang me afterwards to offer congratulations. The next day, I learned that the film had attracted approximately one million viewers—a very respectable number for a late-night British television programme unsuitable for young audiences.

As one might imagine, reviews appeared in quite a number of the main British broadsheet newspapers—many quite complimentary, and some less so. One of the papers waxed very snide indeed, and, clearly upset by my conclusion that much sexual fantasy derives from early childhood trauma, accused me of knowing less about psychology than a first-year undergraduate! I must confess that this remark rather stung me, but I took it in my stride.

Two responses, in particular, pleased me greatly. Several days after the transmission of the film, while walking through the car park of the Tavistock Clinic where I then worked (in the Tavistock

Marital Studies Institute), a very senior member of staff, known for his conservatism, approached me and, quite unexpectedly, wrapped his arms around me with great enthusiasm, hugging me tightly. Although I had known this man for many years, I do not think that we had ever so much as shaken hands previously. But, apparently, he enjoyed the film greatly, and he waxed rhapsodic about how I had made an important contribution to the field of psychology.

And some days after this, a woman rang me out of the blue. She had found my telephone number, presumably through directory enquiries. She thanked me for having made this film and then proceeded to explain that for the whole of her adult life she had experienced immense shame over what she regarded as her apparently unusual sexual fantasies. She told me that she had no idea why she had these particular fantasies, and this troubled her greatly. But now that she had watched *Britain's Sexual Fantasies* on television, she understood the origin and the meaning of her private thoughts for the very first time. This lady did not share the content of her fantasies with me, and I certainly did not ask her to do so. Instead, I told her that I deeply appreciated her telephone call, and that it pleased me to know that this forty-seven-minute film had proved of some value.

CHAPTER TEN

How to make 120,000 people happy in just ten weeks

Ah! *Vanitas Vanitatum*! Which of us is happy in this world?
Which of us has his desire? or, having it, is satisfied?

William Makepeace Thackeray, *Vanity Fair: A Novel without a Hero*,
Chapter LXVII, 1848
[Thackeray, 1848, p. 624]

Part One: 2002–2005

I am seated on a sleek leather banquette, discreetly tucked away in the alcove of a bustling, sun-streaked restaurant in Waterloo, South London, just a stone's throw from the Old Vic Theatre, lunching with a very dynamic Welshwoman called Patricia Llewellyn—"Pat" to her friends—one of Great Britain's most enterprising independent television producers. I have known Pat for some time, having met her through her partner, Ben Adler, also a television executive, with whom I had worked on a project years previously. Pat founded a thriving company, Optomen Television, which supplies programmes to the major terrestrial broadcasters in the United Kingdom, such as the British Broadcasting Corporation and Channel Four Television, and recently she has begun to conquer the world as well. Hugely creative, energetic, and successful—not to mention charmingly self-effacing—Pat has specialised in making cookery programmes, and, in her time, she has discovered some of Great Britain's major chefs, most particularly Jamie Oliver—"The Naked Chef"—now a super-chef—and, also the culinary experts Clarissa Dickson Wright and Jennifer Paterson, better known as the "Two Fat Ladies". More recently, she has served as the brains behind several series of restaurant transformation programmes featuring the increasingly popular entrepreneur, ex-footballer Gordon Ramsay, the twenty-first-century equivalent of Julia Child or Delia Smith . . . with bite.

As I have never become a master of the culinary arts, I remain very uncertain as to why this high priestess of *haute cuisine* has not only invited me to lunch, but seems intent on paying for it as well.

Over roast suckling pig, an admittedly unusual, though tasty, choice, as well as not one, but two bottles of Retro 55, Pat explains that, although cookery programmes and gardening programmes will never go out of fashion, all of her senior chums at the B.B.C. have told her that *psychology* will soon become a growth area, and some of the executives in the commissioning department—those benighted individuals who decide which programmes will eventually be transmitted into our homes—have even begun to speak of psychology as "the new gardening". Never one to miss an opportunity, Pat decides to pick my brains, knowing me to be a media-friendly mental health professional who has already worked in radio and television for quite some time.

Chewing on our delicious food, Pat and I engage in conversation about what sort of psychology programme I might like to make. I respond instantly that I would love to write and present a multi-part documentary on the history of psychology, covering all of the great heroes and heroines in the field, surveying their major contributions. I try to sound as engaged as possible, but, as a trained clinician, I can tell, quite quickly, that in spite of her sympathetic head nods, Pat really has little interest in bringing Sigmund Freud, Carl Gustav Jung, and Alfred Adler to the big screen. After all, none of them had bequeathed any memorable Austrian or Swiss recipes. I can see that Pat's interest has begun to wane, and, in a kittenish way, she desperately attempts to stifle her yawns. A little voice inside my head tells me that this might be a good moment to mention that one-time bestseller, *Freud's Own Cookbook*, co-written by the popular Jungian analyst Dr James Hillman (Hillman and Boer, 1985), which contains recipes for such delectable delicacies as "Banana O." and "Little

Hansburgers"; but decorum triumphs, and I swallow my thoughts with another sip of wine.

Pat then explains that *she* has an idea that might be of interest. Clearly, she had asked me about my own dream plans merely to humour me. This "free" lunch has had a secret agenda all along. It seems that some wag had recently proclaimed Swindon—a grim industrial town in the backwaters of England—as the most depressed location in the country. Would it not be wonderful, Pat beams, if she could send a team of psychotherapists into Swindon to cheer up the entire population? Would this be possible? Ethical? Crazy? According to Pat, this could be not only a socially responsible piece of television, but compulsive viewing as well—a sort of modern-day Freud meets *Beat the Clock*. Can the shrinks cure Swindon's melancholia in a mere matter of weeks?

Needless to say, Pat's idea has an instant appeal and proves to be a great challenge. Even after an excruciatingly long day, having worked with ten private patients, back-to-back, in fifty-minute chunks, I often leave my consulting room feeling that I have made only a small impact on the amelioration of psychic suffering in the United Kingdom. Pat's proposed project speaks instantly to my broader social and political desire to use psychotherapeutic and psychoanalytic ideas to reach a wider audience. But how could I possibly treat the tens of thousands of neurotic individuals in Swindon—a place whose bleakness has not escaped me, having visited there on a multitude of occasions, en route to regular summer holidays in the bucolic Gloucestershire countryside?

I assure Pat that the idea intrigues me and that it would be a treat to brainstorm with her and the Development Team at Optomen Television to see how we might cure Swindon of its misery without needing to bring the entire membership of the British Psychological Society, the Royal College of Psychiatrists, and the United Kingdom Council for Psychotherapy into town as reinforcements. Pat seems deeply relieved by my encouraging, if somewhat bewildered, response. As a cookery expert, she clearly wanted to meet with a workaday clinician to discover, first of all, whether anyone had ever "treated" an entire town before and, second of all, whether it might even be possible. If Pat could conjure up a plan for curing Swindon, this would be her greatest recipe to date.

After a series of meetings with Ms Llewellyn and her staff, we have at last crafted a blueprint for a sure-fire series: a team of five experts, consisting of a mental health professional (possibly me), a town planner, a workplace consultant, a physical trainer, and, perhaps, a social entrepreneur skilled in helping large groups of people to work together, will be shipped into Swindon. The members of the Development Team have generated literally hundreds of ideas as to how we might improve the mental health of the Swindonians, which include importing a fleet of dancing policemen who would make people laugh by doing jigs in the town square; as well as baking the world's largest-ever cake, hundreds of feet long, hundreds of feet wide, and hundreds of feet high, which could then be consumed by every one of the local residents, bringing a new meaning to community activity. In my own rather predictable way, I suggest that we might try to identify those members of the town most in need of psychotherapy and then set up a series of analytically orientated groups that my mental health colleagues and I could facilitate. The television executives look misty-eyed by my very traditional suggestion for promoting happiness, and one of them sneers, "Yes, of course we *could* offer them therapy, but it's not very visual." I explain that Freud did not design psychoanalysis as a spectator sport. The cheeky television buck then replies, "Yes, that may be, but what will we see on screen? Just some chap looking sympathetic? Viewers will turn off in droves."

In any event, I certainly did *not* suggest that we should offer psychotherapy *on camera*. Rather, I had thought that we might provide some short-term interventions *off-screen*, in the hope that this would make an impact, and that the participants could then speak about this experience afterwards, if they so wished.

Clearly, the needs of the television producer and the needs of the psychotherapist could not be more divergent, but I have always espoused the view that, although we come from different traditions, we should strive to find ways to collaborate with one another, because, when all is said and done, we in the mental health field can each reach ten patients a day, at the very most, but the television supremos can make contact with hundreds of millions of people worldwide. Perhaps we have something to learn from them.

Eventually, a title emerges for our proposed four-part series: *Making Swindon Happy*. Cheers erupt throughout the Optomen Television offices, and everyone waltzes around the converted chocolate factory with inane grins, predicting that *Making Swindon Happy* will become "cult" television and win all of the awards—Emmys, B.A.F.T.A.s, and the like. Further, we predict that this programme will become so successful that we shall have to repeat it in every downtrodden city in the land, and that we will have created a franchise—*Making*

Scunthorpe Happy, *Making Basildon Happy*, and *Making Puddleby-on-the-Marsh Happy*, to boot. Now all we need is a commission from the B.B.C. for many millions of pounds!

I wait, and wait, and wait.

Indeed, I wait for quite a long time.

Three years later, Patricia Llewellyn invites me out for a dinner with Ben Adler, once her boyfriend, now her husband. In the intervening years, I had the privilege of attending their glamorous wedding, an event so star-studded that the best man began his toast: "Ladies and Gentlemen . . . and Television Presenters . . ." As we settle down to a Japanese meal around the corner from my consulting room in North London's Hampstead, not far from the onetime home of Sigmund Freud himself, Pat and Ben tell me gleefully that, after years of prevaricating, the B.B.C. has finally agreed to fund the project, and they thank me for being so patient. Unfortunately, Swindon has fallen by the wayside, because the B.B.C. has decided that Slough, an equally downtrodden town of 120,000 residents, in the county of Berkshire, would better suit their purposes. Thanks to its investment of a lot of money in promoting a sitcom called *The Office*, set in Slough, the B.B.C. could count on viewers having already formed a relationship with the town—so, therefore, the programme will now be called *Making Slough Happy*, and the poor residents of Swindon will have to make do, alas, with antidepressants and the placebo effect.

Although the B.B.C. brass have axed Swindon, replacing it with Slough, it seems that someone liked my screen test, and so I have survived the in-house execution; thus, if I wish, I could be the resident psychotherapist and use my clinical skills to transform the mental health of the Sloughians in just ten short weeks. I should be ecstatic that such a visionary project will now become a televisual reality, but as the waitress brings our sushi and our salmon teriyaki, I find myself quaking, wondering how I shall manage to turn the neurotic misery of Slough into extraordinary happiness—especially as I work full-time in clinical practice, with barely a ten-minute lunch break. Pat and Ben assure me that filming days will be planned to accommodate my clinical timetable, but that I should be prepared to work late into the evening as well as every weekend. Fortunately, a fast train from London's Paddington Station can spirit me easily to Slough in a mere twenty minutes or so; thus, I should be able to make frequent appearances.

Thereafter an endless round of television-related activities begins: meetings with the Producer, meetings with the Executive Producer, meetings with the Assistant Producer, photo-sessions with the B.B.C., photo-sessions with the local newspapers in Slough, appearances on B.B.C. Radio 2, as well as appearances on the local Slough radio station Star F.M., hosted by the impossibly beautiful Angie Walker, who looks like a young Marilyn Monroe. The Production Manager of *Making Slough Happy*, Sarah Gowers, who has the thankless task of coordinating all the administrative details of this increasingly behemoth project, telephones me six or seven times a day in order to pin me down to a raft of filming dates, experts meetings, and suchlike. Our conversations always begin thus: "Can you manage Friday morning the 12th, Brett?" "No, sorry, Sarah, I am with patients all morning." "What about Tuesday afternoon, the 16th—any good for you, Brett?" "No, sorry, Sarah, I'm with patients all afternoon." "Well, Brett, can you manage the following Wednesday, late in the evening? We'll send a car for you and pick you up from your office." "Yes, Sarah, actually, that works quite well. It's a deal." Ten minutes later, the telephone rings again, "Sorry, Brett, it's Sarah. One of the other experts can't manage next Wednesday. Any chance we can go back to the Tuesday?" "No, sorry, Sarah, I *still* have my patients." "I just thought that maybe some of them could be cancelled, Brett." "No, sorry, Sarah, you must understand that these people have been coming to see me for years, at these regular times, and I cancel only for funerals, health scares, and family emergencies." "Oh, Brett, I see. Well, I'll have to get back to you."

Eventually, we select a date on which to begin filming, or rather, the Production Manager has selected a date—a Saturday in May—and she tells me in no uncertain terms that because the vast majority of the other team members can manage this date, it cannot be altered. Unfortunately, I had already registered to attend a three-day conference in Dublin—the annual meeting of the International Association for Forensic Psychotherapy, at which I must deliver a keynote address. Although I have already paid my subscription and booked my flight and also my hotel, I will have to leave the conference midway through in order to return to England on time, and then, once back home, wend my way quite speedily to Slough.

I travel to Dublin, deliver my pre-conference dinner speech on the Thursday night, catch up with long-standing colleagues in the forensic mental health field, and then attend most of the sessions on the Friday, during which time the Executive Producer bombards me with hourly faxes and telephone calls at my hotel to brief me on the running order of filming for the first day. I elect to stay for the main conference dinner on the Friday night, especially as the incoming President has asked me to make a speech praising the contributions of the outgoing President. All my forensic colleagues, many of whom I have not seen for years, decide to party into the small hours of the morning, but by 10.00 p.m. I return, reluctantly, to my hotel, as I must catch a 7.20 a.m. flight from Dublin in order to arrive in Slough by 10.00 a.m. And in order to catch the 7.20 a.m. departure, I must be at the airport by 6.00 a.m. And in order to be at the airport by 6.00 a.m., I must be in a taxi by 5.00 a.m. Therefore, I request a wakeup call for 4.00 a.m. Of course, owing to the excitement and anxiety of the forthcoming shoot—a major four-part B.B.C. television series—I cannot fall asleep easily, and so I read through my briefing notes again and again in preparation for the filming, and I iron my shirts with care, as there will not be time to do anything domestic once I have arrived in Slough. By 3.00 a.m., I drift into semi-consciousness, only to be awakened by the shrill ring of the telephone one hour later. I feel wretched and groggy, rather like a frightened first-year undergraduate who has "pulled an all-nighter" in order to finish my term paper minutes before the deadline. As I revive myself in the hotel shower, I curse Pat and Ben, I curse the B.B.C., and I curse myself for having agreed to undertake some thirty days of filming, which will absorb every hour of my non-clinical time over most of the next three months—intruding upon precious domestic time—and all for a social experiment with a very uncertain outcome.

After a worryingly bumpy flight, albeit a mercifully short one, I arrive at Heathrow Airport at 8.50 a.m., relieved that Sarah Gowers has, indeed, dispatched a very fancy car to take me directly to Slough. Sarah had hoped that by providing me with a private driver, I would arrive "fresh" for the first day of filming. Sadly, she did not reckon on the fact that I had managed only one hour of sleep. Perhaps I should have left the conference the night before, but having already booked, and having yearned to see many lifelong colleagues, I opted for this particular arrangement.

Before I meet the residents of Slough, fifty of whom have signed up for a course of intensive life-transformation, I must film a series of "travelling shots" of me arriving in Slough for the first time. The driver has strict instructions to drop me off on the motorway, where

I shall meet Sam Maynard, one of the two Producer-Directors, along with a fleet of assistants. Martin, the sound man, laces a microphone through my shirt, which clips onto my tie, and shuttles me into yet another B.B.C. chauffeured car. Sarah, the Assistant Producer (one of three Sarahs on the core team), drives us onto the motorway, while Sam, perched in the front seat, turns round and shoves his camera right up against my face for a close-up and asks me, "So, Brett, are you nervous?" I know that Sam would like me to answer "yes", so that when he comes to edit the footage, he can build up some dramatic tension; and I already know from past experience with editors that the voice-over (which for this programme will be spoken by the Academy Award-winning actor Jim Broadbent) will probably sound something like this: "To help make the residents of Slough happier, we've called in leading psychotherapist Brett Kahr. No stranger to helping people in trouble, Brett is the Resident Psychotherapist on B.B.C. Radio. But *can* he work his magic on the people of Berkshire?" I reply that I *do* have butterflies in my stomach, never having undertaken a project of this magnitude before. Actually, I seem not unduly nervous, but having slept only one hour and having just disembarked from a choppy flight, I am, instead, exhausted, though endeavouring to be buoyant.

Because television directors fear technical hitches, such as passing airplanes that interfere with the sound quality or film that becomes somehow damaged, every sequence must be shot, and re-shot, and then re-shot once again, until we have several "takes" in the can. I spend the next half hour explaining to Sam, in different intonations, that I have butterflies in my stomach, owing to the novelty of this challenging adventure. It all seems very silly, not least because Sam then jumps out of the car and positions himself at the side of the motorway with his camera. He instructs Sarah, the driver, to turn back on herself and to come up the motorway again and again, at least two times, so that he can shoot a sequence of my car arriving in Slough. Apparently, a mere shot of me in the back seat will not provide the viewers at home with sufficient evidence that I have come to Slough from elsewhere. In television land, my arrival must be *seen*. And though the shot of my car entering Slough will occupy only two or three seconds of on-air time—certainly no more—we spend yet another half hour driving up and down, up and down, until Sam satisfies himself that he has captured a glimpse of me through a smoky-glass window, dashing by at lightning speed.

Eventually, I arrive at a huge mansion not far from Slough itself—Caversham House—once home to the G.C.H.Q. (Government Communications Headquarters) during World War II and subsequently the offices of B.B.C. Radio Berkshire. Once there, I meet my fellow experts (now six in total): a talented young economist who believes that governments should devote their time to improving subjective well-being rather than to gross national product; a social entrepreneur who received the O.B.E. [Officer of the Most Excellent Order of the British Empire] decoration from Her Majesty the Queen for having turned the downtrodden London satellite of Bromley-by-Bow into a thriving creative community; two glamorous workplace consultants who have made quite an impact at transforming the culture of various office environments; a statistically-minded research psychologist, who will have the onerous task of conducting empirical work throughout our project, testing and retesting the levels of happiness of the natives of Slough on a number of standardised questionnaires; and yours truly as the provider of a depth-psychological contribution whose precise nature we have not yet quite determined. Nicola Moody, a former high commissioner within the B.B.C. and now a freelance Executive Producer for Optomen Television, greets us and briefs us on our task. For the first day of filming, we must meet the "Slough 50"—those men and women who have volunteered to work with the six of us at close quarters over the next few months, during which time we, the experts, must improve their lives, almost beyond recognition, and boost their baseline happiness ratings to states of near delirium.

Dr Richard Stevens, the research psychologist and himself the author of a good student guide to the work of Sigmund Freud (Stevens, 1983a) and a comparable introductory tome on the work of Erik Erikson (Stevens, 1983b), has already administered one round of pre-intervention questionnaires to the Slough 50. Apparently, these people suffer from so much depression that their baseline happiness before the project seems to be on a par with the inhabitants of most Third World countries. We have our task cut out for us, as we must now spread joy and sunshine, change the culture of their offices, improve their family relationships, transform their sex lives, lift their depressions, and get the residents of Slough to hum together as a creative community. The Slough 50 will serve as ambassadors, and they will be our links to the remaining 119,950 or so residents of Slough, many of whom will feature in the programme as well.

As the sole mental health clinician among the six experts, I have negotiated that I will provide as much off-camera psychotherapy and group psychotherapy to the Slough 50 as I can physically muster in the time available—in all likelihood, short-term psychodynamically orientated psychotherapy. We have not yet established which residents will come to see me, nor where, nor, indeed, at what frequency. Nicola has decided, quite rightly, that I must meet them first.

But in view of the fact that I cannot, and will not, practise actual psychotherapy on camera in front of a potentially limitless audience of multiple millions, the producers have insisted that we must find another role for me—one that will utilise my psychological knowledge and skills, and will also be "visual", and will not compromise the code of clinical confidentiality.

Nicola Moody, the Executive Producer, tells me that a "little bird" has informed her that, in my spare time, I compose songs and play the piano and sing, and that I have written music for the theatre—all true. Perhaps I could create a Slough Choir? After all, I could not only use my psychotherapeutic capacities to promote group cohesion, but I could also deploy my musical skills to help the people of Slough to find their voices. I suddenly remember that, throughout much of the 1990s, I did serve, first as Musical Director, and next as author, of several annual Tavistock Clinic pantomimes, and then, in 1997, I became the first Musical Director of the Tavistock Clinic Choir. I reasoned that if I could manage to extract some tuneful sounds from a group of predominantly silent British health service psychoanalysts and psychotherapists, I might just stand a chance at getting the residents of Slough to warble as well.

And so, after some coaxing, I agree that I shall attempt to become "The Singing Psychotherapist", and in my first meeting with the Slough 50 I invite them all to join me in learning the jaunty anthem of happiness, "Put On a Happy Face", from the popular Broadway musical *Bye Bye Birdie*. After our first rendition, with me on piano, the previously grey group of Sloughians suddenly erupts in peals of laughter and jubilation, and before long the heights of happiness seem within immediate reach. By the end of the first day of filming, I have had good conversations with all fifty key participants, and we have established a date for the first rehearsal of the Slough Choir. It seems that I have also agreed to write a pop song that will be performed at a big concert in the Slough town centre on the final day of filming, and which will serve as the climax to the four-part television series.

As I head back to London at the end of the day, this time on the train (as Sarah Gowers needs to keep a tight eye on the budget), I can just about hear Jim Broadbent's voice-over narration in my mind: "Well, Brett has rashly agreed to write a pop song for the residents of Slough. But can he pull it off? Will the Slough 50 disappoint him? Will they be able to sing on key? Will it all prove to be a great disaster? Tune in at nine o'clock next week."

Part Two: 2005–2020

My "Letter from London" about *Making Slough Happy*, originally published in 2006 (Kahr, 2006b), ended at this point. Professor Peter Rudnytsky, then Editor of the psychoanalytic journal *American Imago*, kept encouraging me to write the sequel, describing what had happened during my months in Slough and what had then transpired as a result of the broadcast of the four one-hour television specials on the B.B.C. Having failed miserably to find a way to summarise such a rich experience in only three thousand words, and, quite frankly, having "overdosed" on all things Slough, I needed to embark upon more fresh pieces of writing at the time. I also reasoned that since many millions of people had already watched the programmes on television, I did not really need to provide an account. Thus, I failed to produce an article at that time.

But in the interest of completeness and in order to round out the story for those people who did not have a chance to watch the television series, I shall now provide a *very* brief overview of what we did in Slough. As I write this some fifteen years after my visits to Berkshire, I have elected to pen this portion in the past tense, in contrast to the first part of the essay, written more freshly in the present tense.

Although Optomen Television had originally engaged me to introduce the residents of Slough to the art of psychotherapy, it soon became apparent that owing to the very large number of Sloughians—roughly 120,000 in total—any free treatment that I could provide would be merely a token gesture. However, the producers and I thought that it might be worthwhile to see whether any psychotherapy could be undertaken outside the familiarity and security of my London consulting room.

At the very outset of my sojourns, one of the "Slough 50", a robust and charming young man, approached me and asked me for a psychotherapy consultation. The producers found us a private office, and we sat down to talk. This gentleman, whom I shall call "Mehmet", told me that although he enjoys his family life, his job, his relations with his girlfriend, as well as a broad circle of friends, he decided to apply for a spot on this television programme because he hoped that one of the experts could help him conquer a crippling anxiety—namely, a fear of the London Underground! Although he had lived in Slough his entire life, he felt that his phobia of the "tube" had prevented him from ever moving to London and had kept him a virtual prisoner in Slough.

Mehmet and I began to discuss his fear of travelling on public transport in our nation's capital, and he told me that although he and his family rarely visited London, due to financial restrictions, he had, on occasion, ridden the tube as a little boy. I asked him *when* the fear of the underground first emerged, and he explained to me in no uncertain terms: "Oh, maybe seven years ago." Naturally, I wondered what had occurred in his life seven years previously, and he sighed that he could not recall much of any note, claiming that, back in 1998, he simply went about his business, socialising, working, and getting on with life, much as he did in 2005, the year in which we made *Making Slough Happy*. In spite of numerous investigations on my part, I could not find *any* particular trigger that would have accounted for the onset of Mehmet's phobia at that particular time.

In the absence of being able to provide an instant or clever answer, I simply permitted the free-associative process to unfold, and I entreated Mehmet to talk about whatever thoughts and images popped into his mind. A very engaging person, he spoke freely and happily, painting a very helpful portrait of his current life, of his colleagues at work, of his partner, and of his relatives. At one point, Mehmet mentioned that he had a large constellation of siblings, describing himself as "one of eight". But half an hour later in the conversation, Mehmet made another comment about his many brothers and sisters, and this time he made a passing reference to "the seven of us". As someone who enjoys obsessing over minute details in the psychotherapeutic narrative, I wondered whether I had misheard Mehmet the first time round. Did he have six siblings ("the seven of us"), or did he have seven ("one of eight")? This seeming discrepancy troubled me, and I asked for clarification.

Mehmet replied with some hesitation, "Ah, did I confuse you? Well, I'm not surprised. You see, we *were* eight, but *now* we're seven. So I guess that means that I have six brothers and sisters. But sometimes, I still think that I have *seven* siblings. Sorry about that." In a soft, understated voice, I asked Mehmet what had happened, having guessed already that he must have suffered a sibling bereavement somewhere along the line. Mehmet turned his head downwards and told me that, several years ago, his eldest sister, "Zofia", had dropped dead of a heart attack at the age of twenty-five. This death came as a huge and sudden shock, and, according to Mehmet, his relatives still find it very difficult to talk about this much missed young woman.

I asked whether Mehmet could tell me anything more about the circumstances of Zofia's death. "Yes, of course", he replied, "she was just coming back from her first day in her new job". "In Slough?" I wondered. "Oh no", he rebutted, "in London". Apparently, Zofia had only just relocated from Slough to London in order to take up a position in a financial institution, and all the relatives bristled with pride, not least as she had become the first person in the family to work in such a highly paid position. I commiserated with Mehmet on this loss and commented that I could see from his expressions and could hear in his voice that he still felt quite sad at the death of his big sister—understandably so. Mehmet nodded in appreciation of my very simple statement, acknowledging his bereavement. I then inquired if he knew where Zofia had died, and when. "Yes, she died on Wednesday, 18th March, 1998, at about 6.30 in the evening", he explained. "The date is still very much at the forefront of your mind", I noted. "Yes, very much so", he replied, "I will never forget her."

I continued to engage Mehmet on this matter and commented that if Zofia had died on a Wednesday, at 6.30 p.m., perhaps she had only recently finished work. "Yes, she was walking on the street, back towards her new flat", he explained, "and then, the heart attack took her from us". "Where did she work?", I inquired. "Oh, in some big banking house in the City of London", he told me. "And where was her flat?" I asked. "Oh, in Stoke Newington, in North London", he offered.

With all of this important information to hand, I then asked Mehmet whether he knew *how* Zofia travelled to and from the office. He told me that he simply did not know. Mehmet thought that she might have taken a taxi, or that she might have walked. As a Londoner, I explained that a daily taxi from the City to Stoke Newington would be quite expensive, and that walking would take an extremely long time. Perhaps, I wondered, she might have used public transport. Suddenly, Mehmet burst into tears and blubbed, "I suppose she took the underground. Do you think she took the underground?" I told him that I could not be certain, but I mentioned that most people newly arrived in London from the provinces, especially young people who cannot yet afford a car, will ride the tube, and that it seemed to me highly possible that his sister might have done so as well. Tears streamed down Mehmet's cheeks as he reflected on his sister, but, to my surprise, he still made no connection whatsoever between his own phobia of the underground and the possibility that his sister might have died from a heart attack shortly after having emerged from a tube station!

I then reminded Mehmet, rather gently, that, at the outset of our conversation he had told me that he stopped going to London approximately seven years previously—in 1998—the very year of Zofia's death. At last, Mehmet's eyes brightened, and he gasped, "My God, I never thought of that. Jesus Christ, the timing is exact. But I never considered that. You think I can't tolerate the tube because of my sister?" I explained that I could not be certain, but that we might entertain this as a possible hypothesis. He cried a bit more and then he wiped his face and turned to me, "Wow, they told me it might be a bit intense to talk to the 'shrink'. I really didn't see this coming."

Mehmet took a sip of water and then he breathed a deep sigh. He thanked me for speaking to him and told me that he would like to try an experiment. Next week, he would take his girlfriend to London for a romantic adventure, and at some point he would be brave and would purchase tickets for the underground. I wished him well, underscoring that I would be very happy to speak to him again in future, should he find that useful, and I thanked him for his candour and for his hard work during what I knew to be his very first conversation with a mental health professional.

Two weeks later, one of the assistant producers of the television programme came running towards me and clapped me on the back, describing me as a miracle worker. Apparently, Mehmet had indeed gone to London with his partner, and, as promised, he managed the tube with few difficulties, for the first time in seven years. He took his girlfriend all over London, and apparently they had a ball!

I certainly did not feel like a miracle worker. Although moved by my consultation with Mehmet, I could not believe the simplicity of our conversation. His sister had died seven years ago, while working in London, after having left Slough; and shortly thereafter Mehmet developed a tube phobia that prevented him from seeking employment in London and kept him imprisoned in Slough. It all made great sense, and I did not have to engage in any particularly deep analysis. Of course, in the context of this private consultation, sponsored by a British Broadcasting Corporation television project, analysis would not be possible or desirable; but in one simple, confidential conversation I helped a young man to talk about a painful bereavement that still caused him great anguish.

In many respects, I had not appreciated that Slough, though separated from London by merely a short train ride, could not be more different from the cosmopolitan, sophisticated world that I inhabited daily in Hampstead, North London, and had done for years and years. Although North London boasts a veritable army of psychotherapists and psychologists, Slough had, at that time, only one psychotherapist, and he spent most of his time working at a London clinic! So, many Sloughians had little emotional vocabulary and, like Freud's early patients, felt psychologically very starved. Hence, a simple conversation about a sibling death provided immense relief and allowed a young man to resolve a long-standing symptom. If only the rest of psychotherapeutic practice proved so simple and straightforward!

Having undertaken this consultation with Mehmet, it soon became clear to me that, although I could try to offer forty-nine more consultations of this variety to the "Slough 50", this would prove to be a very time-consuming endeavour, and, moreover, none of this material could be shown on the television programme, owing to the demands of clinical confidentiality. If the B.B.C. wished to use me, we would still have to find something for me to do that would not involve psychotherapeutic sessions. One of the producers, trained in Greek and Latin, jested with me that I had to do something "on camera" as opposed to "*in camera*" (i.e., in private).

Music, of course, became the vehicle and, after many discussions, the producers and I decided that I would, indeed, establish a special Slough Choir. The producers knew that music brought me much happiness and creative pleasure, and they hoped that I would be able to share this enthusiasm with the participants in the television series. All of the choir sessions would be filmed, and we would not be restricted by the demands of confidentiality.

In January 1890, a young Winston Churchill (1890, p. 67) wrote a letter to his mother, Lady Jennie Churchill, in which he decried the value of singing, informing her that, "Papa said he thought singing was a waste of time, so I left the singing class." Sadly, Churchill suffered from a lifetime of depression. One wonders whether he would have become less miserable in adult life had he persisted with singing.

Having already established choirs in a number of different psychiatric inpatient and outpatient settings and having created the first Tavistock Clinic Choir, I not only knew a great deal about the healing benefits of music and song, but I also felt confident that I would be able to conjure something useful for our television programmes; and so, several times a week, I took the train to Slough after I had finished work with my regular analytic patients in London, and I facilitated an evening choir with approximately fifteen of the Slough 50. The group consisted of a good mixture of men and women, including the very old and the very young, as well as the enthusiastic and the depressed. The producers had found me a marvellous large room in a nearby nunnery, replete with an excellent, freshly tuned baby grand piano; and, twice weekly, I seated myself at the keyboard and attempted to get the members of this newly consecrated choir to sing.

With one exception, most of the participants in the Slough Choir had had virtually no musical training, and many of them had but tiny, wafer-thin voices, inhibited by anxiety and by lack of experience in being heard. So, I proceeded slowly and gently, just as I had done with the psychiatric choirs that I had facilitated, and just as I had done with the staff at the Tavistock Clinic, none of whom could sing especially well either, and yet all of whom yearned to do so.

As the weeks unfolded, confidence began to grow, and the *pianissimo* voices gradually swelled to a *mezzo forte*. Naturally, we had some dramas with which to contend. One of the members of the choir, a young housewife, threatened to drop out, as she believed that she could not compete with the other members in terms of volume, pitch, or vocal dexterity. The producers seized upon this woman and filmed her extensively, and I could readily foresee that they hoped to shape a really compelling story-line around her: "Will she continue with the choir and satisfy her dream of singing 'Happy Birthday' to her children, or will she bottle out? And can Brett help?"

Although one might hypothesise that the fear of singing out loud, of using one's voice, and of enjoying one's voice, can be linked to depressive affects and to early discouraging experiences, I had to be careful not to expose this woman's psychological history on television. But I could help her in an ordinary way by offering her private singing lessons at the piano. To my delight, and to the pleasure of the producers, this sweet lady readily took up the offer, and, step by step, I coached her through "Happy Birthday", until she had the confidence to stand on a rostrum, all by herself, and sing the song loudly and proudly at the top of her lungs. Tears and laughter followed in equal amounts as she marvelled at her achievement—something that she regarded as a major breakthrough. Eventually, she returned home and sang happy birthday to her son for the first time ever!

During the weeks and months in which I focused on the Slough Choir, the other experts did magnificent work in their own areas of specialisation. Richard Reeves, a multi-talented graduate of the University of Oxford, who has worked, *inter alia*, as a correspondent for *The Guardian* newspaper and also as a policy adviser, launched himself into the revitalisation of Slough in the most creative and fearless manner, preaching sermons in a house of worship, lecturing on the virtues of happiness with a megaphone on the open streets, and launching a campaign to remove television sets from the homes of the Slough 50 to help them to progress beyond their lives as "couch potatoes". A man of immense popularity and personal charm, he made a big impact in Slough, and he turned his hand to anything and everything with zest and good cheer. Andrew Mawson, a social entrepreneur who had received an O.B.E. from Her Majesty Queen Elizabeth II in the Millennium New Year's Honours List for his work in revitalising the downtrodden district of Bromley-by-Bow, in the London Borough of Tower Hamlets, worked vigorously with the members of local government in Slough to advise on how structural changes could be made to improve transport, industry, economy, and lifestyle. Jessica Pryce-Jones, a dynamic, super-smart woman who founded a high-level workplace consultancy organisation called "iOpener", and her affable colleague Phillippa Chapman, ventured into many of Slough's family businesses and did wonders to sort out conflicts on the factory floor. And Dr Richard Stevens, the distinguished academic psychologist and sometime Head of the Psychology Department at the Open University, undertook a number of activities to engage the people of Slough, launching wonderful outdoor exercise programmes and such. He also designed and supervised the research project that allowed us to collect pre-intervention, peri-intervention, and post-intervention data about the impact of our work on the levels of happiness in Berkshire. I felt very privileged indeed to work with such a formidable team of experts, and I learned an immense amount from all of them.

As the months of filming unfolded, Dr Stevens offered us encouraging news. His mid-term research analysis revealed that, according to the self-report measures of the participants themselves, happiness ratings had increased dramatically. People no longer regarded themselves as depressed or apathetic. The Slough 50 and their families now felt seen and heard, respected and encouraged, and involved in a project that became increasingly community-based and impactful. Buoyed by these encouraging results, the experts and the production team became more and more hopeful that we might actually help to achieve something uplifting, worthwhile, and, perhaps, enduring.

Travel and timetabling proved to be a challenge for all of the experts. None of us lived in Slough, and all of us had other professional and domestic commitments that prevented us from moving to Berkshire for the three months of filming. As a practising clinician, I had perhaps the most restricted timetable of all, as I would not cancel any of my regular patients to undertake filming; and as I have already indicated, the producers thoughtfully accommodated my availability and scheduled my shoots in the evenings and on weekends. In consequence, I often missed seeing Andrew, Jess, Philippa, and the two Richards—my fellow experts—except for our occasional team meetings in which we would review our progress. It soon became quite clear that each of us had embarked on very separate interventions. At one team meeting, I wondered whether the time had come for us all to join forces and plan a large "closing" event that would integrate our skills and capacities and would serve as a hopefully inspiring ending to the final television programme in this four-part series. Drawing upon my musical training, I suggested that we put on a show!

With tremendous enthusiasm and encouragement, the other experts agreed that we should indeed unite, and so we set about creating a day of celebration. Andrew Mawson agreed to supervise the physical transformation of Slough town centre into a giant performing space with a large raised stage; Richard Reeves and Richard Stevens volunteered to mobilise individuals and groups from the town to participate as street entertainers, acrobats, dancers, and vendors; Jessica Pryce-Jones and Philippa Chapman promised to enlist the help of the local industries; and the accomplished team of television executives and researchers would provide much-needed administrative assistance and support. I offered to compose a special song for the Slough Choir and to supervise its rehearsal and staging.

Over the years, I have written songs for West End theatre artists and for performers overseas, all of whom have excellent, professionally trained voices with a wide vocal range. I knew that, on this occasion, I would have to create something far more simple for the Slough Choir: something that would encapsulate the essence of *Making Slough Happy*, a televisual experiment in psychological and social transformation. My frequent train journeys from Paddington Station in London to Slough and back, afforded me some protected time in which to compose a hopefully catchy tune with singable lyrics.

Eventually, it occurred to me that if we could bring people together in a large community project, if we could offer special support and carefully tailored interventions to people in need, and if we could boost happiness ratings in Slough, why could this model not become a template for other towns and cities throughout Great Britain and beyond? Perhaps, over time, we *could* make Slough happy, and then Swindon, and then Basingstoke, and then Crewe. Perhaps, over time, we could *change the world*. And so, in a moment of arguably hypo-manic enthusiasm, I penned the following song. The printed lyrics of this *pièce d'occasion* hardly do justice to the peppiness of the tune and to the rich vocal harmonies, but, hopefully, in the absence of hearing the music, readers can still gauge something of the rhythm.

> *We're Gonna Change The World*
>
> Though we are facing a planet that's troubling,
> Pulses are racing, adrenaline's bubbling,
> We are ablaze with unbeatable energy,
> Ready to change the world.
>
> Battered and bruised but our soul is uncrushable,
> Crazed and confused but our voice is unhushable,
> Singing in unison, singing in harmony,
> Ready to change the world.
>
> We're gonna change the world,
> Aren't we?
> We're gonna change the world.
> Turning our town into something terrific
> By helping our sisters in need,
> Embracing our brothers of every colour and creed.
>
> In spite of our scars we will not let them censure us.
> Reach for the stars, we are bold and adventurous.
> Maybe we'll stumble, but nevertheless,
> We're going to give it a try.
>
> We're gonna change the world,
> Aren't we?
> We're gonna change the world.
> Turning our town into something terrific
> By helping our sisters in need,
> Embracing our brothers of every colour and creed.

We can improve each acre that we inhabit,
Life is a banquet with bounty beyond compare.
Jump out of bed, there's plenty of love so grab it.
People, it's time to declare:

Stand and be heard even though you are ill at ease,
Passions are stirred, we have great possibilities,
Poised on the brink of a brighter horizon,
Ready to change the world.

We're gonna . . .
We're gonna change the world,
Aren't we?
We're gonna change the world.
Turning our town into something terrific
By helping our sisters in need,
Embracing our brothers of every colour and creed.

We're gonna . . . change . . . the . . .
We're gonna change the world,
Change the world.

After setting the song to music and polishing the lyrics, I then demonstrated the number to my fellow experts, on camera, and to my delight, Andrew, Jess, Philippa, Richard, and Richard all graciously consented to participate in a final event, which would culminate in a performance of "We're Gonna Change the World". Jessica Pryce-Jones, with whom I had developed a fond connection, confessed that she had previously trained as a flautist, and that although she had not had much time to make music in recent years, she would unearth her flute from the back of a cupboard and would join us as one of the musicians. We then set about our various tasks, giving ourselves approximately two weeks to prepare for what we hoped would be a climactic finale.

Shortly thereafter, I met once again with the Slough Choir, and I taught them the song. I think they enjoyed the fact that I had written something especially for them, and they sang with bravura. Regrettably, in spite of their valiant efforts, the dozen or so members of the Slough Choir could hardly make a sufficiently impactful sound to fill the town square. And I feared that we would look rather sparse on the enormous stage that Andrew Mawson and his team would be constructing. It soon became clear that we might need reinforcements, and so we decided to recruit citizens from the wider Slough community to supplement our numbers and make this finale more full, more theatrical, and more group-orientated. The Slough Choir began co-opting their relatives and friends; the members of the production team started to round up people from the streets; and we all twisted arms. Before long, our tiny Slough Choir had swelled into a large group of perhaps a hundred singers, including a bevy of angelic-voiced children from the local primary school!

I knew that I would need help at this point, as one lone clinician-musician could not possibly manage to rehearse a choir of this size, especially as I had to return to London for my next day of sessions with patients. And so, I spoke to our ever cheerful Production Manager Sarah Gowers and told her that I needed to enlist the services of an extremely talented musician to help rehearse, conduct, orchestrate, and co-ordinate this big number. After hemming and hawing, Sarah managed to work wonders with the programme budget, and she succeeded in earmarking a fee for a musical consultant to support me and the Slough Choir. With funding in place, I telephoned my old friend, John Gladstone Smith, one of the most accomplished musicians in London's West End and one of the most psychologically healthy to boot. During his long and distinguished career, John has worked for Andrew Lloyd Webber and has served as Musical Director for many of Baron Lloyd Webber's productions. I, too, have had the privilege of working with John on a number of more modest projects, as has my wife, a full-time singer. I trust John unreservedly, and I knew that the Slough Choir and its new recruits would warm to him greatly and that he would deliver exactly what we needed.

Shortly thereafter, John and I convened at Paddington Station, and we took the train to Slough, planning our rehearsal programme en route. I then introduced him to the members of the Slough Choir, waiting eagerly at the nunnery, and I seated him behind the piano and let him begin to work his magic. As a West End musical director, John often has the task of taking a group of extremely talented professional singers and making them sound even better. He brought all of that know-how to bear upon the Slough Choir, and after several rehearsals, he helped me to turn those meagre voices into bountiful instruments. He also assembled a team of local musicians to create a band, and he even found time to work with Jessica Pryce-Jones, who would be joining us on flute.

After a week of rehearsals, the big day arrived. John and I took a very early morning train to Slough, and we headed straight for the town centre. To my delight, the television production crew had worked through the night with the local townspeople, and they had transformed an otherwise dreary public square into the most impressive of performing spaces, replete with stage, banners, streamers, audio speakers, and lights. Eventually, the crowds started to appear, with dancers of every ethnicity, street musicians, jugglers, clowns, and men on stilts. The sleepy town soon came to life in the most starbust-like fashion, and everyone immersed themselves in the increasingly cheerful party atmosphere. Towards the end of the afternoon, the Slough Choir took to the stage, in front of an audience of several thousand local people, with the cameras recording our every move. I made a short speech, introducing the choir and the *Making Slough Happy* project, and then, joined by my fellow experts and by the members of the choir, we launched into our song. The enthusiastic crowds greeted our little musical effort with loud cheers, and I took great pleasure in seeing the happy faces of the members of the Slough Choir, many of whom never thought that they would have the courage to sing out loud, let alone to sing in public!

Did we make Slough happy? Apparently, we did.

After we had completed our ten weeks of filming, Dr Richard Stevens re-interviewed the Slough 50 to evaluate whether our interventions had helped, and it pleases me to report that, in every case, people claimed to have benefited hugely, and their self-ratings on Richard's various specially designed questionnaires revealed large increases in happiness levels. Thankfully, we had done something right.

After several months of feverish, round-the-clock editing, the British Broadcasting Corporation trailered the programme and then launched a publicity campaign. As an experienced broadcaster, the B.B.C. had me appear on many radio programmes in the days leading up to transmission, talking about the project, about the importance of happiness for long-term mental and physical health, and about what can be done to ameliorate sadness and depression. Eventually, *Making Slough Happy* aired over four successive weeks, beginning on Tuesday, 15 November 2005. We enjoyed the highly visible 9.00 p.m. slot on the television channel B.B.C. 2, which guaranteed a substantial number of viewers—nearly two million in total for each episode. I confess that we had a very mixed reaction from the notoriously cynical British press. Although we had many favourable reviews, a number of journalists, who regarded us as rather imperialist, made cutting swipes at the programme, attacking the London-based experts for descending, as we did, on the unsuspecting residents of Slough.

Others found us too peppy and accused us of shoving happiness down everyone's throats. However, as the series progressed, some of the more jaded reporters began to revise their views, and after the fourth week of transmissions one of our most outspoken critics apologised to us in print in a major national newspaper for having misjudged our efforts so quickly and so prematurely. This reporter had now watched our work over four hour-long episodes, had become increasingly immersed in the human stories of transformation, and had much enjoyed our finale concert. It seems that people could at last appreciate that rain-sodden British misery need not be a permanent state of mind.

After the programme ended, Jessica Pryce-Jones invited the experts to facilitate a training day at the Saïd Business School at the University of Oxford, where we talked about our methodology to a group of very intelligent professionals from a variety of disciplines who wished to take our work further. We discovered that happiness, though at first derided as a rather sappy concept, had now become part of the public discourse.

The B.B.C. produced a book as a "tie-in" with the television series, entitled *How to Be Happy*, written by the highly respected journalist Liz Hoggard (2005) and based heavily upon interviews with the experts. Designed to be read by the general public, the front cover bore a shiny orange "smiley" face, with the inscription: "LIFE-CHANGING INSIGHTS FROM THE TV SERIES MAKING SLOUGH HAPPY". Not having glanced at this book in over fourteen years, I recently opened up a page at random in the middle of the book, and, in a chapter on promotion of greater happiness in families, I read the following passage, extracted from one of Ms Hoggard's (2005) many conversations with me:

> The key element in raising happy children is to love them uncondi-
> tionally, but also offer boundaries. "Children need boundaries, but
> boundaries are very different from discipline", says BBC happiness
> expert Brett Kahr. He believes that the word "discipline" has an
> inherently punitive quality to it, and overtones of a master–slave
> relationship. Truly loving parents will always want to set bounda-
> ries rather than discipline their child. In practice, this means grant-
> ing them considerable autonomy while setting clear rules about
> what is and isn't permissible, then stepping back and letting them
> get on with it. All children find it easier to develop their potential
> if they know that, no matter what happens, they have a safe emo-
> tional base in the family. [2005, p. 121]

Mostly Hoggard, derived from a thought or two by Kahr, this book reached a very wide audience and, hopefully, offered some sage advice. At any rate, having treated far too many patients crushed in childhood in the name of "discipline", it pleases me that I could speak out in this way.

Serious discussions about happiness continued to filter into British public discourse. Eventually, in 2010, shortly after his election as Prime Minister of the United Kingdom, David Cameron announced that happiness would form part of his political platform, and that the government would devote itself to studying happiness, including its economic and health-care benefits, as well as its psychological benefits. The subject has even attracted serious attention in medical publications such as The Lancet (e.g., Easterly, 2011). In our small way, we had helped to bring attention to the newly emerging field of "positive psychology" (e.g., Carr, 2004; Layard, 2005; Gilbert, 2006; Linley, Joseph, Harrington, and Wood, 2006; Diener and Biswas-Diener, 2008; Baylis, 2009; David, Boniwell, and Conley, 2013), and to demonstrate that happiness can be boosted by a number of means, whether musical, psychotherapeutical, or what have you. The subject has now spawned the creation of an International Association of Positive Psychology; and even Jigme Khesar Namgyel Wangchuck, His Majesty The King of Bhutan, no less, has argued that, in evaluating the health of a country, one must take account not only of Gross National Product but, also, of "Gross National Happiness" (Khesar, 2013, p. vii).

My fellow experts all went on to do distinguished work in the public sphere. Richard Reeves (2007) produced a major biography of John Stuart Mill, having always admired Mill's work as a champion of women's rights; and then, in 2010, Richard became a Special Adviser to Nick Clegg, the Deputy Prime Minister of the United Kingdom. Richard's experiences in Slough have no doubt informed his important work for the government. Now the recipient of a Ph.D. in philosophy, Reeves currently works as a Senior Fellow in Economic Studies at the Brookings Institution "think tank" in Washington, D.C. And Andrew Mawson, already an O.B.E., became elected as a life peer in the House of Lords in 2007, now styled as Baron Mawson of Bromley-by-Bow in the London Borough of Tower Hamlets. He also published a very important study of The Social Entrepreneur: Making Communities Work (Mawson, 2008). Richard Stevens continued his important teaching in psychology at the Open University; Jessica Pryce-Jones and Philippa Chapman made "iOpener" increasingly successful as a consulting agency, and Jess has written a lovely book on *Happiness at Work: Maximizing Your Psychological Capital for Success* (Pryce-Jones, 2010). I continue to remain speechless with admiration for the very important public contributions made by each of these visionary individuals, and I remain honoured to have had this opportunity to collaborate with them.

After I finished my work on the Slough project, I received a number of very kind invitations to speak at national conferences, most of which I had to refuse, with great regret, having decided that I had done quite enough juggling for the time being. Instead, I focused full-time on my clinical practice and have remained thus ensconced ever since. I certainly know that one can improve someone else's happiness by singing songs, by dancing, by exercising, by eating good food, and by relating to loving people; but I also know that *profound* characterological change often requires more intensive psychological intervention of the sort that I have trained to provide, and thus I have come to the conclusion that I can best contribute to the growth of happiness in the United Kingdom by persevering in my daily psychoanalytic work. I still contribute to various media projects from time to time, but the core of my diary and of my thinking time will always be my psychotherapeutic practice.

I did have one very amusing experience post-Slough that I would like to share. Perhaps three or four weeks after the broadcast of the final episode, I delivered an evening lecture to a group of young singing students at the University of London in the heart of Bloomsbury. The group consisted of twelve students—eleven women and one man. At the end of this class, which met on a Friday evening, the students invited me out to have a short drink at a nearby pub frequented by undergraduates from University College London. I accepted with pleasure. The single male student on the course had to leave to catch his train, and thus I found myself, a middle-aged man, surrounded by eleven beautiful young women. We found a large table on the upstairs floor of the pub, and we all began to talk animatedly about music, singing, and related matters. Nearby, three young male students sat in their rugby jerseys, with pints of beer in their hands, all looking rather miserable, devoid of any female companionship on a Friday night. These young men kept staring at me and whispering. I felt rather uncomfortable as I imagined them wondering, "How the hell does that old, bespectacled man manage to have eleven female groupies?"

Eventually, we had all finished our drinks, and I got up from the table to leave the pub. As I walked past the three single men, one of them called out, "Hey, Brett!" I panicked, wondering how on earth he knew my name. "Nice job in Slough!", he shouted above the din of the pub. I smiled, thanked this chap, and felt very pleased to know that our television programme had reached a young audience.

Randolph Churchill (1955, p. 213), son of Sir Winston Churchill, once wrote to his father, "by being happy, make those who love you happy too". Though easy to lampoon as a sentimental concept, happiness has now become an object of serious study, and it has also become a key policy item on the agenda of many presidents and prime ministers worldwide. I feel pleased to have made a very small contribution to the public foregrounding of happiness, and I take great satisfaction that others with more vision and talent can now develop this subject further in such a multitude of creative ways.

CHAPTER ELEVEN

A night at the opera:
the Freudians at Covent Garden

Donde hay música, no puede haber cosa mala.
[Where music is, there can no ill thing be.]

"Sancho Panza", in Miguel de Cervantes Saavedra, *El ingenioso hidalgo
don Quixote de la Mancha*, Segunda Parte, 1615

Although Great Britain boasts more than *eight thousand* psychotherapists registered with either the British Psychoanalytic
Council or the United Kingdom Council for Psychotherapy—
the two principal professional bodies for psychotherapists in this
country—we have, at present, only a tiny handful of fully accredited *marital* psychotherapists, or, as we have become known more
recently, "couple psychoanalytic psychotherapists". After much spirited debate, our tiny, intrepid band changed its name from the Society
of Psychoanalytical Marital Psychotherapists (the official grouping of
the graduates of the Tavistock Centre's training in marital psychotherapy) to the Society of Couple Psychoanalytic Psychotherapists
(then, subsequently, to the British Society of Couple Psychotherapists
and Counsellors, and, ultimately, to the Alumni Department of Tavistock Relationships at the Tavistock Institute of Medical Psychology)
in an effort to reflect the fact that many of the marital couples with
whom we work nowadays may never have exchanged jewellery or

144

paperwork or may, in fact, be gay or lesbian. So, the term "marital psychotherapy" has come to be superseded by the more progressive moniker "couple psychotherapy", at least in the United Kingdom. Our American colleagues, so I understand, still refer to themselves as "M.F.T."s: Marital and Family Therapists.

As couple psychotherapists in Great Britain, we undertake important work, helping often deeply troubled spouses by offering long-term psychoanalytically orientated psychotherapy. In doing so, we hope that we may assist couples to recapture the joys that they had once experienced as a marital partnership. Why, then, do we have barely forty fully accredited clinical psychotherapy members in our professional organisation, especially when we have a population of some 45,000,000 adults, most of whom live in a marital or co-habiting arrangement? Our training at Tavistock Relationships, part of the Tavistock Institute of Medical Psychology, demands a great deal of time and effort, like any intensive psychoanalytic formation. The clinical trainees generally undergo five or six years of study—and often longer—in order to complete their post-graduate diploma, treating at least six couples successfully in long-term psychoanalytic psychotherapy. Many of the students on the training will already have graduated from an individual psychoanalytic training, so we do *not* attract, on the whole, young, energetic students; rather, we appeal to older, hopefully wiser, trainees who will, however, also be burdened by extensive domestic and professional commitments. This explains, to a certain extent, our relatively small numbers.

One might understand the dearth of marital practitioners in Great Britain by recourse to external factors (such as age, time commitment, cost, etc.), but I suspect that there may be a far more important reason why colleagues often neglect marital work as a possible field of specialisation. Not only does couple work force us to question the strength and creativity of our own marital relationship, but, as couple psychotherapists, we must spend a great deal of our working lives in the presence of warring couples, depressed couples, hypersexual couples, hyposexual couples, mentally ill couples, forensic couples, bereaved couples, and the like. Not only does the nature of the work stretch our psychological digestive capacities, but it also requires us to tolerate being a "third" party in an oedipal triangle; and, as many of us may already have felt excluded from such triangular experiences as infants and children, we may find ourselves avoiding the marital situation as a defence against having to tolerate triangulation.

Whatever the ultimate explanation for the sheer paucity of couple psychoanalytic psychotherapists in Great Britain, those few of us who have made a lifelong, passionate commitment to the work continue to struggle to generate interest in our field, both among our individual psychoanalytic colleagues and among members of the public, many of whom might benefit from our services, yet who, because of our small numbers, do not even know of our existence.

Some years ago, my very charismatic colleague, Mrs Pauline Hodson, then Chair of the Society of Couple Psychoanalytic Psychotherapists, twisted my arm and encouraged me to serve on the Executive Committee of our dogged group of marital workers. Knowing of my involvement in the media, as a presenter of both radio programmes and television programmes dealing with mental health issues, Pauline thought that I might be able to make a contribution to the "public face" of couple psychoanalysis in Great Britain. At our first committee meeting, one of my colleagues suggested that we mount an academic conference for the general public, full of worthy papers about "What is Couple Psychotherapy?", "Why Should One Undergo Couple Psychotherapy Instead of Individual Psychotherapy?", "How Do Transference and Countertransference Issues Become Manifest in Our Work?", and so forth. I realised that such a conference would be highly meritorious—a sober parade of up-to-the minute British psychoanalytic clinical thought on the marital relationship—but that such a day-conference would hardly pull punters in from off the streets. I humbly suggested that if we wished to prize people away from their e-mails, their television sets, their health clubs, and their iPads, we would have to create a more cunning, more inviting means of exploring the world of marital woe.

Having organised theatrical events in the past—including a charity gala designed to raise money for a child mental health organisation, hosted in the presence of Prince Charles, His Royal Highness The Prince of Wales (Kahr, 1999b)—I felt confident that I could draw upon my earlier experiences in order to concoct a more novel means of introducing psychoanalytic marital concepts to the general public than the typical academic–clinical conference. After extensive planning and discussion with colleagues in both the psychoanalytic community and the theatrical community, I stumbled upon what I thought might be a rather interesting conception.

It occurred to me that the worlds of literature, drama, opera, and musical theatre contain many fine representations of rich, intricate, and often troubled couple relationships, ranging from "Romeo" and

"Juliet" in William Shakespeare's timeless play, to "George" and "Martha" in Edward Albee's *Who's Afraid of Virginia Woolf?*; and in the musical world one cannot help but wonder about the unconscious nature of the attraction between "Alfredo", the aristocrat, and "Violetta", the courtesan, in Giuseppe Verdi's and Francesco Maria Piave's opera *La Traviata*; or perhaps, similarly, one might wish to theorise about the powerful dynamics that prompted "Maria" and "Tony" to become so enmeshed in Leonard Bernstein's, Stephen Sondheim's, and Arthur Laurents's masterpiece, *West Side Story*. I reasoned that if we could engage a talented core group of actors and singers to perform highlights from some of the great works of drama, opera, and musical theatre, we could then witness the complexities of some iconic, yet convoluted, couple relationships unfold before our very eyes. And, to help us to understand the vicissitudes of such intimate partnerships, we could assemble, similarly, a team of qualified couple psychoanalytic psychotherapists to offer clinical commentary on these dramatic and musical vignettes.

Before I became a mental health professional, I had trained as a musician, and although I work full-time in the psychological field, I have always devoted a small percentage of my energies to music, either as a composer or as a lecturer on musical topics. I have, therefore, over the years, come to know a great many people in the musical world, and so I decided that, in the spirit of being a loyal couple psychotherapist, I would attempt to forge a marital alliance between psychoanalysis and music, thus bringing these two often disparate worlds into closer collaboration.

I presented my notion of producing a "musico-psychological" concert evening to some of my contacts at London's Royal Opera House; and although such a performance would be rather a far cry from their usual fare, the enlightened officials at Covent Garden responded with cheeriness and enthusiasm to my suggestion of mounting a "special event", to be hosted in the Royal Opera House's smaller space, the Linbury Studio Theatre (known as R.O.H. 2), which boasts 394 seats and fifty-six standing-room places. I reasoned that if we could manage to sell tickets to a psychoanalytic event at Great Britain's premiere cultural institution and obtain press coverage in the process, we would then be able to publicise couple psychoanalytic psychotherapy to a hitherto untapped audience.

With the Royal Opera House on board, affording us the privilege of using their studio theatre on a Sunday evening, thereby not interfering with any of the opera company's ongoing productions, it

took little persuading to enlist the services of a talented team of singers, actors, directors, musicians, and psychotherapists to mount an
evening entitled "Couples in Counterpoint", during which we could
explore the psychodynamics of couple relationships in a hopefully
creative and unusual manner—a far cry from the usual academic-
style gathering to which we have all become so very accustomed over
the last century.

I thus formed a working party, spearheaded by the West End
theatre director Lisa Forrell, the daughter of the American psychoanalyst Mildred Forrell, a senior member of the New York Freudian Society (subsequently renamed The Contemporary Freudian
Society); and after much animated dialogue, we eventually decided
that we would focus our evening on the nature of couple interactions as portrayed in the American musical theatre—in part because
Lisa has worked extensively in the musical theatre world and has
many helpful and willing comrades in this field. Before long, we
had organised a very exciting series of auditions and soon found
a dream cast of talented West End performers to assist us in our
endeavour. Jessica Martin, a well-known star of theatre and television in Great Britain, perhaps best remembered for her leading role
in the West End musical *Me and My Girl*, came on board at once,
followed swiftly by Andy Morton, a brilliant operatic tenor who
had sung on a recording of my music some years earlier. Andy
agreed to undertake the exhausting rehearsal period, in spite of the
fact that he had a number of performances as "Nemorino" in Opera
North's production of Gaetano Donizetti's classic opera *L'Elisir
d'Amore*, based in Leeds, many miles away from London. A true
trouper, Andy took the train to London on his days off and committed himself enthusiastically to extra rehearsal.

John Addison and Lydia Griffiths, two juvenile leads who had
starred, respectively, as "Marius" and "Éponine" in the West End
production of Sir Cameron Mackintosh's long-running musical *Les
Misérables*, rounded out our singing ensemble. And Nigel Lilley, an
outstanding musician, who had, most recently, worked on the West
End production of the hit Broadway musical *Wicked*, supervised the
vocal coaching and served as our musical director.

We all enjoyed a stroke of good fortune when we succeeded
in securing the participation of the Broadway and West End diva
Kim Criswell, an American-born singer who has recorded over forty
albums during the course of a distinguished international career.
Winner of the Helen Hayes Award and nominee for the Laurence

Olivier Award, Miss Criswell has performed in many of the world's great opera houses and concert halls, ranging from the Teatro alla Scala in Milan, to the Théâtre du Châtelet in Paris, to La Fenice in Venice, to Carnegie Hall in New York City, to the Wigmore Hall and the Royal Albert Hall in London. A specialist in the American musical theatre songbook, Miss Criswell played the leading role of "Ruth Sherwood" in Leonard Bernstein's *Wonderful Town* with the Berlin Philharmoniker, conducted by Sir Simon Rattle, and starred in the West End revival of Irving Berlin's *Annie Get Your Gun*, to great acclaim.

In conjunction with Lisa Forrell, our vivacious director, we put together a great line-up of songs:

1. "Together" (from the musical *Gypsy*, with music by Jule Styne and lyrics by Stephen Sondheim), performed by John Addison, Lydia Griffiths, Jessica Martin, and Andy Morton.

2. "One Hand, One Heart" (from the musical *West Side Story*, with music by Leonard Bernstein and lyrics by Stephen Sondheim), performed by John Addison and Lydia Griffiths.

3. "On My Own" (from the musical *Les Misérables*, with music by Claude-Michel Schönberg and lyrics by Alain Boublil, Herbert Kretzmer, Jean-Marc Natel, Trevor Nunn, and John Caird), performed by Lydia Griffiths.

4. "Could I Leave You?" (from the musical *Follies*, with music and lyrics by Stephen Sondheim), performed by Jessica Martin.

5. "I Won't Send Roses" (from the musical *Mack and Mabel*, with music and lyrics by Jerry Herman), performed by Andy Morton, and reprised by Jessica Martin.

6. "Soliloquy" (from the musical *Carousel*, with music by Richard Rodgers and lyrics by Oscar Hammerstein II), performed by John Addison.

7. Medley (from the musical *Annie Get Your Gun*, with music and lyrics by Irving Berlin), performed by Kim Criswell and Andy Morton, comprising, "The Girl That I Marry" [Mr Morton], "You Can't Get a Man with a Gun" [Miss Criswell], "They Say It's Wonderful" [Miss Criswell and Mr Morton], "Anything You Can Do" [Miss Criswell and Mr Morton], "An Old Fashioned Wedding" [Mr Morton and Miss Criswell].

8. Surprise Finale.

Essentially, we decided that we would have the actors perform these wonderful, legendary songs, and then invite a team of marital psychotherapists to offer commentary on stage, as a means of helping the audience to acquire a better sense of how we speak and how we think. Fortunately, I managed to recruit three senior marital psychotherapeutic colleagues to join me on the platform: Dr Christopher Clulow, the recently retired Director of the Tavistock Marital Studies Institute and its successor institution, the Tavistock Centre for Couple Relationships; Mrs Pauline Hodson, the Chair of the Society of Couple Psychoanalytic Psychotherapists; and Mrs Helen Tarsh, past Chair of the Society of Psychoanalytical Marital Psychotherapists.

In order to illustrate what the clinicians contributed to the evening, let me describe how we handled one of the songs. After an opening number, our two talented juveniles, John Addison and Lydia Griffiths, recreated the classic roles of "Tony" and "Maria" from *West Side Story* and sang a beautiful, tender rendition of the well-known ballad "One Hand, One Heart". Lisa Forrell, the Director of "Couples in Counterpoint", explained to the audience that, from a theatrical point of view, "Tony" and "Maria" represent the epitome of "romantic love"—two young teenagers who triumph over parental prejudice and heal the bonds of racial hatred by forging a passionate liaison. Lisa then asked the panel of couple psychotherapists whether we would concur. Straightaway, the four couple clinicians engaged in spirited disagreement with one another, albeit in a friendly and, hopefully, coherent manner.

I began the discussions by acknowledging that although "One Hand, One Heart" cannot fail to grip the listener with its sentiments and sweetness, one must not forget Tony will soon be shot to death and Maria deeply bereaved—reminiscent of the fate of their Shakespearean counterparts "Romeo" and "Juliet"—and that, perhaps, the romantic connection between the two juvenile leads in *West Side Story* may not be a simple expression of "love" but, rather, an attempt to forge a primitive symbiotic merger as a means of avoiding a terrifying external and internal world and as a defence against an accurate perception of an impending tragedy. Indeed, Tony and Maria intone with teenage passion, "Make of our hands one hand,/Make of our hearts one heart." As a romantic sentiment, it would be difficult to surpass the wish to meld into one's lover; but as an expression of a characterological state, their desire to make two hands one and two hearts one might indicate something more psychologically vulnerable and fragile—namely, the need to fuse together as a means of combating depression, emptiness, and persecutory anxiety. My colleague Pauline Hodson expressed an alternative viewpoint. She argued that, in order for healthy adult intimacy to emerge, one *must* have a period of losing one's bodily boundaries and falling in love in a primitive, teenage manner. With our stall thus set out, the other panellists joined us in a vibrant fashion as our clinical quartet discussed such couple psychoanalytic concepts as shared defence structure, unconscious marital wishes and fears, shared marital phantasy, splitting and projective identification, and so forth.

As the evening unfolded, we examined "tender love" from *West Side Story*, "unrequited love" from *Les Misérables*, "bitter love" from *Follies*, "defensive love" from *Mack and Mabel*, as well as "anticipatory parental love" from *Carousel* as the character of "Billy Bigelow" contemplates the arrival of his first child in the famous "Soliloquy". We particularly wished to include a song about a young man becoming a father, because the birth of the first child represents one of the most common family events that threaten to disequilibrate the fabric of marital life, and in our work as couple psychotherapists and couple psychoanalysts we see a very large number of people whose marriages begin to founder in the immediate aftermath of the transition to parenthood.

The four marital psychotherapists on stage at the Royal Opera House offered a variety of psychodynamic observations about all aspects of these songs. At times we agreed and at times we disagreed in a thoughtful, collegial manner, thus modelling for the members of the general public the ways in which psychotherapists enjoy a capacity to learn from one another. We also wanted to portray ourselves as independent-minded thinkers, thus quashing a popular cultural anxiety that psychoanalysts and psychotherapists blindly apply orthodox theory to every single patient in a dogmatic, nomothetic manner.

Additionally, Pauline Hodson and I conducted a mock marital therapy session with Andy Morton, who portrayed the silent film director "Mack Sennett", and with Jessica Martin, who played the silent film star "Mabel Normand", in the Jerry Herman musical *Mack and Mabel*. After they sang "I Won't Send Roses", a song about two people who "love" each other but who cannot move beyond the "dating" phase and risk real intimacy, Pauline and I engaged "Mack" and "Mabel" in a recreation of a psychoanalytic session on stage. We worked with the actors for approximately ten minutes, during which time we offered the audience a small taste of how we welcome couples into the consulting room, how we speak, how we interact, how we formulate interpretations, and how we conceptualise. This segment proved one of the most popular and successful of the whole evening, offering a more privileged glimpse into the nature of our work, without any risk of breaching confidentiality, which would have resulted if we had spoken about real patients.

The evening concluded with a medley of songs from the infectiously tuneful Broadway musical *Annie Get Your Gun*, featuring our diva Kim Criswell. A story about the nineteenth-century Midwestern sharpshooter "Annie Oakley" and her rival "Frank Butler", *Annie Get Your Gun* represents the apotheosis of healthy romantic love. Beginning with Frank Butler's ballad "The Girl That I Marry", a paean to idealised love, and Annie Oakley's charm number "You Can't Get a Man with a Gun", a communication about her phallic, castrating posture, the audience enjoyed the opportunity of watching this couple embark upon an important psychological journey in which the character of Frank began to remove women from the pedestal, while his female counterpart, Annie, dared to surrender her rifle. Together, the couple allowed themselves to risk the vulnerability of intimate relatedness in the sweeping romantic ballad "They Say It's Wonderful". Once Frank and Annie could begin to retrieve their projections and examine one another in a more reality-orientated fashion, they then found themselves having to face the challenge of envy and competition, expressed in the exuberant duet "Anything You Can Do", before resolving their aggressivity, and before coming to respect their differences in the thoughtful and lilting duet "An Old Fashioned Wedding". Kim Criswell and Andy Morton brought down the house with their medley—brilliantly sung and stunningly acted.

We concluded the evening with a rendition of one of my own compositions, a comedic number entitled "The Divorce Song", which I sang with Miss Criswell, with yours truly on the piano. Afterwards, the entire cast of actors and clinicians performed a reprise of Irving Berlin's "They Say It's Wonderful", with the audience joining in.

In spite of the uncertainty of such a new type of theatrical venture, we succeeded in filling each of the 394 seats as well as the fifty-six standing places; and, with regret, we had to turn away large numbers of keen individuals who had not managed to book in time. I suspect that we could have sold double the number of tickets in the end. The audience included many colleagues from numerous other psychotherapeutic institutions such as the Association of Child Psychotherapists, the British Association for Sexual and Relational Therapy, the British Association of Psychotherapists, the British Psychoanalytical Society, the London Centre for Psychotherapy, Nafsiyat, the Oxford Psychotherapy Society, Relate, the School of Psychotherapy and Counselling at Regent's College, the Tavistock Society of Psychotherapists, and the Wessex Psychotherapy Society, as well as American colleagues from the New York Freudian Society and from other psychoanalytic groupings. Additionally, we attracted prominent members of other professions, including a brace of barristers and Q.C.s [Queen's Counsels] from the law, distinguished practitioners of medicine, numerous enterprising television producers, representatives from some of the nation's leading newspapers, as well as noted figures from British cultural life, such as Lady Rattle [Candace Allen] and also Lord Hollick [Clive Hollick], the Chair of London's South Bank Centre. Lord Smith [Chris Smith], the former Arts Minister in Prime Minister Tony Blair's Labour government, had purchased a ticket but, sadly, could not attend at the last minute; nevertheless, he generously sent a donation. So, at least two peers of the realm now possess a much more intimate knowledge of marital psychoanalysis.

All in all, the event exceeded our expectations. Not only did we achieve our primary aim of publicising marital psychotherapy as a discipline and modality, but we also managed to acquire some goodly press coverage, and we even earned a surplus for the coffers of the Society of Couple Psychoanalytic Psychotherapists, which we used to sponsor future educational activities. As a direct result of our opera house evening on "Couples in Counterpoint", our training body, the Tavistock Centre for Couple Relationships, received a number of new requests from potential students, and the Couple Psychotherapy Service, our clinical outreach arm, fielded several potential new referrals from couples eager to embark upon a course of marital psychotherapy.

Although I cannot speak with any authority about the public perception of psychoanalytic mental health professionals in the United States of America or elsewhere, I can confirm that, in Great Britain, we still remain objects of suspicion and derision among the general public, in spite of our century-long existence. I remain committed to the notion that mental health professionals must become accessible, approachable, and available; and although we must never lose our dignity or our gravitas, we must endeavour to find better ways of publicising our organisations and our services, mindful of the fact that our future patients will all have grown up in the post-internet era. One young colleague, for instance, told me that he would never visit a psychotherapist who did *not* have his or her own website. I suspect that this view will become increasingly common among the patients of tomorrow, and we should therefore not be embarrassed about drawing upon our reservoirs of creativity in an attempt to design newer, and even more theatrical, means of reaching the man and woman in the street.

Indeed, our more "outward" stance allowed our tiny cadre of thirty-five or so qualified members in the Society of Couple Psychoanalytic Psychotherapists to re-evaluate the composition of our own professional organisation; and, in 2009, we voted to change our name to the British Society of Couple Psychotherapists and Counsellors. This rebranding not only gave us greater national prominence, but also permitted us to welcome highly trained couple psychodynamic counsellors into the membership, many of whom had also qualified in psychoanalytically orientated psychosexual therapy from the Tavistock Centre for Couple Relationships. Thus, our tiny little troop of thirty-five individuals gradually swelled to over 250 members, providing us with a sufficiently secure base from which to promote couple psychotherapeutic services in Great Britain.

Since our night at the opera, couple psychotherapy has continued to flourish in the United Kingdom, spurred greatly by the visionary leadership of Susanna Abse, the first Chief Executive Officer of Tavistock Relationships (the successor organisation to the Tavistock Centre for Couple Relationships), and, thereafter, by Andrew Balfour, the distinguished psychologist and couple psychotherapist who currently occupies that role. Each of these colleagues has forged important relationships with parliamentarians and has undertaken visionary work at promoting couple mental health far and wide.

I trust that this brief account of a "musico-psychological" experiment—a marital collaboration between psychotherapists and singers—may serve as a small piece of inspiration to colleagues in other branches of the mental health field who may wish to explore different models for transmitting our knowledge—other than the long-standing tried-and-tested (and perhaps tired) staple of the conference and the journal article. We may surprise ourselves by cultivating some new friends and by enjoying some new sources of inspiration for our work.

CHAPTER TWELVE

Defending "Lady Macbeth": testimony of an expert witness

> In Westminster Hall I danced a dance,
> Like a semi-despondent fury;
> For I thought I never should hit on a chance
> Of addressing a British jury.
>
> "The Learned Judge", in William Schwenck Gilbert and
> Arthur Sullivan, "The Judge's Song", *Trial by Jury*, 1875

The telephone rang.

"Brett, would you be free next Sunday night to be an expert witness in the 'Lady Macbeth' murder trial at the Royal Courts of Justice? I'm defending her."

"Excuse me?"

"It's an event for charity. The Criminal Bar Association . . . to raise money for young barristers. It will be great fun."

The caller did not identify herself. She did not have to. I recognised the unmistakeable Scottish lilt immediately as that of Helena Kennedy, Q.C., Baroness Kennedy of the Shaws, one of the finest legal minds in Great Britain or, indeed, anywhere. I have the pleasure and privilege of having known Helena for many years through our mutual interest in the forensic mental health field. A great advocate of psychotherapy and psychoanalysis for offender patients, Helena

155

has fostered a closer collaboration between mental health profession-als and the law and has defended many grossly battered women in criminal trials. An inspiring human rights lawyer as well as a crimi-nal lawyer, Helena sits in the House of Lords as a Labour Peer and has performed yeoman service for our country as a leading social reformer. I certainly could not refuse her unusual invitation.

"Come to my house next Saturday morning at 10.30 a.m., and we'll work on our defence. 'Lady Macbeth' will be there too." Helena put down the telephone receiver, and I instantly became panic-stricken, wondering what on earth I had just agreed to do.

After a cup of coffee and a slice of toast with Helena and her hus-band, the pre-eminent maxillo-facial surgeon Professor Iain Hutch-ison, a pioneer in facial reconstruction for men and women who have suffered from devastating cancers and injuries, Helena and I repaired to her sitting room with the beautiful Maxine Peake, a bril-liant up-and-coming actress who had recently distinguished herself in two major television series of a forensic nature, namely, the five-part British Broadcasting Corporation drama *Criminal Justice II* about a young housewife who, anally raped by her husband, stabs him to death, and, also, the two-part *See No Evil: The Moors Murders*, an award-winning dramatisation of the life of Myra Hindley, one of the most notorious killers in British history. As we sat down on Helena's sofas, surrounded by personalised photographs from Prince Charles, Oprah Winfrey, and a host of political leaders, Helena explained that the Criminal Bar Association would be staging a "literary–historical" trial of both "Lord Macbeth" and "Lady Macbeth", with real Queen's Counsellors defending and prosecuting. The witnesses would be portrayed by leading Shakespearean actors, and the expert witness testimony would be provided by real-life mental health professionals. Maxine Peake would play Lady Macbeth, and Matthew Macfadyen, a huge star of British film and television who had appeared opposite Keira Knightley as "Fitzwilliam Darcy" in the big-screen version of *Pride and Prejudice*, would play Macbeth, the Scottish monarch. Max-ine giggled charmingly at the prospect of being married to Matthew Macfadyen, because the two of them have worked together several times previously; indeed, he played the very husband who had raped her in the *Criminal Justice II* drama, whom she then skewered to death with a kitchen knife.

Maxine and I stared in awe as Baroness Kennedy, Q.C., prepared the defence of Lady Macbeth. We felt very honoured to watch one of the world's leading lawyers embarking upon a court case, albeit a fictional one. The trial would be quite serious nevertheless, following all court protocols, but we would also have fun, and we would have to pepper our scripts with copious "in-jokes", not least because we would be staging the trial in front of some seven hundred top criminal judges and barristers in the Great Hall at the Royal Courts of Justice, a towering and terrifying institution on The Strand, in Central London, whose chilly interior with a ceiling nearly one hundred feet in height almost resembles the entrance of Westminster Abbey.

Helena decided that, in order to defend Lady Macbeth from her murder charge, we would have to investigate whether we could plead diminished responsibility, owing to the fact that her husband Macbeth had treated her brutally over many long years prior to the murders of "Duncan" and "Banquo". My "expert witness" testimony would be valuable in establishing that Lady Macbeth suffered from a number of interrelated mental illnesses. Although such testimony would ordinarily be provided by a forensic psychiatrist, Baroness Kennedy told me that she had chosen me for this purpose because of my experience as a mental health professional who has worked extensively in the media, and who would be able to play along with *both* the seriousness *and* the light-heartedness of the event. Although not a forensic psychiatrist, I have worked extensively in the forensic psychotherapy field and, indeed, I have edited a monograph series of books on forensic mental health for many years, so I do have, I trust, a reasonable knowledge of the territory.

After "interviewing" Lady Macbeth, we decided that, in my testimony, I would assert that she meets the formal D.S.M.–IV diagnostic criteria for: (1) Major Depressive Disorder, Recurrent Type; (2) Post-Traumatic Stress Disorder; (3) Obsessive-Compulsive Personality Disorder; and (4) Sleepwalking Disorder. Additionally, I would argue that, owing to the loss of her only child, Lady Macbeth also suffers from a severe Bereavement reaction. On the witness stand, I would have to justify my diagnosis and then prepare for cross-examination by Macbeth's barrister, the formidable Robert Marshall-Andrews, Q.C., a sometime Member of Parliament and one of the most accomplished lawyers in the English courts, as well as by Anthony Arlidge, Q.C., a grand old man of British criminal law, prosecuting for the Crown. Although the speeches delivered by the actors playing Macbeth, Lady Macbeth, and the other dramatic parts would all be carefully drafted by an award-winning television writer, Peter Moffat, there would be no time to script the cross-examination of the expert mental health witnesses, so I would have to leap into the fray and do my very best.

Baroness Kennedy, Maxine Peake, and I parted company at lunchtime on the Saturday and arranged that we would all congregate the following day at the Royal Courts of Justice for a long rehearsal commencing at noon, prior to the trial in front of seven hundred legal stars at 6.30 p.m. After my meeting with these two dynamic women, I raced into the centre of town and purchased D.V.D.s of Roman Polanski's film *The Tragedy of Macbeth* and of the more recent movie version of *Macbeth* starring the Australian actor Sam Worthington. Although I had read through the play several times after having received Helena's invitation, I thought that a Macbeth film-fest might help to prepare me even more fully. As I watched the stunning Francesca Annis play "Lady Macbeth" in the Roman Polanski version, I realised that we would have a challenging time defending the Scottish queen, because she hardly comes across as a battered wife—quite the opposite, in fact. Suddenly, my blood pressure began to rise, and I wondered why on earth I had consented to participate in a fictional murder trial!

On the appointed day of our unique event, I arrived at the Royal Courts of Justice at 11.50 a.m., and, to my surprise, I found the gates completely locked, with no Q.C.s or Shakespearean actors anywhere in sight. Obviously, after decades of running a psychoanalytic practice, I have rather good timekeeping. The same cannot be said for actors on a Sunday afternoon. Eventually, a custodian unlocked the chains on the enormous fortress-like gates, and I walked into the Great Hall and stared in amazement at the imposing ceilings. I must confess that I felt rather dwarfed. Indeed, I imagine that any real criminal hauled into the Royal Courts of Justice, unless completely psychopathic and impervious to anxiety, would feel very petrified indeed.

Eventually, the cast started to assemble. Maxine Peake, our Lady Macbeth, arrived first; and although I suppose that an expert witness ought not to hug and kiss a defendant, we embraced one another, having got on rather well the previous day at Baroness Kennedy's home. Then Matthew Macfadyen walked into the hall, looking very regal as the Thane. Throughout the day, a whole string of incredibly familiar faces appeared: Martin Shaw, who had, years earlier, portrayed "Banquo" in the Roman Polanski film, and who has since become one of our most distinguished actors, had agreed to play the Judge; Kevin

McKidd, a Scottish thespian who had scored a great sensation in the television drama *Rome* and who subsequently appeared with a *faux* American accent in *Grey's Anatomy*, had arrived to play "Banquo", replacing popular television star Rupert Penry-Jones at the last minute, owing to the latter's indisposition, having contracted gastritis in Delhi; Toby Stephens, son of Dame Maggie Smith and one of the rising breed of new Shakespearean stars, had agreed to take on the role of "Hamlet"; and Simon Russell Beale, another icon of the British stage, graciously joined the cast in order to make a guest appearance as William Shakespeare. Phil Davis, an extraordinary comic with a long pedigree in classical drama, arrived, joined by stalwarts Roger Lloyd Pack and Toby Jones, who would band together mischievously as the three witches. And, as if this would not be enough to sate the theatrical cravings of the judges and barristers, none other than Sir Derek Jacobi appeared in a natty suit and tie, fully prepared to play the ghost of Hamlet's father!

As the day wore on, I sat mesmerised in the vast hall as these leading lights of the British stage and screen cavorted on the platform of the makeshift courtroom, reciting monologues from Shakespeare's plays, alternating between serious renditions of their speeches and quite humorous asides. I could not believe my good fortune in spending the day with these remarkable practitioners of drama. I found each of them to be extremely kindly, interested, and straightforward, like all top professionals, irrespective of their field. Most of them had given up their Sunday to support the Criminal Bar Association's charity; and many had worked with the writer Peter Moffat previously and thus enjoyed doing him a favour. At any rate, none of them moaned or complained. They delighted at seeing the Macbeths in the "dock", and they played along accordingly.

At 6.00 p.m. we opened the doors, and in poured the cream of the British legal profession, dressed in dark suits and evening gowns, waiting to see Miss Kennedy, Mr Marshall-Andrews, and Mr Arlidge take to the stage in full regalia—robes and wigs—to defend or to prosecute the Macbeths. I stood high up in the gallery, near the robing rooms, staring down at the audience as they entered, rehearsing my diagnostic formulation like a mantra: "Her Ladyship meets the formal diagnostic criteria for a Major Depressive Disorder, Recurrent Type, compounded by Post-Traumatic Stress Disorder, specifically, the Battered Woman's Syndrome . . ." The expert witnesses would not be required until quite late in the trial; in the meanwhile, I would have to pace in the wings for a very long time.

Shortly after 6.30 p.m., Christopher James, a real-life Court Clerk, walked onto the platform, followed by Miss Kennedy and Mr Marshall-Andrews, the barristers for the defendants, and by Mr Arlidge, the barrister for the Crown. Maxine and Matthew took their places in the dock with neutral facial expressions that would have made a classical Freudian analyst proud. The Court Clerk then banged his gavel with bravado and cried out, "All rise", at which point seven hundred lawyers stood, and in walked Martin Shaw in an imposing judge's robe. A chill descended upon the assembled crowd. The trial had now begun, and the nervous mental health professionals, waiting to give evidence, would have to contain our fear. Though tempted to bolt, I took a deep breath and watched the trial unfold.

"Are you, Macbeth, Thane of Glamis, Thane of Cawdor, King of Scotland?", barked the Court Clerk. "Yes", replied Macbeth. "Are you Lady Macbeth?", Mr James demanded. "Yes", answered the Scottish queen.

The Court Clerk then exclaimed, "You have entered pleas of not guilty to the murders of Duncan and Banquo. Is that right?" "Yes", replied Matthew and Maxine in unison. The Clerk then swore in the entire audience *en masse* as the jury!

Bob Marshall-Andrews, the Q.C. defending Lord Macbeth, requested immediately that the case be dismissed on jurisdictional grounds, owing to the fact that one cannot try Scottish people in an English court. The Judge refused, provoking huge ripples of laughter throughout the audience.

The Macbeths' porter then gave evidence, followed by the three witches, each turning in a hugely comic performance. Then the defence called Banquo to the stand, but the prosecution objected on the grounds that a dead man cannot testify. Mr Marshall-Andrews, with sleight of hand, then summoned "Hamlet", the Prince of Denmark, who offered elegant evidence that dead men *can* indeed speak, at which point the unparalleled Sir Derek Jacobi burst onto the balcony of the Great Hall, hovering perhaps fifty feet above the distinguished audience, and bellowed some verses as the ghost of Hamlet's father in the most beautiful, stentorian tones. The sudden, unexpected appearance of Sir Derek, known to the entire country for his remarkable work in the dramatisation of *I, Claudius*, one of the most memorable series in all of television history, caused a frisson of deep excitement throughout the entire room.

Bob Marshall-Andrews then called his client Macbeth, who promptly admitted, in an ironic voice, to the murder of one "Tybalt" and, also, to the slaying of the two princes in the Tower of London! Martin Shaw, the Judge, looked horrified as Macbeth confessed to several *new* murders, whereupon the Judge then promptly asked Marshall-Andrews whether his client had gone mad. "Precisely", gloated Mr Marshall-Andrews, having already begun to lay the ground for a plea of diminished responsibility!

Next, Lady Macbeth took the stand, and Baroness Kennedy examined her with thoroughness and shrewdness, establishing that in an eleventh-century marriage such as this, the woman had no rights, and lived in terror of her brutal husband. Maxine Peake turned in a delicious performance as Lady Macbeth and played her role with passion and brio. One soon forgot Lady Macbeth's evident complicity in the murder of King Duncan, and one could not help but feel saddened by her plight as a battered wife, bereaved of child. I now realise only too clearly how sentiment and affect can transform the attitudes of jurors in court. The line between legal evidence and show business may, in fact, be greyer than one might ever imagine.

Eventually, the defence counsel summoned the two expert witnesses. First, a very distinguished real-life forensic psychiatrist from Broadmoor Hospital, a special hospital for the criminally insane in Berkshire—home to many serial killers—gave "evidence" that Lord Macbeth suffered from diminished responsibility, triggered in part by post-traumatic stress disorder acquired while in battle against the Norwegians. But then, in cross-examination, Baroness Kennedy "discredited" my worthy colleague's testimony when she ascertained that the psychiatrist is, in fact, a real-life friend of a noted judge who just happens to be a trustee of the charity sponsored by the Criminal Bar Association. This revelation of the psychiatrist's partiality and conflict of interest produced further gales of laughter.

Then the Court Clerk boomed, "Call Professor Kahr. Call Professor Kahr", whereupon I nervously mounted the stairs to the witness box, theatrical lights shining in my eyes, mercifully occluding the sight of seven hundred lawyers in front of me. I later discovered that, during the psychological testimony, all of the actors had snuck out into the auditorium to watch the proceedings. I doubt that I would have spoken my lines very coherently had I known that Sir Derek Jacobi sat in judgement!

I read my report, and I responded to all of Baroness Kennedy's clarificatory questions. "In view of your diagnosis, Professor Kahr, is there an abnormality of mind?", inquired Helena. "Most certainly", I replied. "Such as to diminish responsibility for murder?", she wondered. "Most definitely", I concluded. This all seemed straight-forward enough.

Then Bob Marshall-Andrews and Anthony Arlidge began their cross-examinations, and my heart began to pound. In foghorn voice, Mr Marshall-Andrews thundered, "Professor Kahr, I put it to you that you are not here to give expert testimony, but that you are a friend of the beautiful Maxine Peake . . . I mean Lady Macbeth . . . and that your evidence is thereby prejudiced." "No", I retorted in resolute fashion. Marshall-Andrews continued to bellow, without any trace of irony in his voice, "And that you are here solely because you hope to be invited to give expert testimony in the upcoming case of Richard III." The audience guffawed, and, with straight face, I issued a firm denial. Marshall-Andrews continued, "We have already established that the previous psychiatric witness is a friend of one of the judges. I put it to you that you are here as a friend of Baroness Kennedy." I stared Mr Marshall-Andrews squarely in the face and, uttering a line handed to me before the start of the trial by the Baroness, I stated slowly and resolutely, "I am here as a friend of the *Court*." Once again, the audience laughed in merry fashion at our rather serious japery.

Then Mr Arlidge, in sneery tones, began his attack: "Major Depressive Disorder, Recurrent Type . . . Post-Traumatic Stress Disorder . . . Sleepwalking Disorder . . . I put it to you that this is nothing more than psycho-mumbo-jumbo, and that you just read out any diagnosis that you could find in a textbook. Isn't that right?" "No", I spluttered. "Isn't that right, Professor?" "No, that is untrue. Her Ladyship meets the full diagnostic criteria of the aforementioned conditions as outlined in the *Diagnostic and Statistical Manual of Mental Disorders*." Arlidge would not be deterred, "I say that is nothing but rubbish. You just copied these disorders out of a book. Is there any illness from which Lady Macbeth does *not* suffer?" "Yes", I quipped, now in full playful mode: "Her Ladyship reveals no evidence whatsoever of either male pattern baldness or erectile dysfunction." At this point the entire audience, and the barristers as well, chortled with good humour. I doubt that we could have scripted a better-timed exit-line, and as the laughter died down, the Judge dismissed me from the witness stand, to my huge relief.

Simon Russell Beale, one of the greatest classical actors of our time, then took to the stage in the guise of William Shakespeare, explaining how he had created the character of Macbeth. When asked to state his name for the record, he replied, cheekily, "Edward de Vere, Earl of Oxford", noting that both Mark Twain and Sigmund

Freud knew the real truth of his identity. Beale rambled in the most charming fashion, reciting fragments from a variety of Shakespearean speeches, none necessarily related to the Macbeths but all quite riveting, nevertheless.

Eventually, the Judge called upon the jury to deliver its verdict, and the foreman declared both Matthew and Maxine innocent of all charges, to resounding applause. Upon hearing the verdict, Judge Martin Shaw then wryly jested, "I now move to sentencing", evoking more mirth from the judges and barristers and, indeed, from all those on stage. In spite of the fact that the jury had pronounced the Macbeths innocent, the Judge, clearly enjoying himself, intoned, "Lady Macbeth, I sentence you to hundreds of years of lazy stereotyping designed to ensure women who stick their heads above the parapet are shot down quickly. Macbeth, I sentence you to life imprisonment during which term I am entirely confident your capacity for violent crime will be nurtured and seriously enhanced." And then, turning to the Court Clerk, the Judge instructed, "Take them up", in other words, to the cells with them.

The trial then ended, and all of the Shakespearean actors and barristers returned to the stage for a curtain call. I remained in my seat in the audience, but my fellow "expert witness" insisted that we, too, should take a curtain call, and with deep absurdity, I found myself sandwiched between Derek Jacobi and Simon Russell Beale, bowing to the assembled crowd.

In summary, we all had a lovely evening and managed to raise a great deal of money from ticket sales and donations for a worthwhile educational charity, helping to prepare young criminal barristers who will, in the future, defend the innocent and convict the guilty. I felt very privileged to have had this inside glimpse of the British justice system at such close range, even if we dared to intersperse the seriousness of an historico-literary murder trial with such jollity and humour.

Above all, I am pleased to have had a chance to talk to so many substantial members of the theatrical profession and the legal profession. At first, I felt rather sheepish that, compared to the actors and the lawyers, we in the psychotherapeutic professions would be dismissed as little more than "Johnny Come Latelys".

But Maxine Peake allayed my fears almost immediately and told me that she wished she could be a psychotherapist, as it must be far more interesting than theatre and television. And several of the other members of the company had confided to me that they had

had extremely good experiences as clients undergoing psychotherapy and felt very grateful. One member of the cast told me that his son had just begun to train as a psychotherapist, and I passed along my telephone number in case the young chap might need some career advice.

Although some of the more conservative and humourless members of the mental health community might balk at the prospect of giving testimony in an eleventh-century murder trial, I hope that I served as a good representative of our field, attempting to convey the seriousness of psychopathology while still maintaining the capacity to play.

PART III

HISTORICAL ESSAYS

Nescire autem quid ante quam natus sis acciderit, id est semper esse puerum.
[To be ignorant of what occurred before you were born is to remain always a child.]

Marcus Tullius Cicero, *Orator ad M. Brutum*, 46 B.C.E.

CHAPTER THIRTEEN

Four unknown Freud anecdotes

Gone are the living, but the dead remain,
And not neglected; for a hand unseen,
Scattering its bounty, like a summer rain,
Still keeps their graves and their remembrance green.

Henry Wadsworth Longfellow, "The Jewish Cemetery at Newport",
1854, in *The Courtship of Miles Standish, and Other Poems*, 1858
[Longfellow, 1854, p. 159]

Introduction

Some years ago, the journal *Psychoanalysis and History* published a brief communication written by Dr Lydia Marinelli (2009), the distinguished Austrian Freud scholar, about the actual tweed cap that Sigmund Freud wore during his flight from the Nazis. Marinelli reported that, after Freud's death, Anna Freud donated this item from her father's wardrobe to the Sigmund Freud Museum in Vienna, where it remained until 1977, when an American visitor stole the priceless headgear. Extraordinarily, some years later, the thief in question actually posted the cap back to the Berggasse, full of contrition, perhaps having had some psychoanalysis in the meanwhile!

Marinelli's little *pièce d'occasion*, though charming and evocative, also serves as a potent reminder that, for those of us interested in the life of the founder of psychoanalysis, no biographical detail seems too insignificant. In fact, we greatly enjoy reading stories about Freud's cap, fascinated by every single aspect of his life. Perhaps a genius deserves such attention. Perhaps his story remains so inspirational that we owe it to Freud and to posterity to capture every piece of trivia. But perhaps our preoccupation with Freud represents no more than a sublimation of our more primordial wish to penetrate the bedroom of our archaic caretakers—"mummy" and "daddy".

Whatever our motivation for researching Freud minutiae—however useful these vignettes may or may not be—they do continue to delight those of us who work within the psychoanalytic domain. Naturally, when the late Professor Margaret Brenman-Gibson, a distinguished psychoanalyst from the Austen Riggs Center in Stockbridge, Massachusetts, told me that the late Professor Erik Erikson had told *her* an unpublished story about Freud, I listened attentively, and then I wrote it down in a notebook immediately thereafter so that I would remember it accurately. Similarly, when I met a woman at a social gathering who told me that, back in the 1930s, her uncle—a sex offender—had travelled to Vienna for treatment with Freud, I also listened carefully and jotted down the story, in spite of the lack of more detail. And when one of my former students, the late Mrs Hilde Schoenfeld, invited me to tea with her honorary nonagenarian aunt, Frau Olga Rosenberg, whose husband had once delivered a carpet to Freud's home, I accepted the kind offer to meet her with eagerness. And then, when I discovered a book written by the American socialite Miss Elsa Maxwell, which mentions a meeting with Freud—an encounter not known to Freud historians—I became slightly excited, and thought that colleagues might wish to read this memoir for themselves.

More dogged historians than I may still manage to locate some voluble centenarians who had intimate relationships with Freud and his circle, and if so, we await the accounts of these meetings with interest. I have only four very marginal anecdotes to share, and I do so unapologetically, safe in the knowledge that fellow Freudophiles might enjoy these as well, but also because each vignette conveys something about the character of Freud, however slight—a character that informs and that often serves as a model of wisdom and guidance.

Sigmund Freud and the sickly child

During the latter part of 1985, I had the opportunity to hear a lovely story about Sigmund Freud from Professor Margaret Brenman-Gibson, who, in turn, had heard this story from her great mentor and friend, Professor Erik Erikson. Many Freud anecdotes will be repeated so often that one often discovers multiple renderings in a variety of printed sources; but I have not heard this particular story spoken elsewhere, or seen it published in the literature. Although one can so very easily fetishise every single vignette about Freud and hasten into print, I regard this little anecdote, especially, as very heart-warming and as very instructive; and I hope that it will provide some stimulation to readers who share an interest in the history of psychoanalysis.

Professor Erikson knew Freud somewhat, of course, as he and his wife Joan Mowat Serson Erikson lived in Vienna while Erik underwent an analysis with Anna Freud and while Joan herself had an experience of psychoanalysis with Dr Ludwig Jekels. Therefore, Professor Erikson would have heard a great many tales about Freud and his patients at first hand. Apparently, Freud had told Erikson this memorable episode from his clinical practice; and it seems to have exerted such an impact on the youthful Erikson that he still found himself speaking about it many decades later.

Apparently, a certain female patient had arrived at Freud's consulting room for her session. As usual, she lay down upon the couch, and she began to free-associate. On this occasion, however, the analysand seemed quite distressed, and she told Freud that she had left her small child at home with a fever and, in consequence, found herself worrying about the child's health. As a physician, Freud shared the patient's concern and admonished her by asking, "Well, what are you doing here, then?"—or words to that effect. He then sent the patient home so that she could resume her duties as a mother. Professor Erikson communicated this story as an expression of Freud's unique compassion and humanity—placing the needs of an ill child before the practice of psychoanalysis.

One could readily use this Freud story as a starting-point in clinical seminars on psychotherapeutic technique. When I first heard this tale, I, too, shared Professor Erikson's joy in Freud's lovely, caring qualities. However, upon further reflection, one wonders whether Freud had acted too precipitously by sending the patient away. After all, although the lady in question may have appreciated Freud's expression of concern for her child, she may also have felt that Freud had abandoned *her*—the adult patient—by placing the *child's* needs ahead of her own. Similarly, Freud may have underestimated the way in which the female patient had used a concrete image of her own ill child as a means of communicating more readily something about the ill, child-like parts of her own personality.

Furthermore, for all we know, the woman may have felt quite persecuted by her own child and would have welcomed the opportunity for a fortifying psychoanalytic session with Sigmund Freud. It may be that she might also have felt infantilised or, indeed, shamed by Freud sending her away, perhaps fearing that Freud thought her incapable of caring for her own offspring and that he had lambasted her as a neglectful mother who had dared to come to her session. After all, the patient may have had a husband, or a maid, or a nanny, or any number of other adults on hand who might have watched over the child while the mother spent an analytical hour in Freud's office.

Of course, with no knowledge of the patient's history, or of the patient's character structure, or of any of the collateral details of the material, one can only speculate about the merits or demerits of this particular Freud intervention. Furthermore, we do not know whether Erik Erikson reported the story in a fully accurate and nuanced way. Perhaps Freud *had* explored the many meanings of the episode with his patient. Nevertheless, I hope that this brief, and hitherto unpublished, moment from Freud's clinical practice can serve as a stimulus for further discussion about matters of technique.

Sigmund Freud and the case of the paedophile

During the last thirty years or more, numerous authors have written quite critically about Sigmund Freud and the whole question of child sexual abuse. Dr Jeffrey Masson (1984), in particular, had spearheaded a vanguard of critical Freud scholars who have claimed that Freud had turned his back on the abused children of Vienna by having abandoned his so-called "seduction" theory of the neuroses in 1897 in favour of an ostensibly more outlandish theory regarding the fantasmatic oedipal origins of the neuroses. But, as I have indicated elsewhere (Kahr, 1991, 1999e), Freud actually maintained a much greater interest in the realities of child sexual abuse and traumatisation than his critics wish to credit him (e.g., Freud, 1896a, 1896b, 1905, 1917, 1931, 1940).

Although Freud (1907a, p. 56) wrote to his German colleague Dr Karl Abraham that, although "ein Teil der sexuellen Träumen, von denen die Kranken berichten, sind Phantasien, oder können es sein" ["a proportion of the sexual traumas reported by patients are or may be phantasies" (Freud, 1907b, p. 2)], analysands do, nevertheless, recall experiences of genuine abuse, though the distinction between these two categories may not always be easy to appreciate. A few years later, in a letter to his Swiss colleague, Pfarrer Oskar Pfister, Freud (1913a, p. 59) explained, "Ich habe selbst mehrere Fälle von realem Inzest (schwerster Art) analysiert und hergestellt" ["I have myself analysed and cured several cases of real incest (of the most severe kind)" (Freud, 1913b, p. 59)]. We must underscore that Freud made these observations about genuine child sexual abuse long *after* he had, supposedly, abandoned his theory concerning the toxic effects of actual sexual traumata.

We know quite well that Freud continued to believe in the reality of child sexual abuse throughout his long career, and we also know that he struggled to discriminate which cases of abuse could be documented reliably and which ones might be an artefact of the patient's fantasies. It remains less well known that, during World War I, Freud did supervise the treatment of a paedophile who underwent analysis with Freud's younger colleague, Dr Theodor Reik, thus suggesting that Freud knew about the practice of paedophilia (Natterson, 1966).

Freud not only supervised a case of paedophilia treated by a disciple, but he also had direct experience of working with at least one paedophile himself, although he seems never to have published an account of this particular psychoanalysis. On 19 February 1995, I had the opportunity to speak to an English woman, whom I first met, quite by happenstance, at a social gathering in London. When I revealed to her my profession, she became quite enthused, and she mentioned that her uncle had undergone analysis with Freud in Vienna in the 1930s. She related the details of her uncle, a convicted paedophile, who seems to have appeared before an enlightened British judge, who told the man that he could either go to prison or else emigrate to Vienna for an analysis with Professor Freud. The paedophile chose the latter option, and he did indeed have such an experience with Freud.

I quizzed my interlocutor thoroughly, and although, to the best of our knowledge, no written documentation of her late uncle's trip to Vienna has survived, this woman spoke at great length about the family history, and about the uncle's favourable experience with Freud (Anonymous, personal communication, 19 February 1995). In the absence of archival data, one does not know how much store to place in the recollections of the niece of one of Freud's patients, treated more than half a century previously, but my encounter with this woman deserves to be chronicled as yet one more suggestion that Freud did, indeed, acknowledge the realities of child abuse even after the so-called abandonment of the seduction theory, in spite of what his critics might sometimes have us believe.

Sigmund Freud and the carpet merchant

In 1992, I had the privilege of meeting Mrs Hilde Schoenfeld, an elderly woman who had decided to train as a psychotherapist late in life. We first became acquainted shortly after she had begun her clinical studies, and I had the pleasure of serving first as her lecturer and then, later, as her clinical supervisor. Hilde stood out among the intake of candidates not only because of her advanced years, but, most particularly, because of her magnificent smile, which lit up the entire room.

A refugee from Berlin, Mrs Schoenfeld had fled from Nazi Germany on a *Kindertransport* train roughly half a century earlier, and she gradually established a rich family life for herself in England. After a full professional career as a teacher, Hilde sought to extend her learning by undertaking a psychotherapy training programme. Although of retirement age, Hilde chose to continue her personal development by enrolling on our course, very much to her credit.

After teaching a psychohistory seminar to Hilde and her colleagues, I soon became a regular instructor, and I had the privilege of facilitating Hilde's group on many subsequent occasions, offering workshops on the psychoses and other forms of severe psychopathology. While the horrors of child abuse and the ravages of mental illness caused many of Hilde's colleagues to wince, she, by contrast, embraced the course material with sensitivity and enthusiasm, and she contributed both extensively and helpfully to our classroom deliberations.

As I often peppered my lectures with German psychoanalytic terms, Hilde could spot at once that we shared a similar cultural background, and she guessed correctly from my surname and from my pronunciation of certain Freudian terminology that my family had come from Vienna several generations previously. The German–Austrian connection solidified a bond between us, and she enjoyed reminiscing to me about life in Berlin in the 1930s.

In the final year of her training, Hilde came to me for clinical supervision, and she proved to be a most responsive, eager, and committed supervisee; and I took great pleasure in helping her to prepare her final case history, which she submitted successfully, qualifying as a psychoanalytic psychotherapist in 1996. I recently had the opportunity to re-read Hilde's case study, and this brought back a flood of fond memories of our supervisory work together and, most particularly, of Hilde's tremendous compassion for her patient, as well as her dedication to her new profession.

I also recall the guilt that I used to feel that I have no lift in the office building in which I work. Although visitors need climb only two flights of not very steep stairs in order to reach my consulting room, Hilde, probably nearing seventy years of age at the time, used to enter my office puffing and panting. Nonetheless, she wanted to make the journey, and I know that she felt immense pride in qualifying at a time in life when other ageing people devote themselves exclusively to retirement and, often, to grandparenthood.

Before her death in 2002, Hilde treated me to a most special experience at her warm and gracious home in North London. For some time, she had promised to introduce me to her nonagenarian friend, Frau Olga Rosenberg, a very elderly Viennese refugee who had become a guardian angel to Hilde for much of her life. Hilde used to call her "Tante Oli" ["Aunt Oli"]. She particularly wanted me to meet Frau Rosenberg, not only because of my own Viennese heritage, but also because Frau Rosenberg's late husband, Herr Sándor Rosenberg, a carpet merchant in Vienna during the 1930s, had once met Sigmund Freud.

Hilde organised the most splendid and wickedly calorific Central European *Jause*—"high tea"—at which I met Frau Rosenberg and also Hilde's very beautiful daughter, Stephanie Schoenfeld, a talented actress. Tante Oli reminisced enchantingly about her late husband's brief but nonetheless memorable encounter with Professor Freud, which, I believe, merits capturing in print.

The Rosenbergs owned a carpet shop in Vienna before World War Two. One day, Freud's youngest daughter, Anna Freud, entered in search of a present for her father. Never renowned for her sartorial splendour, Anna Freud often looked quite shabby, dressed rather like a peasant, and Tante Oli thought she must be a beggar in search of some loose coins! Frau Rosenberg almost gave her the money in the "beggar's bowl", which Viennese tradespeople used to keep in their shops for precisely that purpose. Before long, the poorly clad Fräulein Freud introduced herself as the daughter of the esteemed founder of psychoanalysis, Professor Sigmund Freud, and she then purchased an Oriental carpet as a gift for her father.

Delighted to have sold a carpet to one of Vienna's most esteemed families, Herr Rosenberg delivered the item personally to Freud's home in the Berggasse, where he had the opportunity to meet the father of psychoanalysis in person. Evidently a most charismatic man, Rosenberg regaled Freud with a joke, and the Professor responded with great appreciation, describing Herr Rosenberg's pleasantry as *"ein schöner Witz"*, which means, literally, "a beautiful joke".

Although this little vignette hardly breaks new ground in our understanding of Sigmund Freud, it confirms his stature and celebrity, in view of the fact that such a brief encounter would still be remembered more than sixty years later. I hope, moreover, that this vignette also illustrates something essential about Hilde Schoenfeld—namely, her appreciation for history and biography, her respect for scholarship, her prosocial desire to link people together, and her wish to be helpful. She brought all of these qualities to bear on her important work as a telephone counsellor with abused children at ChildLine, and in her labours as a private practitioner of psychotherapy.

Hilde never expected to have a long career in mental health and had no thoughts of writing books or serving on committees. She entered our field for her own personal growth. As one of my elderly students at another training institution once confessed to me, "I am doing this course because I *have to*. It is the only way I can feel of value to myself and to others." I hope that Hilde Schoenfeld can serve as a role model for other women and men of advanced years who can still make important contributions to the psychotherapy community.

Sigmund Freud and the socialite

Today, the name of Elsa Maxwell will be known only to the very elderly or to those familiar with American cultural history during the middle years of the twentieth century. But in her heyday Elsa Maxwell would have required no introduction. A successful songwriter, a newspaper columnist, a compulsive socialite, a sometime film star, and, above all, a consummate hostess who entertained virtually everyone of renown, Elsa Maxwell hobnobbed with fellow songwriters Irving Berlin, Noël Coward, and George Gershwin. Her extremely great friend and colleague Cole Porter immortalised her in several of his own compositions, such as "Tomorrow", from his 1938 musical *Leave it to Me*; "I'm Throwing a Ball Tonight", from his 1940 musical *Panama Hattie*; and "Farming", from his 1941 musical *Let's Face It!*. Porter also paid an affectionate, if sarcastic, tribute to Miss Maxwell in a song written, not for a Broadway show, but, rather, as a private birthday present, given at one of Maxwell's Paris parties in the 1920s. Entitled "I'm Dining with Elsa", the witty composition contains the encapsulating quatrain: "I've got Bromo Seltzer/To take when dinner ends,/For I'm dining with Elsa/And her ninety-nine most intimate friends!" Fellow songsmith Irving Berlin commemorated her, likewise, with a prominent reference in his song "The Hostess with the Mostes' on the Ball" from the 1950 musical *Call Me Madam*. And Noël Coward lampooned her affectionately in his 1938 song "I Went to a Marvellous Party", first introduced on stage in 1939 by the comedienne Beatrice Lillie in Coward's revue *Set to Music*; and in the same year, Richard Rodgers and Lorenz Hart referenced Miss Maxwell in their jaunty song "I Like to Recognize the Tune" from the Broadway show *Too Many Girls* (cf. Staggs, 2012). Miss Maxwell received not only "name checks" in the aforementioned songs, but she also formed the basis for a character, one "Eva Standing", a high-level hostess, in the 1935 Broadway musical *Jubilee*, with music and lyrics by Cole Porter and with a libretto by the esteemed writer Moss Hart (cf. Mordden, 2010).

She also cavorted with novelists and dramatists such as Ernest Hemingway, Aldous Huxley, William Somerset Maugham, and George Bernard Shaw, and lounged with actors such as John Barrymore, Fanny Brice, Charlie Chaplin, Gary Cooper, Greta Garbo, and Rita Hayworth. In fact, Miss Maxwell had the responsibility of introducing Rita Hayworth to the playboy socialite Aly Khan shortly after the screen goddess's marriage to Orson Welles; and, notoriously, Hayworth would leave Welles for Khan not long thereafter. Maxwell also met Salvador Dalí, Albert Einstein, Dwight Eisenhower, and Adolf Hitler, and she even enjoyed a great penchant for crossdressing in men's clothing, impersonating, *inter alia*, Aristide Briand, Benjamin Franklin, and Herbert Hoover. Apparently, Miss Maxwell also harboured a significant sexual passion for the opera diva Maria Callas, whom she befriended with ardour (Galatopoulos, 1998).

Elsa Maxwell knew *everyone*, and, clearly, she had a deep-seated need to ensure that everyone would know *her*, however slightly. Unsurprisingly, Maxwell's list of trophy encounters would not be complete without a consultation in Vienna with Professor Sigmund Freud.

In her autobiography, Miss Maxwell (1954, p. 18) wrote, "I've been told a psychiatrist could have a field day with me, but I'm inclined to doubt it. My analysis would be completed in one quick session because I know, almost to the minute, the two incidents that freed me of the complications that clutter up the lives of most people—money and sex." She then explained, "I never had a sexual experience, nor did I ever want one" (Maxwell, 1954, p. 18), and that, "I saw so much unhappiness in the marriages of friends that I was content to have chosen music and laughter as substitutes for husbands and lovers" (Maxwell, 1954, p. 19). In this context, Miss Maxwell then summarised her visit to the founder of psychoanalysis in one short paragraph.

According to Elsa Maxwell (1954),

> At least one authority gave me a passing grade in emotional development. In 1931, I met the great Sigmund Freud in Vienna. He must have been amused by my talk, for he engaged me in conversation for fully a half hour. Freud asked me about my background. When I told him, he nodded and murmured: "A healthy woman who will never suffer from neuroses . . ." I didn't know then what neuroses were. [p. 20]

As if to confirm the diagnosis, Miss Maxwell included a photograph of Freud in her book with the following caption: "*Freud. He told me I would never suffer*" (Maxwell, 1954, between pp. 182 and 183).

Elsa Maxwell's name does not appear in Freud's (1992) *Kürzeste Chronik*—his list of visitors and key diary events—for 1931, nor indeed, for any other year. Freud did, however, record many other events from 1931, such as his X-ray from a certain Dr Presser; his medical consultation with Professor Dr med. Hans Pichler; a surgical procedure in the Auersperg Sanatorium; his wife Martha Freud's attack of influenza; his son Oliver Freud's fortieth birthday; his evenings with colleagues Dr Siegfried Bernfeld and Dr Sándor Radó; the deaths of Mathilde Breuer and Arthur Schnitzler; his session with the sculptor Oscar Nemon; the announcement of the translations of his works into Japanese and Spanish; the seventieth birthday of his wife; as well as his own seventy-fifth birthday, *inter alia*. Perhaps the half hour with Elsa Maxwell did not merit a mention. Indeed, I have never come across the name of Elsa Maxwell in the Freud literature. In view of the circles in which Miss Maxwell travelled, and in view of her remarkable persistence of character, I have no reason to doubt the authenticity of this thirty-minute encounter. But, owing to the relative obscurity of Miss Maxwell's memoir—at least in psychoanalytic circles—this account has escaped the attentions of Freud scholars. On the basis of such a short recitation, one cannot draw any conclusions from Maxwell's report, although students of Freud's personality will wonder, of course, whether the jolly socialite, ostensibly free of neuroses, had the capacity to appreciate Freud's considerable sense of irony.

Scrutinising Freud's body

Sigmund Freud loved little details. In a letter to Eduard Silberstein, his old friend from adolescent years, Freud (1910a, p. 213) pleaded, "Ich wüßte gerne im Einzelnen, wie es Dir geht" ["I should very much like to hear in detail how things are with you" (Freud, 1910b, p. 185)]. A few short weeks later, Freud (1910c, p. 36) wrote to his Swiss colleague, Pfarrer Oskar Pfister,

> diese psychoanalytischen Dinge erst in einer gewissen Vollständigkeit und Ausführlichkeit begreiflich, sowie die Analyse selbst erst geht, wenn der Patient von den ersetzenden Abstraktionen zu den kleinen Details herabsteigt.
>
> [these psycho-analytic matters are intelligible only if presented in pretty full and complete detail, just as an analysis really gets going only when the patient descends to minute details from the abstractions which are their surrogate.] [Freud, 1910d, p. 38]

His interest in detail became extremely well known among his pupils. Indeed, in an obituary of Freud, written for *The International Journal of Psycho-Analysis*, Dr Ernest Jones (1940, p. 2) underscored the maestro's "unfailing interest in the small things as well as in the great".

As a clinician, I have derived enormous benefit from Sigmund Freud's observations that every miniscule detail of human psychology, no matter how arcane or obscure, can be of value. Freud became increasingly preoccupied with detail, as his essay on "Der Moses des Michelangelo" ["The Moses of Michelangelo"] (Anonymous [Sigmund Freud], 1914)—to cite but one example—reveals only too clearly. For Freud, it mattered greatly why Michelangelo Buonarroti sculpted the arms of Moses as he did and why he interlaced the fingers of Moses in his marble beard in such a particular fashion. Towards the end of his life, Freud (1937a, p. 463) noted, in his classic paper "Konstruktionen in der Analyse" ["Constructions in Analysis"], that, when offering a construction to a patient, "Wir wollen diesen Punkt eingehend behandeln" ["The point must be gone into in detail" (Freud, 1937b, p. 262)].

Of course, in spite of Freud's love of detail, he also knew that one could overestimate the detail, perhaps in a morbid manner. In his analysis of the seventeenth-century Bavarian painter Christoph Haizmann, a gentleman ostensibly possessed by the Devil, Freud (1923a, p. 22) cautioned of "die Gefahr, Kleinigkeiten zu überschätzen" ["the danger of overvaluing trifles" (Freud, 1923b, p. 93)].

I leave it to the reader to decide whether the careful preservation of these Freudian minutiae represents something of interest or, rather, merely an eccentric preoccupation with the parental body, which, in spite of years of analysis, continues to persist.

Why Freud turned down $25,000: mental health professionals in the witness box

> What is the use of Americans, if they bring no money? They are not good for anything else.
>
> Professor Sigmund Freud, Letter to Dr Ernest Jones,
> 25 September, 1924
> [Freud, 1924b, p. 552]

On 21 May 1924, two wealthy, academically precocious American teenagers attempted to commit the "perfect crime" (Darrow, 1932, p. 228). Nathan Leopold, Jr, aged nineteen, son of Nathan F. Leopold, Sr, a millionaire box manufacturer, and Richard Loeb, aged eighteen, son of Albert H. Loeb, an extremely prosperous Vice-President of Sears, Roebuck and Company, kidnapped fourteen-year-old Robert Franks as he journeyed home from the Harvard School for Boys in the exclusive Hyde Park district of Chicago, Illinois. The following morning, the victim's father, property tycoon Jacob Franks, received a ransom letter by special delivery, demanding $10,000 in unmarked twenty-dollar bills and fifty-dollar bills; but before Mr Franks could respond, the police had already located Bobby Franks's naked body, soaked in blood, abandoned in a marsh on the South Side of Chicago, with his skull bludgeoned by a chisel (Baatz, 2008).

Although intent on committing the perfect crime, Nathan Leopold, Jr had, nevertheless, dropped his specially manufactured horn-rimmed spectacles at the scene—a symptomatic gesture, indicative, perhaps, of the wish to be apprehended and treated. After consulting with Almer Coe and Company, the oculist who had made the eyeglasses, the Cook County police eventually captured the killers (Darrow, 1932). Both scions of successful Jewish families, whose joint estimated wealth amounted to fifteen million dollars, Leopold and Loeb excited tremendous anti-Semitic bloodlust among the American populace, who clamoured for the execution of these two young culprits (Tierney, 1979). Each fiercely intelligent, Loeb had become the youngest person ever to graduate from the University of Michigan, while Leopold held a similar distinction as the youngest ever baccalaureate from the University of Chicago, graduating with Phi Beta Kappa honours; in fact, he had already commenced his postgraduate studies at the University of Chicago Law School. Nathan Leopold, in particular, shone as an academic, having studied fourteen languages, both classical and modern, as well as philosophy, enjoying a particular penchant for the works of Friedrich Nietzsche. He also delivered regular addresses to ornithological organisations based on his encyclopaedic knowledge of birds. Additionally, he had become known as an "advanced botanist" (Darrow, 1932, p. 231). The press had a field day with such unusual, colourful, and brainy murderers.

In desperation, the family of Richard Loeb approached Clarence Seward Darrow, the famous lawyer, in the hope that he would represent the accused and save them from a sentence of death by hanging. Though physically weary, suffering from neuralgia and rheumatism, and wary of the tide of public opinion against Leopold and Loeb, the sixty-seven-year-old Darrow agreed to handle the case; and, of course, he proved to be the perfect lawyer to advocate on behalf of the boys. A vocal opponent of capital punishment, Darrow (1922) had only recently published a pioneering and compassionate book, *Crime: Its Cause and Treatment*, a hitherto unappreciated classic that anticipates many of the philosophical tenets of contemporary psychoanalytic forensic psychotherapy by insisting on compassionate treatment for offenders and by recognising that criminals will have suffered from abusive backgrounds. In his feisty polemic, Darrow spoke about the causal role of poverty and deprivation in the genesis of criminal behaviour; and he also argued strenuously for prison reform and believed passionately that the general public must take responsibility for criminals. As a trial lawyer, Darrow endeavoured, in pioneering fashion, to introduce the psychological-motivational dimension into the courtroom itself.

Expert psychiatric testimony would be needed prior to the commencement of the trial in July of 1924, and, thus, Darrow sought out a group of witnesses to participate in this spectacularly public case. The prosecution had already secured the services of several eminent Chicago psychiatrists, and so Darrow, not to be outdone, sent his colleague, Walter Bachrach, a relation of the Loeb family, to the annual meeting of the American Psychiatric Association in Atlantic City, New Jersey, to enlist the support of Dr Bernard Glueck, Sr, Dr William Healy, and Dr William Alanson White, three titans of American psychoanalytic psychiatry, all of whom specialised in forensic work.

In view of the sensational scandal surrounding the case, and the pleas from the families of the accused, Colonel Robert Rutherford McCormick, the libertarian co-editor and co-publisher of the *Chicago Tribune* newspaper, called upon his staff reporter George Seldes to contact Professor Sigmund Freud in Vienna and to invite him to come to Chicago to serve as an expert witness in the infamous murder trial of these two privileged boys. Robert McCormick—a relation of Medill McCormick, a devotee of Dr Carl Gustav Jung—may have harboured sympathies for the depth psychologies, and consequently he instructed George Seldes: "Offer Freud 25,000 dollars or anything he name come Chicago psychoanalyze (i.e. the murderers)" (quoted in Jones, 1957, p. 103).

Although Freud could have used the money fruitfully to sponsor the growing psychoanalytic movement, he declined the invitation from the *Chicago Tribune*. Diagnosed with carcinoma of the jaw one year earlier (Schur, 1972; Romm, 1983) and never a great fan of the United States of America (e.g., Freud, 1921; cf. Falzeder, 2012), Freud remained in Vienna, having responded to Seldes by letter on 29 June 1924:

> Your telegram reached me belatedly because of being wrongly addressed. In reply I would say that I cannot be supposed to be prepared to provide an expert opinion about persons and a deed when I have only newspaper reports to go on and have no opportunity to make a personal examination. An invitation from the Hearst Press to come to New York for the duration of the trial I have had to decline for reasons of health. [Freud, 1924a, p. 103]

It seems that William Randolph Hearst, the phenomenally wealthy newspaper tycoon, whose life would inspire the character of "Charles Foster Kane" in Orson Welles's classic film *Citizen Kane*, had already attempted to lure Freud to New York for the very same purpose. Hearst had told Freud that he could claim whatever fee he desired and had even offered to charter a special ocean liner for Freud's express use (Jones, 1957).

Certainly, Freud's cancer would have served as a powerful deterrent, but, he may, of course, have had reasons other than illness for refusing such a lavish fee. We do not know whether he regarded the invitations of McCormick and Hearst as genuine or, rather, as callous publicity stunts, because, to the best of our knowledge, no documentation survives that sheds light on the fuller reasons for Freud's refusal. The *Chicago Tribune* had offered to arrange for a radio broadcast of the trial, whereas the *Evening American* had hoped to turn the capacious stadium Comiskey Park, the home of the Chicago White Sox baseball team, into an open-air courtroom. Thus, Freud may have worried that he might become embroiled in a media circus.

Fortunately, Darrow, known in the press as the "Old Lion", managed very well indeed without Freud's intervention. Dr Bernard Glueck, Sr, a New York prison psychiatrist, Dr William Healy, an expert in juvenile delinquency, and Dr William Alanson White, the director of St. Elizabeths Hospital for the Insane in the District of Columbia, testified successfully, albeit for the rather more modest fee of $250 per doctor, per day (Weinberg and Weinberg, 1980). The London-born judge, the Honorable John Caverly, capitulated to Darrow's pleading and, after having listened to his masterful twelve-hour summation, delivered over the course of three days, sentenced Leopold and Loeb to life imprisonment, in spite of the fact that Caverly had the right to condemn the murderers to death (Gurko, 1965; Tierney, 1979).

Happily, Freud's unwillingness to become an expert witness for the defence did not prevent Clarence Darrow from participating, some years later, as one of the speakers in the special banquet for some 200 guests, at the Ritz-Carlton Hotel in New York City, in honour of Freud's seventy-fifth birthday in 1931. On that occasion, Dr William Alanson White delivered the principal address, and Darrow provided his own tribute to Freud, as did the novelist Theodore Dreiser and other speakers (Jones, 1957).

One wonders, of course, what Freud might have had to say about Leopold and Loeb, and whether his insights would have helped to facilitate the development of the field of forensic psychotherapy, that branch of mental health which approaches the treatment of offender patients through the use of psychoanalytic concepts and techniques.

Naturally, we cannot know. We also remain mystified as to the undisclosed motives of Freud's refusal of a blank cheque to come to the United States of America in a private ocean liner. Though Freud's cancer did deter him from making a long journey, his illness did not confine him to his bed; in fact, Freud continued to work devastatingly lengthy days and nights, treating patients, writing books and papers, and tending to the increasing complexities of the international psychoanalytic movement.

So, did cancer prevent Freud from testifying for Clarence Darrow, or could anti-American prejudice be blamed? (Roazen, 1995; Prochnik, 2006; Falzeder, 2012). Or did Freud fear the prospect of dealing with a case of murder (cf. Wolff, 1988), perhaps for countertransferential reasons? After all, many mental health professionals shy away from the complexities and burdens of forensic work. Perhaps Freud simply worried about the impact of collaborating with potentially crass and unethical mass media?

Several months after the Leopold–Loeb trial, Samuel Goldwyn, the American film mogul, travelled to Europe to meet with Freud, hoping to offer him the princely sum of $100,000 to serve as a consultant to a proposed film about great love stories from history, beginning with that of Mark Antony and Cleopatra. Not only did Freud turn down the offer of a consultancy as well as the gargantuan fee, but he refused even to meet with Goldwyn in person, in spite of the latter's long journey to Europe (Jones, 1957).

Shortly thereafter, Freud expressed deeper concern still when he discovered that two close disciples, Dr Karl Abraham and Dr Hanns Sachs, had begun to offer their advisory services to a German film company, the Universum Film Aktiengesellschaft (U.F.A.), for a movie about psychoanalysis, entitled *Geheimnisse einer Seele* [*Secrets of a Soul*], directed by the noted Austrian filmmaker Georg Wilhelm Pabst (Chodorkoff and Baxter, 1974; Ries, 1995). Though ultimately the director produced a film quite favourable towards psychoanalysis, Freud (1925) remained wary and, also, concerned that the filmmakers had seduced both Abraham and Sachs. Clearly, Freud's reluctance to participate in either the Leopold–Loeb trial or the Samuel Goldwyn film, and now, the U.F.A. film as well, betokens someone with an aversion to engage with the popular media.

Naturally, Freud did not have the luxury to explore the media in the way in which we do today. After all, psychoanalysis and psychotherapy have since become extremely well-established fixtures of both the clinical and the cultural landscapes—so much so that one injudicious piece of consultancy would hardly cause the edifice of modern psychology to crumble. But back in the 1920s, Freud, by contrast, had to protect the scientific integrity of the fledgling discipline of psychoanalysis in order to prevent its dilution and disgrace. But, one must wonder, did he protect the integrity of psychoanalysis too much, at the expense of its public dissemination?

In July of 2004, I became the Resident Psychotherapist for B.B.C. Radio 2 and Spokesperson for the B.B.C. mental health campaign "Life 2 Live", in which capacity I had the privilege of broadcasting with a psychoanalytic accent to approximately 15,000,000 British people weekly. In undertaking this work, I followed in the venerable tradition of figures such as Dr Donald Winnicott, who had essentially pioneered good psychoanalytic media psychology in Great Britain (e.g., Kahr, 2015, 2018b), creating a body of work elaborated upon by other important mental health broadcasters such as the late Dr Anthony Storr and the late Professor Anthony Clare. One cannot help but wonder *if* Freud had collaborated responsibly with Darrow, whether the field of forensic psychotherapy would have become better established much sooner; and *if* Freud had worked with Samuel Goldwyn and with Georg Wilhelm Pabst, whether the appointment of a Resident Psychotherapist on Radio 2 in the year 2004 would have seemed "old hat" rather than innovative, reaching, as it did, for the first time, British people who live in areas devoid of psychotherapists or psychoanalysts.

Every responsible mental health professional must, of course, tread cautiously before joining forces with the mass media. But one must also avoid allowing one's thoughtfulness and judiciousness to develop into an inhibitionistic symptom of phobic proportions (Kahr, 2001b), thus denying proponents of psychoanalysis the opportunity to use the media effectively in order to promote the work for which we have trained over many long decades.

PART IV

THE MIND OF THE PSYCHOTHERAPIST

No stir in the air, no stir in the sea,
The ship was still as she could be,
Her sails from heaven received no motion,
Her keel was steady in the ocean.

Robert Southey, "The Inchcape Rock", 1803

CHAPTER FIFTEEN

Musings of a musicophiliac

Ich hört' ein Bächlein rauschen
Wohl aus dem Felsenquell.
[I heard a brooklet splashing
From its rocky source.]

Wilhelm Müller, "Wohin?", 1820, lines 1-2

Although Sigmund Freud never played a musical instrument and, by all accounts, did not particularly relish most musical performances (Freud, 1957), the vast majority of mental health professionals whom I know, both professionally and socially, cherish musical experience deeply. In one clinical organisation to which I belong, we boast an eminent classical composer who has written pieces for the British Royal family, but who now practises full-time as a clinician. In another of my professional organisations, we count as one of our members a retired operatic baritone, who also works full-time with patients. And in still another organisation for which I have long served as a Tutor and Training Therapist, two of my colleagues have participated in a jazz ensemble that has recorded a much-admired suite of music in memory of the late Dr John Bowlby. Many of my psychological colleagues have married musicians; and my own spouse has sung professionally for the whole of her career. Indeed, as a frequent concert-goer in London, I would be hard pressed to recall a recent visit to the Barbican Centre, the English National Opera, the Royal Opera House, or the Wigmore Hall—temples of British classical music—at which I did not encounter one or more psychological professionals (whether psychotherapists, psychologists, psychoanalysts, or psychiatrists) during the interval.

Perhaps psychological workers have a natural affinity for music, in part because both mental health professionals and, also, musicians possess an acutely developed auditory capacity and, moreover, a heightened sensitivity to sound and its importance. Elsewhere I have written about the crucial role of the psychotherapist's voice as a curative ingredient in clinical practice, based, in part, on observations of some of my cherished mental health colleagues who have speaking voices that I would describe as colourful, textured, layered, and rich and therefore capable of attuning to the subtleties of affective states within the session through a careful modulation of vocal pitch, cadence, key signature, and rhythm (Kahr, 2005b).

As a musician myself, trained first as a classical pianist and subsequently as a classical singer (in my spare time), musicality has always played an important role in my daytime work as a psychotherapist. From my earliest student days as an intern in a psychiatric hospital, I attempted to use music therapeutically as a means of making contact with severely regressed, catatonic schizophrenic individuals. In the early nineteenth century, Dr James Cowles Prichard (1835, p. 296), the pioneering English alienist, observed that, "The good effects of music in madness have been chiefly extolled by persons who were themselves devotedly fond of it." I would agree with Prichard's observation entirely; and I suppose that I came to find music a helpful adjunct to psychological work, in part, because of my own love of music in all its forms.

I shall never forget the first time I stepped onto the ward of a psychogeriatric unit in a ramshackle provincial psychiatric institution, more than thirty-five years ago. Most of the patients suffered from the gross psychomotor effects of tardive dyskinesia, and many could not, therefore, control their tongue movements; hence, their tongues dangled out of their mouths, dripping copious amounts of saliva, contributing to a greater sense of "freakishness", "bizarreness", and alienation. As a neophyte, the sight of so many elderly tardive dyskinesics frightened me, and after failing miserably to make contact with these individuals through traditional verbal means, I sought refuge behind the battered, out-of-tune upright piano, tucked in the corner of the Day Room, whose dust-covered keyboard suggested that this old instrument had suffered from the very same kind of neglect experienced by the patients themselves. With trepidation, I seated myself on the cold plastic chair and began to play some songs from the 1890s and 1900s, which, I reasoned, would be known to these geriatric patients, many of whom had spent the bulk of their lives on this very forgotten long-stay ward.

As I launched into an impromptu rendition of the old classic jaunty waltz of 1892, "Daisy Bell" (better known nowadays as "A Bicycle Built for Two"), I suddenly saw three nurses running in my direction. "Damn", I thought, "my first day in a psychiatric institution, and I've blown it already." I soon turned round from the keyboard and observed the nurses crouching over an elderly catatonic patient called "Joe". Apparently, something in my performance had caused Joe to burst out singing, warbling at the top of his lungs: "Daisy, Daisy, give me your answer do/I'm half crazy all for the love of you." One of the nurses called to me in disbelief, "What did you do to him?" I shrugged my shoulders innocently, as the nurse replied, "This man has not uttered a single word in forty years—*literally*—and now he's singing. How can this be?" Thus, on my very first day of work in the mental health field, I learned only too powerfully that music has the capacity to reach patients in a way in which words cannot do quite so easily.

Although I now work full-time in classical psychoanalytic practice, music has continued to play an important role not only in my private life but, also, in my professional work. I do not mind revealing that, during much of my twenties, I worked as a pianist in a multitude of settings, out of hours; the money that I earned from these endeavours provided a much-needed supplement to my clinical income and helped considerably to pay for my own personal five-times-weekly psychoanalysis. But, above all, I found ways to use music in my professional work with individuals and groups. Although principally a "talking therapist" who practises along traditional, boundaried psychoanalytic lines, suffused by classical Freudianism, Kleinianism, Winnicottianism, attachment theory, and relational psychoanalysis, I have always tried to preserve arenas in which I could engage with people therapeutically through the use of music.

For instance, when I began to work with schizophrenic and manic-depressive patients at yet another psychiatric hospital in the backwaters of rural England, I had the great good fortune to be apprenticed to an enlightened Consultant Psychiatrist. This distinguished gentleman encouraged my fledgling efforts in the practice of psychoanalytic psychotherapy with psychotic individuals, which taught me an unparalleled amount. However, I soon noticed that while the patients benefited from their fifty minutes of daily individual psychotherapy, they had virtually nothing else to do in the remaining twenty-three hours and ten minutes of the day. With the blessing of my Consultant, I decided to establish a weekly therapeutic music and singing group, as well as a weekly therapeutic songwriting group, in which all patients (apart, of course, from those with whom I worked in individual psychotherapy or group psychotherapy) could join me and a team of extremely dedicated and life-enhancing psychiatric nurses and occupational therapists for playing, singing, and listening to music and, for the more able patients, an experience of writing songs together. This therapeutic music work proved extremely rewarding, and although I do not have the space here to describe my musico-psychological practice in detail, I did succeed in bringing several other catatonic schizophrenic patients "back to life", facilitating their return from mutism by helping them to sing.

I continued to host these groups for psychotic men and women, in both inpatient and outpatient community mental health settings, while I persevered with my own more formal trainings in the verbal psychotherapies. And though the challenge of talking therapy always compelled me and satisfied me professionally, I did also manage to complete a Diploma in the Creative Arts Therapies from the London College of Dance, which provided me with the foundation and supervision for undertaking musico-therapeutic work in a more considered and reflective manner.

As my career became more established, I accepted, first, a post as a Lecturer and then as a Senior Lecturer (the British equivalents of the American Assistant Professor and Associate Professor), and worked exclusively as a verbal psychoanalytic practitioner. All of this allowed very little time for me to undertake musical sessions or groups in a psychiatric facility. Nevertheless, I still found myself drawn to musical subjects and to musical personalities.

On one memorable morning in 1987, I had the very pleasant opportunity to have tea with the late Mrs Marion Milner, one of the icons of British psychoanalysis, who delighted me with reminiscences of her dear friend and mentor, none other than Dr Donald Winnicott (personal communication, 24 October 1987). During our conversation, Marion leaned over to me conspiratorially and whispered, "Did you know that Donald had a secret career wish?" "No", I replied in eager expectation. "Well", she murmured, "he once told me that he always hoped to write an operetta in the style of Gilbert and Sullivan." As I have long worshipped the wit and playfulness of Sir William Schwenck Gilbert and Sir Arthur Sullivan, I knew at that moment that I would have to study Winnicott much more carefully, and thus began my love affair with the great British paediatrician, child psychiatrist, and psychoanalyst, which resulted, rather unexpectedly, in the publication of several books about his life and work (Kahr, 2001a, 2002a, 2016), including the first biography of the man (Kahr, 1996a).

To my delight, I eventually discovered that Winnicott had played classical piano in his youth, rather well in fact, and that he enjoyed a wide musical palate, from Ludwig van Beethoven to the Beatles. He even entertained students at his seminars by playing on his John Broadwood piano and by singing to them as a treat after a presentation of a child psychiatric case history. My discovery of Winnicott's own musicianship proved a great source of relief and identification, for here I had found a role model of someone who could use music creatively, healthily, entertainingly, and educationally, for the benefit of his students and colleagues and, also, for himself. Indeed, in order to prepare for the arrival of each new patient, he would often finish a clinical session, rush upstairs to his keyboard, bang out a few chords, and then greet the next analysand with a clearer mind (Winnicott, 1978; Kahr, 1995a).

As the decades unfolded, I tried to find other ways to combine my joint interests in psychology and music. For several years I served as the Musical Director and then as the author of the annual Pantomime at the Tavistock Clinic, where I trained and then taught, eventually establishing a choir for psychiatrists, psychoanalysts, social workers, psychologists, psychotherapists, and administrative staff. The challenge of emboldening a group of essentially reticent mental health professionals to sing with more resonant, open mouths proved one of the greatest of my career thus far; but in the end we succeeded in loosening some of the characterological inhibitions that interfere with singing, and eventually our Tavistock Clinic Choir even performed at various psychoanalytic book launch events.

Not only has musical composition, study, and performance provided great creative sustenance outside the consulting room, but my knowledge of music has often proved extremely helpful within the consulting room while practising traditional verbal psychotherapy. I shall offer three brief vignettes from sessions with patients who free-associated verbally, while reclining on the couch, in which musical experiences proved unexpectedly helpful and transformative.

Vignette 1:   Mr SS

I had worked with Mr SS, an intelligent, articulate, and likeable gentleman referred for mild depression, for approximately one year, at a frequency of three times weekly. Mr SS used the couch, and he participated very actively in the psychoanalytic process, attending with great punctuality, sharing intimate pieces of biography, and so forth; but somehow, I could see no shifts in his external life: he still found his boss persecutory, he still experienced his job as unsatisfying, he still argued with his wife, and he still complained about his children. Furthermore, he struggled mightily with inhibited creativity. Secretly, he wished to become a novelist in his spare time, but he did absolutely nothing about this and rarely ever attempted to put pen to paper. In spite of Mr SS's seeming cooperativeness with the process, I could not help but wonder whether I had missed something crucial or, whether, in spite of the ostensibly positive transference, we had reached some sort of psychotherapeutic impasse.

Round about this time, I had set myself the private musical task of attempting to learn the two tenor roles of "Belmonte" and "Pedrillo" from Wolfgang Amadeus Mozart's incomparable opera *Die Entführung aus dem Serail* [*The Abduction from the Seraglio*]. The vocal tessitura of Mozart's writing for this *Singspiel* challenges even professional opera singers, and I certainly found myself struggling to develop my breath control so that I could better perform the long vocal lines, replete with Mozart's often diabolical musical runs. With the aid of my very supportive singing coach, I tackled a number of the solo arias, as well as Pedrillo's famous Allegro Duetto with "Osmin", the drinking song "Vivat Bacchus! Bacchus lebe!", in which Pedrillo attempts to intoxicate the jailer Osmin in order to free his beloved "Blonde" and her mistress "Konstanze" from the clutches of the Pasha "Selim".

Mozart's Bacchanalian tribute delighted me above all the other arias, in part, because it moves at such a fast tempo that the tenor has a greater chance of finishing without complete exhaustion and without having to strain for the high A's that characterise the other tenor contributions in this opera. Indeed, I found myself humming this drinking song during many odd moments of the day.

To my surprise, although I do not usually think about music while facilitating a clinical session with a patient, the drinking song kept popping into my mind during silences in my work with my patient Mr SS. At one point, this "musical countertransference" became so peskily insistent that I had to work very hard to banish Mozart from my mind. In attempting to analyse my countertransference, I first thought that Mr SS must be boring me so much that I had to rely on the vivacity of Mozart to help enliven me in the session, but no matter how hard I tried, I could not banish the first nine bars of music from my head. Curiously, I did not find myself humming Mozart silently with any other patient.

Eventually, the penny dropped. Perhaps I could not escape the repetitive strains of "Vivat Bacchus! Bacchus lebe!", in part, because of its *lyrics*: a veritable Mozartian love letter to the virtually erotic joys of wine, verging on alcoholism. During our sessions, Mr SS had never mentioned drinking to me; but perhaps I had missed something quite substantial.

The next time that Mr SS began to talk about how he wished that he could become a novelist but did not have the patience to sit down at his computer after supper to write, I decided that I would investigate his creative inhibition more deeply. Instead of interpreting his fears of success, his guilt, his terror of finding himself emptied of stories, I asked, quite simply, "Well, what *do* you do after supper?" He immediately replied, "Well, I have some wine, and I read the newspaper." "How much wine?" I wondered aloud. "Oh," he responded, "maybe two bottles per night."

Before long, an entire furtive history of near-clinical alcoholism emerged—one that had caused Mr SS a great deal of shame. Somehow, he had developed the capacity to absorb two bottles of wine nightly, and yet this large amount of drinking did not seem to interfere with his performance at his job, at least not in any grossly overt way. After the secret became manifest, Mr SS arrived at his next session with a hangover—the first time that he had done so in a whole year of work—in order to bring the alcoholism into the room at last.

In the space of such a brief clinical vignette, I shall not, of course, trace the subtle contours of how the patient and I worked with this new material; but now, several years later, the alcoholism has receded, and Mr SS's life has improved along many different dimensions, including the development of his creativity. Although I dare say that the revelation of the furtive alcoholic enactments would have emerged at some point during our work, my own unconscious mind must have sensed something about the patient, outside my conscious awareness; and the opportune happenstance of learning the Mozart drinking song proved to be an unexpectedly helpful means of "picking up" something in the ether of the countertransference that had not yet become manifest in a more direct, verbal manner.

Nowadays, whenever I might find myself humming a musical fragment *sotto voce* in sessions, I treat these musical countertransferential punctuations as important clues to undigested pieces of the patient's psychological experience. And although I do not share my own personal musical associations with my patients, I do use them to inform my lines of investigation, almost always with very encouraging results.

Vignette 2:   Mrs TT

I have worked with Mrs TT for many, many long years, also at a frequency of three times weekly. Like Mr SS, she, too, uses the couch. Mrs TT had originally come to see me because of violent psychosomatic pains in virtually every part of her body, which have now disappeared completely. Mrs TT seems to have suffered no gross physical or sexual trauma as a little girl, but she did endure what she described as "a million tiny cuts" at the hands of two depressed parents who often failed to hold her in mind and who would sometimes not even remember her birthday. Mrs TT had the capacity to instil an air of great heaviness and great hopelessness whenever she entered the consulting room.

Although married, Mrs TT led an extremely bleak life, both externally and internally; she never went to the theatre, or to the cinema, or to concerts, even though she lives in Central London. Instead, she would go to work at a fairly menial job, one well beneath her cognitive capabilities; and, after leaving the office, she would return home and spend the evening watching hours of mindless television.

During our first year of treatment, Mrs TT went to the theatre to see the new Andrew Lloyd Webber musical *The Beautiful Game*, at the Cambridge Theatre, in the heart of London's West End. She did not want to go at all, because she thought that she hated the theatre or indeed anything joyful; but her boss at work had booked tickets as a Christmas present for the whole office. And so Mrs TT went to see the show; and she told me the next day how much, to her surprise, she had enjoyed it. But after this brief mention, she never referred to the musical again.

Scroll ahead six years. By this point, the crippling psychosomatic pains had begun to diminish, but even so Mrs TT still lived a very arid extracurricular life and rarely if ever went out to socialise. I felt, of course, quite glad that the psychosomatic symptoms had ameliorated, but still quite sad that, in spite of our prolonged labours, Mrs TT seemed to experience so little pleasure.

In one of her sessions I tried, yet again, to explore what prevented the patient from leading a more satisfying life. Despondently, Mrs TT threw up her arms in resignation, muttering, "What's the point, I hate everything. I hate the cinema, it's so stupid. I hate reading, it's so boring. And my parents never took me to the theatre, so I never learned to like it." I reminded her that, many years previously, she had attended a performance of the Andrew Lloyd Webber musical *The Beautiful Game* at the Cambridge Theatre as part of a work outing with her boss and other colleagues, and that she had had a surprisingly good evening.

Mrs TT craned her head round to peer at me, looking utterly dumbstruck. "God", she cried, "that must've been six years ago. I can't believe that you still remember the name of the show, the composer, and the theatre. Do you study your notes all the time?" I replied quite simply, "Perhaps it's impossible for you to imagine that someone might actually take an interest in the details of your life, might actually remember an important event in your life, and might even be able to recall something about you without recourse to written notes." This comment obviously touched a chord, and for the very first time Mrs TT began to cry.

Like most mental health professionals, I do try to have a good memory for the intricate, detailed fabric of the biographies of my patients, and I strive to remember the names of patients' siblings, friends, work colleagues, and the like. But I must confess that, on this occasion, my musical life outside the consulting room certainly came to my aid.

What Mrs TT could not, and did not, know is that a very dear friend and old musical colleague of mine had actually served as the conductor for the Andrew Lloyd Webber musical *The Beautiful Game*, and through him I had the privilege of attending the opening night performance and the opening night party, and then returned several more times to see my friend conduct the show. In fact, my musical friend has, from time to time, given me some lessons in conducting (another interest of mine), and once he kindly permitted me to sit in the orchestra pit, watching him conduct the show at very close quarters. Thus, in view of all this personal experience with *The Beautiful Game*, I doubt that I could have forgotten the name of the show, the name of the composer, or the name of the theatre.

No doubt every psychoanalytic worker will have a comparable experience, whether musical or not, in which we draw upon our own semantic memory banks to assist us in recalling details from the lives of our clients, patients, and analysands. In this case, my own private knowledge of a particular musical theatre show served me well in helping my patient to realise that, for whatever reason, an important event from her own life could be held successfully in mind.

Vignette 3:   Mr UU

Another patient, Mr UU, had entered twice-weekly psychoanalytic psychotherapy in the wake of a work-related trauma that had left him rather shaky and confused about his future career. Mr UU used projective mechanisms extensively, and he blamed all his work failures on his evil colleagues who "had it in" for him. It did not take long to realise that Mr UU exuded a great deal of unprocessed, uncontained murderous rage—so much so that he proved quite incapable of uttering a kindly or tender word about anyone or anything.

One day, Mr UU spoke with considerable vitriol, lambasting a former work colleague, a certain Ms VV. As I had heard stories about some fifteen or twenty of Mr UU's different office colleagues over recent weeks, I wanted to clarify that I fully appreciated the specific details about Ms VV. I believe that I said something along the following lines: "If I remember correctly, Ms VV is the person that you described in your last session as 'that envious bitch'." Perhaps I had made a technical mistake in attempting such a clarification, but Mr UU flew off the handle, and he began to fume, "I *never* called her a bitch. I *never* called her a bitch. She's actually a very nice person." I stated that perhaps he harboured great anger towards me for having *seemingly* misunderstood him, but Mr UU refused to engage with me. Instead, he seethed and repeated, "She's a nice person. I *never* called her a bitch."

As I began to reflect on the session, wondering whether I could have handled it differently, I became increasingly convinced that Mr UU *had*, indeed, referred to Ms VV as a bitch, but, that, for some reason, Mr UU found it very difficult to "own" his aggression. It always had to be projected elsewhere for safekeeping.

In the very next session, Mr UU told me, free-associatively, that for some strange reason the lyrics to an old song had just popped into his mind. He asked me whether I knew the song called "My Ship", and he then proceeded to recite the first few lines of the lyric:

> My ship has sails that are made of steel,
> The decks are trimmed with gold.

I smiled privately to myself, because I know this song very well indeed, and perhaps many readers will also recognise this piece.

With music by the legendary composer Kurt Weill, and with lyrics by the renowned poet Ira Gershwin, "My Ship" first appeared in the famous 1941 Broadway musical *Lady in the Dark*, which starred the British actress Gertrude Lawrence. Psychoanalytic devotees will appreciate, of course, that *Lady in the Dark* holds an important place in both clinical and entertainment history as the first musical theatre piece about psychoanalysis, based, in large measure, upon playwright Moss Hart's own personal psychoanalysis with the distinguished New York practitioner Dr Lawrence Kubie. Mr UU will certainly not have known that I have played this song on the piano since my adolescence, and I had even published a paper about *Lady in the Dark* in *The Psychoanalytic Review* (Kahr, 2000).

After eliciting free associations from Mr UU about why *this* particular song—"My Ship"—had popped into his head, I took the liberty of informing Mr UU, very diplomatically, of course, that he had committed a parapraxis. I said to my patient, "You have just quoted the lyric as "My ship has sails that are made of *steel*", when, in fact, if memory serves me correctly, I believe that the author actually wrote, "My ship has sails that are made of *silk*." I expected Mr UU to engage in a disputation with me and wondered whether I had stuck my neck out too far. But to his credit Mr UU calmed himself, and he replied, "Yes, you're right. It is *silk*, not *steel*. I wonder why I turned something so lovely as silk into something so hard as steel?"

Gingerly, I commented that, perhaps, after his work-related trauma, he needed to gird himself and become angry and steely, as an understandable means of protecting himself, whereas, if he had remained all vulnerable and silky, then somebody could perhaps hurt him again. I also noted that when mentioning colleagues such as Ms VV, he would often become readily confused as to whether he experienced other people as silky or steely, kindly or bitchy, and that, perhaps, he might sometimes feel that way about me too.

At this point, Mr UU suddenly relaxed his tense body, and he breathed a very audible sigh of relief, pleased, at last, that someone could notice the internal steeliness of him, and that he could finally begin to recognise his own murderousness. Eventually, Mr UU began to speak much more directly about many painful experiences of sexual abuse and emotional neglect from which he had suffered as a child, and this proved essential for the unfolding of our psychotherapeutic work.

Not every mental health practitioner has enjoyed his or her own private musical soundtrack. Professor Leo Rangell, the distinguished American psychoanalyst, for example, suffered from a rare condition known as "musical hallucinosis" during his final years, hearing music in his mind unceasingly in the wake of cardiac surgery. Understandably, Rangell (2009, p. 47) often found this "inward singing" to be very disruptive, but he eventually learned to exert some conscious control over his musical hallucinosis by concentrating on other activities and mental engagements. The octogenarian Rangell still practised as a psychoanalyst and came to appreciate that if the musical hallucinosis became noticeable in a session, he had begun to listen to his patient less intensively. For Rangell, suffering from a surgically induced neuro-audiological disorder, the presence of music in his mind represented not a clue but, rather, a distraction. Music in the mind may, therefore, be either a help or a hindrance to the clinical practitioner.

* * *

Sigmund Freud bequeathed a complicated legacy to his successors in relation to music. Someday we may obtain a greater appreciation of Freud's relative lack of musical enthusiasm. Even though he did not play an instrument, he could, nevertheless, work therapeutically with composers such as Alban Berg (Grun, 1971; Oberlerchner and Tögel, 2015; cf. Berg, 1923) and Gustav Mahler (Freud, 1935a). One need not be especially musical in order to enhance the creativity of others, but I hope that I have underscored, through this very personal testimonial, not only the ways in which my own love of music has become a source of extra-clinical sustenance for me, but also the ways in which I have used music therapeutically and have deployed my private knowledge of music to good effect in the practice of verbal psychotherapy. No doubt every colleague reading this contribution will have his or her own area of specialist knowledge that often comes in handy in the course of plying our craft.

In the minds of our ancient Greek forebears, the god Apollo held many responsibilities. Often depicted with lyre in hand, Apollo served, of course, as the god of music, but the Greeks also regarded him as the god of healing. It cannot be accidental, one supposes, that music and healing enjoy such a natural historical relationship, and I can only hope that, as a profession, we might all dare to become a bit more "musical" in our approach to our clinical work, whether by analysing our patients' fears of using their voices to greater effect, by analysing their inhibitions against joy, or even by studying singing technique ourselves to allow us, as clinicians, to speak with a greater vocal palette, so that we may better attune to the very particular shifting mood states that we encounter on a frequent basis in the course of psychoanalytic investigations.

CHAPTER SIXTEEN

I suffer from Karnacitis

Timeo hominem unius libri.
[I fear a man who knows only one book.]

Attributed variously to Saint Thomas Aquinas
and to Augustine of Hippo

Quite a few years ago I read an obituary of the American author, intellectual, and critic, Susan Sontag, who, after a multi-decade battle against cancer, died from leukaemia on 28 December 2004, at the age of seventy-one. Although sad to hear of the great suffering endured by this creative writer, I did breathe a little sigh of relief and recognition when I discovered that, at the time of her death, Sontag reputedly kept some 15,000 books in her Manhattan apartment. Although I do not have a New York apartment, I do, nonetheless, possess a ridiculously large number of professional books, and I thought to myself, just as the chronic dipsomaniac must do upon sitting down at that first meeting of Alcoholics Anonymous, "Hooray, I am not alone."

I first discovered H. Karnac (Books) at 58, Gloucester Road, London S.W.7, in either the latter part of 1982 or the early months of 1983, while still a student, having stumbled upon an advertisement for the shop in *The International Journal of Psycho-Analysis*. I do recall that, upon entering the rather unprepossessing premises, I saw no psychology volumes at all—only the usual selection of cookery and gardening fare. I staved off my rising sense of disappointment as I walked towards the very back of the shop, wondering whether I had in fact come to the wrong location; but then, happily, I spied a bust of Sigmund Freud perched near a dimly lit and unmarked staircase, which led to the basement. As I entered into the musty underground grotto, I felt as though I had discovered Ali Baba's magical cave—an entire room filled to bursting with multiple copies of every psycho-analytic book imaginable. I immediately regressed to an infantile state, surrounded by too much milk, not knowing which nipple to choose. I suppose I must have spent twenty pounds or so (a small fortune to a student in those days), though I regret I cannot remember which books I actually purchased. It really did not matter, because I returned again and again and again, eventually striking up a rapport with the charming owner, Mr Harry Karnac, who had first begun to stock psychoanalytic books many decades earlier, at the suggestion of the psychoanalyst Dr Clifford Scott, who had a consulting room nearby and who recommended that Mr Karnac ought to sell the popular works of Dr Donald Winnicott. From such modest begin-nings, Karnac himself became quite expert about psychoanalysis, and he soon turned his ordinary shop into the world's first specialist psychotherapeutic booksellers.

As an impecunious young trainee, working part-time as a Research Officer in a backwater psychiatric hospital, I had no idea at all what a crucial role Karnac Books would come to play in my life in the decades that followed. By the time I moved to London in 1986, Harry Karnac had sold the shop to Mr Cesare Sacerdoti, an accomplished businessman, a lover of fine literature, and a passionate advocate of psychoanalysis, who expanded Karnac Books into a more substantial force still by promoting the publishing arm for which Karnac Books has since acquired an international reputation. Harry Karnac did reprint some classic psychoanalytic titles during his tenure, but the bulk of the publication work became the special project of Cesare Sac-erdoti. Not only did Cesare commission and print many new titles, he also opened a second branch of Karnac Books at 118, Finchley Road, in North London, only a stone's throw from the Freud Museum, where I had worked, and from the Tavistock Clinic and Portman Clinic, where I had become a student. I also had my own personal psychoanalysis on nearby Fitzjohns Avenue in North London, and in order to get there from my flat in Pimlico, in South London, I alighted at the Finchley Road underground station, just across the road from the new branch of Karnac Books. So, for many years, I passed by Karnac Books five days a week! After a while, it became a second home, as I would pop in regularly, spending too much money, purchasing too many books, using the shop as a second library by checking references for the academic papers that I had begun to write, and sometimes literally seeking shelter from the rain.

Through my extremely frequent visits to the North London branch of Karnac Books, I also came to know Mr Malcolm Smith quite well, the encyclopaedic guru who ran the Finchley Road shop for many years and who knew the current status of every single book (in print or out of print) without even needing to glance at his computer. A fellow bibliophile, Malcolm would indulge my addiction by letting me have a sneak preview of any second-hand collections that came into the shop. (Karnac Books has, for many years, served as a saviour to the widows and widowers of deceased psychoanalysts, because the shop has purchased many collections from the families of those colleagues no longer with us.) These acquisitions of old out-of-print books became my favourites, and Malcolm would allow me to snag any volumes of great interest before he put the remainder out on the open shelves. One day, both Dr Murray Cox, the noted forensic psychiatrist from Broadmoor Hospital (and also my clinical supervisor at the time) and I spied a rare volume, entitled *Discourse on Hamlet and Hamlet: A Psychoanalytic Inquiry*, written by the New York City psychoanalyst Dr Kurt Eissler (1971), that Malcolm Smith had kept back for our inspection. I yielded to Murray, himself a great Shakespeare scholar, who had more immediate need of Eissler's tome than I did.

In the early 1990s, I had signed a contract with a London-based publisher to write a book on the work of Donald Winnicott, but I became so engrossed with the research for what should have remained a very short biographical chapter that I decided to cancel my contract for a Winnicott primer in order to write a full-length biography instead. The publishers with whom I had begun to work had no interest in a Winnicott biography, and I felt very much at sea. Fortunately, Malcolm Smith introduced me to Cesare Sacerdoti, who not only commissioned the biography of Winnicott with alacrity, but took me out for a crucial lunch during which he helped me with both the structure and the scope of the book, assisting me in finding a way to manage an increasingly behemoth project. Our efforts became rewarded when my first book, *D.W. Winnicott: A Biographical Portrait*, originally published in 1996 (Kahr, 1996a), then appeared in American (Kahr, 1996b), Portuguese (Kahr, 1997), Spanish (Kahr, 1999a), Italian (Kahr, 2005a), and French (Kahr, 2018a) editions, and, to our great delight and surprise, also received the Gradiva Award for Biography in 1997. So, I owe a huge debt to Cesare, who went on to commission two further books on Winnicott from me (Kahr, 2001a, 2002a), and who then appointed me as the Series Editor of the Karnac Books "Forensic Psychotherapy Monograph Series", which has since spawned some nineteen titles, with many more in the pipeline.

By this time, my collection of psychoanalytic books had begun to reach an unwieldy size, as I scoured shops both in England and abroad for choice titles. But throughout this period I always remained faithful to the shop in Finchley Road as the chief supplier of my addiction. I even coined the term "Karnacitis", a new form of psycho-pathology, designed to describe people like me who suffer from this chronic condition, for which no treatment can be found.

With the passage of time, I can report, happily, about the natural course of patients afflicted by Karnacitis. Although the symptoms will never disappear completely, one can learn to manage them.

After Cesare Sacerdoti sold H. Karnac Books Limited in 1999, two American-based psychoanalysts, Dr Judith Feher-Gurewich and Dr Michael Moskowitz, took charge for a short while and kindly encouraged my book-writing and editing work, before handing over the reins to Mr Oliver Rathbone, who developed the business hugely into a successful global imprint that attracted some of the world's best psychoanalytic practitioners as authors. Over the years, Oliver made a huge impact on the development of psychoanalysis and psycho-analytic publishing, commissioning titles not only from classical Freudian psychoanalysts, but also from Jungian analysts, Lacanian psychoanalysts, relational psychoanalysts, and even from cognitive-behavioural psychotherapists—something that his more conservative predecessors would never have allowed.

Oliver kindly invited me to serve as Series Editor for two more book series—namely, "The History of Psychoanalysis Series", in conjunction with Professor Peter Rudnytsky, and also "The Library of Couple and Family Psychoanalysis", which I co-edit with Ms Susanna Abse, Dr Christopher Clulow, and Dr David Scharff. Fortunately, the increased workload and responsibilities of writing my own books and commissioning titles by colleagues permitted me infinitely less time for book-buying, and, thus, my long-standing case of "Karnacitis" became much less severe.

Books serve a multitude of purposes, offering not only health-ful and relational possibilities but, also, retreated and anti-relational ones. As Lucius Annaeus Seneca observed in his *Epistulae morales ad Lucilium*, "distringit librorum multitudo" ["the abundance of books is a distraction"]. And yet books allows us to find a profession or a calling and to immerse ourselves spectacularly. As the Harvard University psychologist Professor Edwin Boring (1956, p. 13) opined in his first editorial in *Contemporary Psychology*, a journal devoted entirely to book reviews: "A science is its books."

Whether the condition known as "Karnacitis" represents some-thing healthful or something obsessional, I shall leave to others to decide. Whatever the final verdict, as my great hero, Dr Donald Win-nicott (1945b, p. 140, fn. 3), once opined, "we are poor indeed if we are only sane"; and I heartily concur that one should have at least a little bit of psychopathology. And so, in that spirit, I recommend Karnacitis as one of the more pleasurable and educational forms of psychological illness.

Postlude

In camera and on camera, or, a maverick's manifesto

> . . . eccentricities of thought and conduct have a special
> philosophic interest, inasmuch as from time to time they turn
> out to be valuable mental variations that initiate new and useful
> developments.
>
> Dr Henry Maudsley, *Natural Causes and Supernatural Seemings*, 1886
> [Maudsley, 1886, p. 151]

In 1948, Dr Lionel Blitzsten, one of the most pre-eminent psychoanalysts in post-war Chicago, Illinois, penned the following lamentation:

> Friday, October 22nd and a more beautiful Indian summer day no
> one could ever want. Yet here I am shut up in my not too ivory
> tower with one window open to let in the breeze, etc., awaiting my
> next couch tenant—one psychiatrist after another, no easy task. At
> the moment I could give it all back to the Indians and exchange it
> for the Indian summer. Reflectively I wonder what possesses any
> sane human being to be a psychiatrist? Can you answer this conundrum? [quoted in Orr, 1961, p. 64]

Many fellow mental health clinicians will appreciate the pleasures
and the privileges of practising psychotherapy and psychoanalysis,

and yet, all of us—no matter how dedicated—will also understand the burdens and will sympathise with Lionel Blitzsten's wish to flee from his "ivory tower" in order to "let in the breeze". But our commitment to each and every "couch tenant"—to use Blitzsten's evocative term—remains unwavering, and while other workers will not hesitate to take a stroll in the warm summer weather, those of use who practise Freudian psychoanalysis remain committed, unwaveringly, to remaining indoors!

Thus, in view of the burden that we place upon ourselves when we enter the mental health profession, we must find ways of playing and stretching our legs—both literally and figuratively—outside our clinical working hours. And through my own interests in music, in history, in media, and in related fields—described in the previous chapters—I have endeavoured, in my own maverick manner, to find forms of pleasure, recreation, and mental stimulation as well, all of which have, I believe, enriched my capacity to engage in culturally rich and creative ways with the material presented by my patients and analysands.

I argue, therefore, that every mental health clinician, whether stodgily mainstream or idiosyncratically maverick, must find a way of retaining his or her commitment to, and integrity for, working "*in camera*" (i.e., in private) as well as "on camera", engaging in some more public form of work, whether televised or not. The essays contained herein not only represent the depth of engagement that we derive from the detail of our private clinical work, but also celebrate how we can transmit some of our specialism and our expertise more widely to a larger audience.

The legendary British psychoanalyst Dr Wilfred Bion once opined that mental health professionals can be quite frightening people to members of the general public. As he explained, "Psychiatrists and psycho-analysts are indeed likely to become perceived more and more by the general public as a threat. Their approach to the mind or character or personality is felt to be something which could undermine government itself" (Bion, 1978, p. 11). Although many might believe that Bion had overstated his case, one must remember that he trained at a time when virtually all members of the general public regarded Freudians with deep suspicion. And even today, with a proliferation of representations of psychoanalysts on television and in film (e.g., Kahr, 2011b), many people might still regard us as having dangerously penetrative insights into the private mind of the other. In view of this, mental health professionals have an obligation to help publicise and popularise our profession in not only a serious, but also a playful manner.

Consequently, my efforts on radio, on television, and in the halls of the Royal Courts of Justice and the Royal Opera House, represent merely a tiny indication of the sort of work that we might undertake after we have bid our couch tenants good evening, have locked the doors to our consulting rooms, and have taken a walk in the breezy air of the outside world.

By interlacing these media-related essays with examples of clinical work and with forays into the historical archives, I hope that I have, in a maverick way, provided some indication of how the clinician with multiple strands of interest can weave among these various pursuits, all of which contribute to a general sense of both professional and personal enrichment. I hope that younger colleagues might find their way to these essays and might obtain some sense of encouragement—indeed permission—to undertake not only the sober investigations of the mental health practitioner *in camera*, but also some of the more joyful and wide-reaching activities of the mental health practitioner *on camera*.

I trust that through these short chapters I have managed to offer a bit of insight into some of the topics that we never learn about in "shrink school"—such as the naked patient (!), the ten-minute gap, tissues, slogans on T-shirts, the choice of a necktie, toppled book shelves, and so forth. I hope that these small contributions might also stimulate some creative ideas among colleagues about what might occur when one brings the worlds of psychotherapy and psychoanalysis to the media. My own forays into media psychology have resulted in the public transmission of psychoanalytic thought but, even more concretely, in the referral of literally hundreds of radio and television producers and writers into long-term therapy with many of my colleagues.

As a maverick clinician, historian, musician, and part-time enthusiast for the possibilities of the media as an integrating force among these patchwork elements, I have derived tremendous pleasure from the knowledge that many of our predecessors had fought hard to become solely themselves. On 24 September 1968, Dr Donald Winnicott, the noted British psychoanalyst, delivered a talk on "The Transmission of Technique" to the 1952 Club—a gathering of young psychoanalysts who had all qualified in that year—at the home of Masud Khan, just around the corner from Harrods. Writing about this seminar in his diary, Khan quoted Winnicott as having spoken of the importance of "being myself quite fearlessly" (quoted in Khan, 1968). In similar vein, I have deeply enjoyed the advice of one of my favourite Austrian authors, the late Joseph Wechsberg. In his riveting memoir entitled *The Vienna I Knew: Memories of a European Childhood*, Wechsberg (1979, p. 155), an émigré, advised, "If you have an accent, speak it proudly."

Inspired by men such as Winnicott and Wechsberg, I can think of no better advice to pass on to my students and to those who will follow in their wake.

ACKNOWLEDGEMENTS

This book owes its genesis entirely to the generosity of Professor Peter Rudnytsky. He and I had first met at a reception, held in the garden of the Freud Museum—Sigmund Freud's London home—back in 1989. Although we had subsequently corresponded by "snail-mail" on a few occasions thereafter, we did not meet again in person until the year 2004, once more at a conference sponsored by the Freud Museum. Over lunch, we caught up on the last fifteen years of our lives.

To my surprise and delight, Peter, then Editor of the scholarly journal *American Imago: Psychoanalysis and the Human Sciences*, co-founded by Freud in 1939 (Sachs, 1939, 1944), kindly invited me to write a quarterly column based on some of my "adventures" as a clinician and mental health broadcaster. Having read *American Imago* avidly since my undergraduate days and having greatly admired Peter's most excellent scholarship (e.g., Rudnytsky, 1987, 1989, 1991, 1993a, 1993b, 2000) and his substantial revivification of the journal during his tenure as Editor, I accepted this kind invitation with gratitude.

Knowing that most of the subscribers to *American Imago* lived in the United States and suspecting that my written contributions might chronicle some of my more idiosyncratic experiences, Peter and I decided to entitle the column "Letter from London"—a name that, we hoped, would allow me the latitude of being the chap from overseas, who might have a somewhat different lens. "Letter from London" also allowed me to pay tribute to the great British broadcaster Alistair Cooke—a journalist whom I had admired since boyhood—who died in 2004 and who had recorded nearly three thousand editions of his "Letter from America" for B.B.C. radio, from 1946 until shortly before his death.

With Peter's kindly encouragement and with his expert editorial eye, I managed to write seventeen "Letters from London", published in *American Imago* between 2005 and 2011. Peter thought that these letters might, perhaps, cohere as a book. Should that be the case, then he deserves the lion's share of the credit for having proved to be the most benevolent and facilitating of colleagues.

I owe a further, profound thanks to my own Training Analyst, the late and much-missed Dr Brendan MacCarthy, former Director of the Child Guidance Training Centre at the Tavistock Clinic, former Director of the London Clinic of Psycho-Analysis, and former President of the British Psycho-Analytical Society. A man of remarkable achievements and an even more remarkable personality—warm, solid, sane, sturdy, and facilitating—he inspired me hugely. As a young trainee undergoing psychoanalysis, I wished at various points that I could be just like him. I shall never forget that, one day, he spoke to me somewhat bemusedly: "You seem to be under the impression that you have to practise psychology in exactly the same way as I do." Needless to say, I experienced this remark as profoundly shrewd and also as deeply liberating, encouraging me to find my own voice rather than imitate his. Of course, I *have* imitated him in many ways, internalising as much as I could of his remarkable qualities; but I would like to think that he also helped me to develop some of my own.

I offer warm thanks to Mr Oliver Rathbone for having commissioned this book, and to his editorial team at Karnac Books, namely, Ms Cecily Blench, Ms Constance Govindin, and Dr Rod Tweedy. After the sale of Karnac Books to Routledge / Taylor and Francis Group, the remarkably congenial Mr Russell George and Dr Elliott Morsia took charge of the typescript. Working with these two respectful and kindly gentlemen has proved to be a great joy. I must also thank Ms Naomi Hill and her team for their ongoing support. And, as ever, I convey my deepest and most heartfelt gratitude to the eternally magnificent Mr Eric King and Mrs Klara Majthényi King of Communication Crafts—the best copy-editors of all—who have the patience of saints. Eric and Klara have worked with me on no fewer than nine of my books for which I count myself deeply fortunate.

My wife Kim, who has always spoken in her own voice and in her own accent, kindly read through these "Letters from London" yet again and offered her frank observations and comments—the sort that only a spouse can make. I thank her for providing an honest ear and, of course, for so much more.

ORIGINAL SOURCES OF THE CHAPTERS

Although each of the principal chapters has already appeared in print in the journal *American Imago: Psychoanalysis and the Human Sciences*, I have updated and revised each essay considerably, occasionally incorporating more detailed and more extensive clinical and theoretical material.

I have, below, provided the original source of each article for those who wish to read or refer to these pieces in their first incarnation.

Prelude
Kahr, Brett (2005). On Practicing Therapy at 1:45 a.m. *American Imago, 62,* 125–131.

Chapter one
Kahr, Brett (2006). The Handshake. *American Imago, 63,* 359–369.

Chapter two
Kahr, Brett (2008). Tissues. *American Imago, 65,* 299–308.

Chapter three
Kahr, Brett (2007). The Ten-Minute Gap. *American Imago, 64,* 567–574.

Chapter four
Kahr, Brett (2010). On Painting the Consulting Room. *American Imago, 67,* 669–675.

Chapter five
Kahr, Brett (2011). The Bookshelf. *American Imago, 68,* 127–134.

Chapter six
Kahr, Brett (2011). Baseball Caps, Overcoats, Orange Suits, and Neckties: On Patients and Their Clothing. *American Imago, 68,* 361–369.

Chapter seven
Kahr, Brett (2005). On Patients Who Remove Their Clothing in Sessions. *American Imago, 62,* 217–223.

Chapter eight
Kahr, Brett (2005). How to Make a Forty-Seven-Minute Television Program in Only Three Years. *American Imago, 62,* 483–491.

Chapter nine
Kahr, Brett (2006). Filming Sexual Fantasies. *American Imago, 63,* 227–233.

Chapter ten
Kahr, Brett (2006). How to Make 120,000 People Happy in Just Ten Weeks. *American Imago, 63,* 485–495.

Chapter eleven
Kahr, Brett (2007). A Night at the Opera: The Freudians at Covent Garden. *American Imago, 64,* 261–272.

Chapter twelve
Kahr, Brett (2010). Defending Lady Macbeth: Testimony of an Expert Witness. *American Imago, 67,* 453–462.

Chapter thirteen
Kahr, Brett (2010). Four Unknown Freud Anecdotes. *American Imago, 67,* 301–312.

Chapter fourteen
Kahr, Brett (2005). Why Freud Turned Down $25,000: Mental Health Professionals in the Witness Box. *American Imago, 62,* 365–371.

Chapter fifteen
Kahr, Brett (2007). Musings of a Musicophiliac. *American Imago, 64,* 95–107.

Chapter sixteen
Kahr, Brett (2006). I Suffer from Karnacitis. *American Imago, 63,* 81–85.

REFERENCES

Adams, John (1775). Diary Entry. 10 December. In John Adams (1961). *Diary and Autobiography of John Adams: Volume 2. Diary 1771–1781*, Lyman H. Butterfield, Leonard C. Faber, and Wendell D. Garrett (Eds.), pp. 224–225. Cambridge, Massachusetts: Belknap Press of Harvard University Press.

Anderson, Mark Lynn (2011). *Twilight of the Idols: Hollywood and the Human Sciences in 1920s America*. Berkeley, California: University of California Press.

Andreasen, Nancy C. (Ed.). (1994). *Schizophrenia: From Mind to Molecule*. Washington, D.C.: American Psychiatric Press.

Anonymous [Sigmund Freud] (1914). Der Moses des Michelangelo. *Imago, 3*, 15–36.

Arfelli, Patrizia (2002). Affective Response and the Analyst's Freedom in Work with Traumatized Adolescents. *American Imago, 59*, 447–458.

Baatz, Simon (2008). *For the Thrill of It: Leopold, Loeb, and the Murder That Shocked Chicago*. New York: Harper/HarperCollins Publishers.

Baily, Lionel (1973). *Gilbert and Sullivan and Their World*. London: Thames and Hudson.

Balint, Michael (1968). *The Basic Fault: Therapeutic Aspects of Regression*. London: Tavistock Publications.

Baylis, Nick (2009). *The Rough Guide to Happiness*. London: Rough Guides.

Berg, Alban (1923). Letter to Helene Berg. 29 November. In Alban Berg, *Briefe an seine Frau*, pp. 532–533. München: Albert Langen/Georg Müller, Georg Müller Verlag, 1965.

Bion, Wilfred R. (1978). *Four Discussions with W.R. Bion*. Strath Tay, Perthshire: Roland Harris Educational Trust/Clunie Press.

Blandford, George Fielding (1871). *Insanity and Its Treatment: Lectures on the Treatment, Medical and Legal, of Insane Patients*. Edinburgh: Oliver and Boyd; London: Simpkin, Marshall, and Company.

Boring, Edwin G. (1956). CP Speaks . . . *Contemporary Psychology*, *1*, 13, 22.

Carlson, Eric T. (1986). The History of Dissociation until 1880. In Jacques M. Quen (Ed.), *Split Minds/Split Brains: Historical and Current Perspectives*, pp. 7–30. New York: New York University Press.

Carlson, Eve B., and Armstrong, Judith (1994). The Diagnosis and Assessment of Dissociative Disorders. In Steven Jay Lynn and Judith W. Rhue (Eds.), *Dissociation: Clinical and Theoretical Perspectives*, pp. 159–174. New York: Guilford Press/Guilford Publications.

Carr, Alan (2004). *Positive Psychology: The Science of Happiness and Human Strengths*. Hove, East Sussex: Brunner-Routledge/Taylor and Francis Group.

Casement, Patrick J. (1982). Some Pressures on the Analyst for Physical Contact During the Re-Living of an Early Trauma. *International Review of Psycho-Analysis*, *9*, 279–286.

Casement, Patrick J. (2000). The Issue of Touch: A Retrospective Overview. *Psychoanalytic Inquiry*, *20*, 160–184.

Chodorkoff, Bernard, and Baxter, Seymour (1974). "Secrets of a Soul": An Early Psychoanalytic Film Venture. *American Imago*, *31*, 319–334.

Churchill, Randolph (1955). Letter to Winston Churchill. n.d. In Martin Gilbert, *In Search of Churchill: A Historian's Journey*, pp. 212–213. Hammersmith, London: HarperCollins Publishers, 1994.

Churchill, Winston (1890). Letter to Jennie Churchill. n.d. January. Quoted in Martin Gilbert, *In Search of Churchill: A Historian's Journey*, p. 67. Hammersmith, London: HarperCollins Publishers, 1994.

Cohen, David (1996). *Alter Egos: Multiple Personalities*. London: Constable London/Constable and Company.

Coltart, Nina (1990). Manners Makyth Man: True or False? In Nina Coltart, *Slouching Towards Bethlehem . . . And Further Psychoanalytic Explorations*, pp. 128–143. London: Free Association Books, 1992.

Crabtree, Adam (1985). *Multiple Man: Explorations in Possession and Multiple Personality*. London and Eastbourne, East Sussex: Holt, Rinehart and Winston.

Danto, Elizabeth Ann (2005). *Freud's Free Clinics: Psychoanalysis and Social Justice, 1918–1938*. New York: Columbia University Press.

Darío, Rubén (1905). *Cantos de vida y esperanza: Los cisnes y otros poemas*. Madrid: Revista de Archivos, Bibliotecas y Museos.

Darrow, Clarence (1922). *Crime: Its Cause and Treatment*. New York: Thomas Y. Crowell Company Publishers.

Darrow, Clarence (1932). *The Story of My Life*. New York: Charles Scribner's Sons.

David, Susan A., Boniwell, Ilona, and Ayers, Amanda Conley (Eds.). (2013). *The Oxford Handbook of Happiness*. Oxford: Oxford University Press.

Davies, William H. (1911). *Songs of Joy and Others*. London: A.C. Fifield.

Diamond, Lisa M. (2008). *Sexual Fluidity: Understanding Women's Love and Desire*. Cambridge, Massachusetts: Harvard University Press.

Diener, Ed, and Biswas-Diener, Robert (2008). *Happiness: Unlocking the Mysteries of Psychological Wealth*. Malden, Massachusetts: Blackwell Publishing.

Doidge, Norman (2007). *The Brain That Changes Itself: Stories of Personal Triumph from the Frontiers of Brain Science*. New York: Viking Penguin/Penguin Group, Penguin Group (USA).

Easterly, William (2011). The Happiness Wars. *The Lancet*, 30 April–6 May, 1483–1484.

Eissler, Kurt R. (1971). *Discourse on Hamlet and Hamlet: A Psychoanalytic Inquiry*. New York: International Universities Press.

Etchegoyen, R. Horacio (1986). *Los fundamentos de la técnica psicoanalítica*. Buenos Aires: Amorrortu editores.

Etchegoyen, R. Horacio (1991). *The Fundamentals of Psychoanalytic Technique*, Patricia Pitchon (Transl.). London: H. Karnac (Books).

Falzeder, Ernst (2012). "A Fat Wad of Dirty Pieces of Paper": Freud on America, Freud in America, Freud and America. In John Burnham (Ed.), *After Freud Left: A Century of Psychoanalysis in America*, pp. 85–109. Chicago, Illinois: University of Chicago Press.

Fenichel, Otto (1945). *The Psychoanalytic Theory of Neurosis*. New York: W.W. Norton and Company.

Field, Tiffany (2001). *Touch*. Cambridge, Massachusetts: Massachusetts Institute of Technology Press.

Fine, Reuben (1985). *The Meaning of Love in Human Experience*. New York: John Wiley and Sons.

Flechsig, Paul (1884a). Zur gynaekologischen Behandlung der Hysterie. [Part I]. *Neurologisches Centralblatt*, 3, 433–439.

Flechsig, Paul (1884b). Zur gynaekologischen Behandlung der Hysterie. [Part II]. *Neurologisches Centralblatt*, 3, 457–468.

Flügel, John C. (1929). Clothes Symbolism and Clothes Ambivalence. *International Journal of Psycho-Analysis*, 10, 205–217.

Flügel, John C. (1930a). *The Psychology of Clothes*. London: Leonard and Virginia Woolf at the Hogarth Press, and the Institute of Psycho-Analysis.

Flügel, John C. (1930b). Sex Differences in Dress. In Norman Haire (Ed.), *Sexual Reform Congress: London 8.–14. IX. 1929. W.L.S.R. World League for Sexual Reform. Weltliga für Sexualreform. Ligue Mondiale pour la réforme sexuelle. Tutmonda ligo por seksaj reformoj. Proceedings of the Third Congress. Bericht des dritten Kongresses. Compte rendu du troisième congrès. Dokumentaro de la tria kongreso*, pp. 461–467. London: Kegan Paul, Trench, Trubner and Company.

Forsyth, David (1922). *The Technique of Psycho-Analysis*. London: Kegan Paul, Trench, Trubner and Company.

Freeman, Lucy (1951). *Fight Against Fears*. New York: Crown Publishers.

Freeman, Lucy (Ed.). (1959). *Troubled Women*. Cleveland, Ohio: World Publishing Company.

Freeman, Lucy (1969a). *Farewell to Fear*. New York: G.P. Putnam's Sons.

Freeman, Lucy (1969b). *The Cry for Love: Understanding and Overcoming Human Depression*. New York: Macmillan Company.

Freeman, Lucy (1969c). *Exploring the Mind of Man: Sigmund Freud and the Age of Psychology*. New York: Grosset and Dunlap Publishers.

Freeman, Lucy (Ed.). (1970). *Celebrities on the Couch: Personal Adventures of Famous People in Psychoanalysis*. Los Angeles, California: Prince/ Stern/Sloan Publishers, and Ravenna Books.

Freeman, Lucy (1971). *The Dream*. New York: Arbor House Publishing Company.

Freeman, Lucy (1972). *The Story of Anna O*. New York: Walker and Company.

Freeman, Lucy (1973). *Your Mind Can Stop the Common Cold*. New York: Peter H. Wyden.

Freeman, Lucy (1978). *What Do Women Want?: Self-Discovery Through Fantasy*. New York: Human Sciences Press.

Freeman, Lucy (1979). *Who is Sylvia?* New York: Arbor House/Arbor House Publishing Company.

Freeman, Lucy (1980). *Freud Rediscovered*. New York: Arbor House/Arbor House Publishing Company.

Freeman, Lucy (1983). Writing of Love and Hate. In Glen Evans (Ed.), *The*

Complete Guide to Writing Nonfiction, pp. 360–365. Cincinnati, Ohio: Writer's Digest Books.

Freeman, Lucy (1984a). *Listening to the Inner Self*. New York: Jason Aronson.

Freeman, Lucy (1984b). The "Seeds" of Murder as Sown "in the Nursery". *Current Issues in Psychoanalytic Practice*, 1, Number 2, 19–28.

Freeman, Lucy (1985). Psychosis: Process and Psychoanalytic Technique. *Current Issues in Psychoanalytic Practice*, 2, Number 2, 95–102.

Freeman, Lucy (1989). *The Beloved Prison: A Journey into the Unknown Self*. New York: St. Martin's Press.

Freeman, Lucy (1992). *Why Norma Jean Killed Marilyn Monroe*. Chicago, Illinois: Global Rights.

Freud, Martin (1957). *Glory Reflected: Sigmund Freud—Man and Father*. London: Angus and Robertson.

Freud, Sigmund (1875a). Letter to Eduard Silberstein. 9 September. In Sigmund Freud, *Jugendbriefe an Eduard Silberstein: 1871–1881*. Walter Boehlich (Ed.), pp. 142–145. Frankfurt am Main: S. Fischer/S. Fischer Verlag, 1989.

Freud, Sigmund (1875b). Letter to Eduard Silberstein. 9 September. In Sigmund Freud, *The Letters of Sigmund Freud to Eduard Silberstein: 1871–1881*. Walter Boehlich (Ed.). Arnold J. Pomerans (Transl.), pp. 125–128. Cambridge, Massachusetts: Belknap Press of Harvard University Press, 1990.

Freud, Sigmund (1886a). Beiträge zur Kasuistik der Hysterie: I. Beobachtung einer hochgradigen Hemianästhesie bei einem hysterischen Manne. *Wiener Medizinische Wochenschrift*. 4 December, pp. 1634–1638.

Freud, Sigmund (1886b). Beiträge zur Kasuistik der Hysterie: II. Beobachtung einer hochgradigen Hemianästhesie bei einem hysterischen Manne. *Wiener Medizinische Wochenschrift*. 11 December, pp. 1674–1676.

Freud, Sigmund (1886c). Observation of a Severe Case of Hemi-Anaesthesia in a Hysterical Male. James Strachey (Transl.). In Sigmund Freud, *The Standard Edition of the Complete Psychological Works of Sigmund Freud: Volume I. (1886–1899). Pre-Psycho-Analytic Publications and Unpublished Drafts*, James Strachey, Anna Freud, Alix Strachey, and Alan Tyson (Eds. and Transls.), pp. 25–31. London: Hogarth Press and the Institute of Psycho-Analysis, 1966.

Freud, Sigmund (1896a). L'Hérédité et l'étiologie des névroses. *Revue Neurologique*, 4, 161–169.

Freud, Sigmund (1896b). Weitere Bemerkungen über die Abwehr-Neuropsychosen. *Neurologisches Centralblatt*, 15, 434–448.

Freud, Sigmund (1905). *Drei Abhandlungen zur Sexualtheorie*. Vienna: Franz Deuticke.

Freud, Sigmund (1907a). Letter to Karl Abraham. 5 July. In Sigmund Freud and Karl Abraham, *Briefwechsel 1907–1925: Vollständige Ausgabe. Band 1: 1907–1914*. Ernst Falzeder and Ludger M. Hermanns (Eds.), pp. 56–59. Vienna: Verlag Turia und Kant, 2009.

Freud, Sigmund (1907b). Letter to Karl Abraham. 5 July. In Sigmund Freud and Karl Abraham, *A Psycho-Analytic Dialogue: The Letters of Sigmund Freud and Karl Abraham. 1907–1926*, Hilda C. Abraham and Ernst L. Freud (Eds.), Bernard Marsh and Hilda C. Abraham (Transls.), pp. 1–4. London: Hogarth Press and the Institute of Psycho-Analysis, 1965.

Freud, Sigmund (1910a). Letter to Eduard Silberstein. 28 April. In Sigmund Freud, *Jugendbriefe an Eduard Silberstein: 1871–1881*, Walter Boehlich (Ed.), p. 213. Frankfurt am Main: S. Fischer/S. Fischer Verlag, 1989.

Freud, Sigmund (1910b). Letter to Eduard Silberstein. 28 April. In Sigmund Freud, *The Letters of Sigmund Freud to Eduard Silberstein: 1871–1881*, Walter Boehlich (Ed.), Arnold J. Pomerans (Transl.), p. 185. Cambridge, Massachusetts: Belknap Press of Harvard University Press, 1990.

Freud, Sigmund (1910c). Letter to Oskar Pfister. 5 June. In Sigmund Freud and Oskar Pfister, *Briefe: 1909–1939*, Ernst L. Freud and Heinrich Meng (Eds.), pp. 36–38. Frankfurt am Main: S. Fischer Verlag, 1963.

Freud, Sigmund (1910d). Letter to Oskar Pfister. 5 June. In Sigmund Freud and Oskar Pfister, *Psycho-Analysis and Faith: The Letters of Sigmund Freud and Oskar Pfister*, Heinrich Meng and Ernst L. Freud (Eds.), Eric Mosbacher (Transl.), pp. 38–40. London: Hogarth Press and the Institute of Psycho-Analysis, 1963.

Freud, Sigmund (1913a). Letter to Oskar Pfister. 1 January. In Sigmund Freud and Oskar Pfister, *Briefe: 1909–1939*, Ernst L. Freud and Heinrich Meng (Eds.), pp. 59–60. Frankfurt am Main: S. Fischer Verlag, 1963.

Freud, Sigmund (1913b). Letter to Oskar Pfister. 1 January. In Sigmund Freud and Oskar Pfister, *Psycho-Analysis and Faith: The Letters of Sigmund Freud and Oskar Pfister*, Heinrich Meng and Ernst L. Freud (Eds.), Eric Mosbacher (Transl.), p. 59. London: Hogarth Press and the Institute of Psycho-Analysis, 1963.

Freud, Sigmund (1917). *Vorlesungen zur Einführung in die Psychoanalyse: Drei Teile. Fehlleistungen. Trauma. Allgemeine Neurosenlehre*. Vienna: Hugo Heller und Compagnie.

Freud, Sigmund (1921). Letter to Ernest Jones. 12 April. In Sigmund Freud and Ernest Jones, *The Complete Correspondence of Sigmund Freud and Ernest Jones: 1908–1939*, R. Andrew Paskauskas (Ed.), Frauke Voss (Transl.), pp. 418–419. Cambridge, Massachusetts: Belknap Press of Harvard University Press, 1993.

Freud, Sigmund (1923a). Eine Teufelsneurose im siebzehnten Jahrhundert. *Imago*, 9, 1–34.

Freud, Sigmund (1923b). A Seventeenth-Century Demonological Neurosis. Edward Glover and James Strachey (Transls.). In Sigmund Freud, *The Standard Edition of the Complete Psychological Works of Sigmund Freud: Volume XIX. (1923–1925). The Ego and the Id and Other Works*, James Strachey, Anna Freud, Alix Strachey, and Alan Tyson (Eds. and Transls.), pp. 72–105. London: Hogarth Press and the Institute of Psycho-Analysis, 1961.

Freud, Sigmund (1924a). Letter to George Seldes. 29 June. In Ernest Jones, *The Life and Work of Sigmund Freud: Volume 3. The Last Phase. 1919–1939*, p. 103. New York: Basic Books, 1957.

Freud, Sigmund (1924b). Letter to Ernest Jones. 25 September. In Sigmund Freud and Ernest Jones, *The Complete Correspondence of Sigmund Freud and Ernest Jones: 1908–1939*, R. Andrew Paskauskas (Ed.), Frauke Voss (Transl.), pp. 552–553. Cambridge, Massachusetts: Belknap Press of Harvard University Press, 1993.

Freud, Sigmund (1925). Letter to Sándor Ferenczi. 14 August. In Sigmund Freud and Sándor Ferenczi, *Briefwechsel: Band III/2. 1925 bis 1933*, Ernst Falzeder, Eva Brabant, Patrizia Giampieri-Deutsch, and André Haynal (Eds.), pp. 48–50. Vienna: Böhlau Verlag/Böhlau Verlag Gesellschaft, 2003.

Freud, Sigmund (1931). Über die weibliche Sexualität. *Internationale Zeitschrift für Psychoanalyse*, 17, 317–332.

Freud, Sigmund (1935). Letter to Theodor Reik. 4 January. In Theodor Reik, *The Haunting Melody: Psychoanalytic Experiences in Life and Music*, pp. 342–343. New York: Farrar, Straus and Young, 1953.

Freud, Sigmund (1937a). Konstruktionen in der Analyse. *Internationale Zeitschrift für Psychoanalyse*, 23, 459–469.

Freud, Sigmund (1937b). Constructions in Analysis. James Strachey (Transl.). In Sigmund Freud, *The Standard Edition of the Complete Psychological Works of Sigmund Freud: Volume XXIII. (1937–1939). Moses and Monotheism. An Outline of Psycho-Analysis and Other Works*, James Strachey, Anna Freud, Alix Strachey, and Alan Tyson (Eds. and Transls.), pp. 257–269. London: Hogarth Press and the Institute of Psycho-Analysis, 1964.

Freud, Sigmund (1940). Abriss der Psychoanalyse. *Internationale Zeitschrift für Psychoanalyse und Imago, 25*, 7–67.

Freud, Sigmund (1992). *The Diary of Sigmund Freud: 1929–1939. A Record of the Final Decade*, Michael Molnar (Ed. and Transl.). London: Hogarth Press.

Freud-Marlé, Lilly (2006). *Mein Onkel Sigmund Freud: Erinnerungen an eine große Familie*, Christfried Tögel (Ed.). Berlin: Aufbau-Verlag.

Friday, Nancy (1973). *My Secret Garden: Women's Sexual Fantasies*. New York: Trident Press/Simon and Schuster.

Friday, Nancy (1975). *Forbidden Flowers: More Women's Sexual Fantasies*. New York: Pocket Books.

Friday, Nancy (1980). *Men in Love: Men's Sexual Fantasies. The Triumph of Love Over Rage*. New York: Delacorte Press.

Friday, Nancy (1991). *Women on Top: How Real Life Has Changed Women's Sexual Fantasies*. New York: Simon and Schuster.

Gabbard, Glen O., and Lester, Eva P. (1995). *Boundaries and Boundary Violations in Psychoanalysis*. New York: Basic Books.

Galatopoulos, Stelios (1998). *Maria Callas: Sacred Monster*. New York: Simon and Schuster.

Galton, Graeme (2006). Bearing Witness to an Abused Patient's Physical Injuries. In Graeme Galton (Ed.), *Touch Papers: Dialogues on Touch in the Psychoanalytic Space*, pp. 69–77. London: Karnac Books.

Gardner, Dorothy E.M. (1969). *Susan Isaacs*. London: Methuen Educational.

Gilbert, Daniel (2006). *Stumbling on Happiness*. London: Harper Press/HarperCollins Publishers.

Gildea, Margaret C.-L. (1980). Some Notes About the Jung Experience in 1931, pp. 122–127. In George E. Gifford, Jr., William McGuire, Margaret C.-L. Gildea, and Robert E. Bosnak, Jung: As Seen by an Editor, a Student, and a Disciple. In Edwin R. Wallace, IV and Lucius C. Pressley (Eds.), *Essays in the History of Psychiatry: A Tenth Anniversary Supplementary Volume to the* Psychiatric Forum, pp. 119–134. Columbia, South Carolina: William S. Hall Psychiatric Institute of the South Carolina Department of Mental Health.

Glover, Edward (1928). *The Technique of Psycho-Analysis*. London: Institute of Psycho-Analysis/Baillière, Tindall and Cox.

Glover, Edward (1955). *The Technique of Psycho-Analysis*. London: Baillière, Tindall and Cox.

Goldberg, Ann (1999). *Sex, Religion, and the Making of Modern Madness: The Eberbach Asylum and German Society, 1815–1849*. New York: Oxford University Press.

Goodwin, Jean M., and Fine, Catherine (1993). Mary Reynolds and Estelle: Somatic Symptoms and Unacknowledged Trauma. In Jean M. Goodwin (Ed.), *Rediscovering Childhood Trauma: Historical Casebook and Clinical Applications*, pp. 119–131. Washington, D.C.: American Psychiatric Press.

Graham, Thomas F. (1967). *Medieval Minds: Mental Health in the Middle Ages*. London: George Allen and Unwin.

Greenson, Ralph R. (1974). The Decline and Fall of the 50-Minute Hour. *Journal of the American Psychoanalytic Association, 22*, 785–791.

Grinker, Roy R. (1940). Reminiscences of a Personal Contact with Freud. *American Journal of Orthopsychiatry, 10*, 850–854.

Grotjahn, Martin (1987). *My Favorite Patient: The Memoirs of a Psychoanalyst*. Frankfurt am Main: Verlag Peter Lang.

Grun, Bernard (1971). Footnote 1. In Alban Berg, *Alban Berg: Letters to His Wife*, Bernard Grun (Ed. and Transl.), p. 335. London: Faber and Faber.

Gurko, Miriam (1965). *Clarence Darrow*. New York: Thomas Y. Crowell Company.

Hacking, Ian (1995). *Rewriting the Soul: Multiple Personality Disorder and the Sciences of Memory*. Princeton, New Jersey: Princeton University Press.

Heppenstall, Rayner (1939). *The Blaze of Noon*. London: Martin Secker and Warburg.

Hillman, James, and Boer, Charles (Eds.). (1985). *Freud's Own Cookbook*. New York: Perennial Library/Harper and Row, Publishers.

Hodson, Pauline L. (2012). *The Business of Therapy: How to Succeed in Private Practice*. Maidenhead, Berkshire: McGraw-Hill/Open University Press/McGraw-Hill Education.

Hoggard, Liz (2005). *How to Be Happy*. London: BBC Books/BBC Worldwide.

Holder, Alex (2000). To Touch or Not to Touch: That is the Question. *Psychoanalytic Inquiry, 20*, 44–64.

Jones, Ernest (1940). Sigmund Freud: 1856–1939. *International Journal of Psycho-Analysis, 21*, 2–26.

Jones, Ernest (1955). *The Life and Work of Sigmund Freud: Volume 2. Years of Maturity. 1901–1919*. New York: Basic Books.

Jones, Ernest (1957). *The Life and Work of Sigmund Freud: Volume 3. The Last Phase. 1919–1939*. New York: Basic Books.

Jung, Carl Gustav (1983). *Jung: Selected Writings*, Anthony Storr (Ed.). London: Fontana Paperbacks.

Kahr, Brett (1985). Freud's Legacy: Climate of Opinion. *Times Higher Education Supplement*, 31 May, pp. 13–14.

Kahr, Brett (1991). The Sexual Molestation of Children: Historical Perspectives. *Journal of Psychohistory*, *19*, 191–214.

Kahr, Brett (1996a). *D.W. Winnicott: A Biographical Portrait*. London: H. Karnac (Books).

Kahr, Brett (1996b). *D.W. Winnicott: A Biographical Portrait*. New York: International Universities Press.

Kahr, Brett (1997). *A Vida e a Obra de D.W. Winnicott: Um Retrato Biográfico*, Carolina Alfaro and Davy Bogomoletz (Transls.). Rio de Janeiro: Exodus Editora.

Kahr, Brett (1999a). *Donald Woods Winnicott: (Retrato y biografía)*, Vivienne A. Sarobe Sopranis (Transl.). Madrid: Asociación Psicoanalítica de Madrid/Biblioteca Nueva, Editorial Biblioteca Nueva.

Kahr, Brett (1999b). The Adventures of a Psychotherapist: How to Write a Musical for Prince Charles in Six Months or Less. *Psychotherapy Review*, *1*, 95–97.

Kahr, Brett (1999c). The Adventures of a Psychotherapist: Lucy Freeman and Her Fight Against Fear. *Psychotherapy Review*, *1*, 199.

Kahr, Brett (1999d). The Adventures of a Psychotherapist: Lucy Freeman's Pioneering Contributions to the Study of Mental Health Journalism. *Psychotherapy Review*, *1*, 244–248.

Kahr, Brett (1999e). Psycho-Analysis and Paedophilia: The Psychodynamics of Young Sex Offenders. Unpublished Typescript.

Kahr, Brett (2000). Psychoanalysis on Stage: Moss Hart's *Lady in the Dark*. *Psychoanalytic Review*, *87*, 377–383.

Kahr, Brett (Ed.). (2001a). *Forensic Psychotherapy and Psychopathology: Winnicottian Perspectives*. London: H. Karnac (Books).

Kahr, Brett (2001b). *Exhibitionism*. Duxford, Cambridge: Icon Books.

Kahr, Brett (Ed.). (2002a). *The Legacy of Winnicott: Essays on Infant and Child Mental Health*. London: H. Karnac (Books)/Other Press.

Kahr, Brett (2002b). Multiple Personality Disorder and Schizophrenia: An Interview with Professor Flora Rheta Schreiber. In Valerie Sinason (Ed.), *Attachment, Trauma and Multiplicity: Working with Dissociative Identity Disorder*, pp. 240–264. London: Brunner-Routledge.

Kahr, Brett (2004). Juvenile Paedophilia: The Psychodynamics of an Adolescent. In Charles W. Socarides and Loretta R. Loeb (Eds.), *The Mind of the Paedophile: Psychoanalytic Perspectives*, pp. 95–119. London: H. Karnac (Books).

Kahr, Brett (2005a). *D.W. Winnicott: Un Ritratto biografico*, Bruno Marchi (Transl.). Rome: La Biblioteca/Edizioni Bari-Roma.

Kahr, Brett (2005b). The Fifteen Key Ingredients of Good Psychotherapy.

In Jane Ryan (Ed.), *How Does Psychotherapy Work?*, pp. 1–14. London: H. Karnac (Books).

Kahr, Brett (2006a). Winnicott's Experiments with Physical Contact: Creative Innovation or Chaotic Impingement? In Graeme Galton (Ed.), Touch Papers: Dialogues on Touch in the Psychoanalytic Space, pp. 1–14. London: Karnac Books.

Kahr, Brett (2006b). How to Make 120,000 People Happy in Just Ten Weeks. *American Imago, 63,* 485–495.

Kahr, Brett (2007). *Sex and the Psyche.* London: Allen Lane/Penguin Books, Penguin Group.

Kahr, Brett (2008a). *Who's Been Sleeping in Your Head?: The Secret World of Sexual Fantasies.* New York: Basic Books/Perseus Books Group.

Kahr, Brett (2008b). *Sex and the Psyche: The Truth About Our Most Secret Fantasies.* London: Penguin Press.

Kahr, Brett (2011a). Multiple Personality Disorder and Schizophrenia: An Interview with Professor Flora Rheta Schreiber. [Revised Version]. In Valerie Sinason (Ed.), *Attachment, Trauma and Multiplicity: Second Edition. Working with Dissociative Identity Disorder*, pp. 204–214. London: Routledge/Taylor and Francis Group; Hove, East Sussex: Routledge/Taylor and Francis Group.

Kahr, Brett (2011b). Dr Paul Weston and the Bloodstained Couch. *International Journal of Psychoanalysis, 92,* 1051–1058.

Kahr, Brett (2014). Media Monasticism and Media Whoredom: The Uncomfortable Marriage Between Psychoanalysis and Public Exposure. Unpublished Typescript.

Kahr, Brett (2015). Lecture on "The Roots of Mental Health Broadcasting". Afternoon Workshop on "Donald Winnicott, the Public Psychoanalyst: Broadcasting Beyond the Consulting Room". International Conference on "Donald Winnicott and the History of the Present: A Celebration of the Collected Works of D.W. Winnicott". The Winnicott Trust, London, in association with the British Psychoanalytical Society, Byron House, Maida Vale, London, and the British Psychoanalytic Association, British Psychotherapy Foundation, London, and the Association of Independent Psychoanalysts, London, at the Board Room, Mary Ward House Conference and Exhibition Centre, Holborn, London. 21 November.

Kahr, Brett (2016). *Tea with Winnicott.* London: Karnac Books.

Kahr, Brett (2017a). From the Treatment of a Compulsive Spitter: A Psychoanalytical Approach to Profound Disability. *British Journal of Psychotherapy, 33,* 31–47.

Kahr, Brett (2017b). Lecture on "'Psychotherapy is Not a Spectator Sport': The Dissemination of Psychoanalysis from Freud to Orbach". Conference on "Psychotherapy is a Cultural Issue: The Influence of Susie Orbach's Work on Theory, Practice and Values". Confer, Woodbridge, Suffolk, at Sixth Floor, Foyles, London. 22 April.

Kahr, Brett (2018a). *D.W. Winnicott: Une Esquisse biographique.* Mage Montagnol (Transl.). Paris: Ithaque / Éditions Ithaque.

Kahr, Brett (2018b). The Public Psychoanalyst: Donald Winnicott as Broadcaster. In Angela Joyce (Ed.), *Donald W. Winnicott and the History of the Present: Understanding the Man and His Work,* pp. 111–121. London: Karnac Books.

Kahr, Brett (2020). *Bombs in the Consulting Room: Surviving Psychological Shrapnel.* London: Routledge/Taylor and Francis Group; Abingdon, Oxfordshire: Routledge/Taylor and Francis Group.

Kardiner, Abram (1977). *My Analysis with Freud: Reminiscences.* New York: W.W. Norton and Company.

Keyes, Daniel (1981). *The Minds of Billy Milligan.* New York: Random House.

Khan, M. Masud R. (1968). Diary Entry. 24 September. *Work Book II: August 20, 1968—April 10, 1969.* In M. Masud R. Khan, *The Work Books of Masud Khan,* Linda Hopkins and Steven Kuchuck (Eds.). London: Routledge/Taylor and Francis Group; Abingdon, Oxfordshire: Routledge/Taylor and Francis Group. [In preparation].

Khesar, Jigme (2013). Foreword. In Susan A. David, Ilona Boniwell, and Amanda Conley Ayers (Eds.). *The Oxford Handbook of Happiness,* pp. vii–viii. Oxford: Oxford University Press.

King, Pearl (2006). Can Touching Be Relevant to Understanding Some Patients in Psychoanalysis? In Graeme Galton (Ed.), *Touch Papers: Dialogues on Touch in the Psychoanalytic Space,* pp. 61–68. London: Karnac Books.

Langs, Robert (1973). *The Technique of Psychoanalytic Psychotherapy: Volume I. The Initial Contact. Theoretical Framework. Understanding the Patient's Communications. The Therapist's Interventions.* New York: Jason Aronson.

Langs, Robert (2006). Strong Adaptive Perspectives on Patient-Therapist Physical Contact. In Graeme Galton (Ed.), *Touch Papers: Dialogues on Touch in the Psychoanalytic Space,* pp. 123–143. London: Karnac Books.

Layard, Richard (2005). *Happiness: Lessons from a New Science.* London: Allen Lane/Penguin Books, Penguin Group.

Levy, Norman B., Mattern, William, and Freedman, Alfred M. (Eds.). (1983). *Psychonephrology 2: Psychological Problems in Kidney Failure and*

Their Treatment. New York: Plenum Medical Book Company/Plenum Publishing Corporation.

Linley, P. Alex; Joseph, Stephen; Harrington, Susan; and Wood, Alex M. (2006). Positive Psychology: Past, Present, and (Possible) Future. *Journal of Positive Psychology*, 1, 3–16.

Longfellow, Henry Wadsworth (1854). The Jewish Cemetery at Newport. In Henry Wadsworth Longfellow, *The Courtship of Miles Standish, and Other Poems*, pp. 157–161. London: W. Kent and Company (Late D. Bogue), 1858.

Mannoni, Maud (1964). *L'Enfant arriéré et sa mère: Étude psychanalytique*. Paris: Éditions du Seuil.

Mannoni, Maud (1973). *The Retarded Child and the Mother: A Psychoanalytic Study*, Alan M. Sheridan Smith (Transl.). London: Tavistock Publications.

Marinelli, Lydia (2009). Fort, Da: The Cap in the Museum, Christopher Barber (Transl.). *Psychoanalysis and History*, 11, 117–120.

Masson, Jeffrey Moussaieff (1984). *The Assault on Truth: Freud's Suppression of the Seduction Theory*. New York: Farrar, Straus and Giroux.

Maudsley, Henry (1886). *Natural Causes and Supernatural Seemings*. London: Kegan Paul, Trench and Company.

Mawson, Andrew (2008). *The Social Entrepreneur: Making Communities Work*. London: Atlantic Books/Grove/Atlantic, Grove Atlantic.

Maxwell, Elsa (1954). *R.S.V.P.: Elsa Maxwell's Own Story*. Boston, Massachusetts: Little, Brown and Company.

May, Rollo (1975). *The Courage to Create*. New York: W.W. Norton and Company.

Menninger, Karl (1958). *Theory of Psychoanalytic Technique*. New York: Basic Books.

Menninger, Karl A. (1988). *The Selected Correspondence of Karl A. Menninger, 1919–1945*, Howard J. Faulkner and Virginia D. Pruitt (Eds.). New Haven, Connecticut: Yale University Press.

Milne, Andrew (1975). *Metternich*. London: University of London Press.

Mordden, Ethan (2010). *The Guest List: How Manhattan Defined American Sophistication—From the Algonquin Round Table to Truman Capote's Ball*. New York: St. Martin's Press.

Morrison, Terri; Conaway, Wayne A.; and Borden, George A. (1994). *Kiss, Bow, or Shake Hands: How to Do Business in Sixty Countries*. Holbrook, Massachusetts: Adams Media Corporation.

Nathan, Debbie (2011). *Sybil Exposed: The Extraordinary Story Behind the Famous Multiple Personality Case*. New York: Free Press/Simon and Schuster.

Natterson, Joseph M. (1966). Theodor Reik: Masochism in Modern Man. In Franz Alexander, Samuel Eisenstein, and Martin Grotjahn (Eds.), *Psychoanalytic Pioneers*, pp. 249–264. New York: Basic Books.

Nemiah, John C. (1979). Dissociative Amnesia: A Clinical and Theoretical Reconsideration. In John F. Kihlstrom and Frederick J. Evans (Eds.), *Functional Disorders of Memory*, pp. 303–323. Hillsdale, New Jersey: Lawrence Erlbaum Associates, Publishers.

Oberlerchner, Herwig, and Tögel, Christfried (2015). Freud in Kärnten—Eine Recherche. *Luzifer-Amor, 28*, Number 55, 158–168.

Orbach, Susie (2006). Too Hot to Touch? In Graeme Galton (Ed.), *Touch Papers: Dialogues on Touch in the Psychoanalytic Space*, pp. xiii-xviii. London: Karnac Books.

Orr, Douglas W. (1961). Lionel Blitzsten, the Teacher. In *N. Lionel Blitzsten, M.D.: Psychoanalyst, Teacher, Friend. 1893–1952*, pp. 21–69. New York: International Universities Press.

Peterson, Emily; Gooch, Nancy Lynn; and Freeman, Lucy (1987). *Nightmare: Uncovering the 56 Strange Personalities of Nancy Lynn Gooch*. New York: Richardson and Steirman.

Prichard, James Cowles (1835). *A Treatise on Insanity and Other Disorders Affecting the Mind*. London: Sherwood, Gilbert, and Piper.

Prochnik, George (2006). *Putnam Camp: Sigmund Freud, James Jackson Putnam, and the Purpose of American Psychology*. New York: Other Press.

Pryce-Jones, Jessica (2010). *Happiness at Work: Maximizing Your Psychological Capital for Success*. Chichester, West Sussex: Wiley-Blackwell/John Wiley and Sons.

Putnam, Frank W. (1994). Dissociative Disorders in Children and Adolescents. In Steven Jay Lynn and Judith W. Rhue (Eds.), *Dissociation: Clinical and Theoretical Perspectives*, pp. 175–189. New York: Guilford Press/Guilford Publications.

Rangell, Leo (2009). *Music in the Head: Living at the Brain-Mind Border*. London: Karnac Books.

Raphael-Leff, Joan (2002). Presence of Mind and Body. In Joan Raphael-Leff (Ed.), *Between Sessions and Beyond the Couch*, pp. 269–290. Colchester, Essex: CPS Psychoanalytic Publications/University of Essex.

Reeves, Richard (2007). *John Stuart Mill: Victorian Firebrand*. London: Atlantic Books/Grove Atlantic.

Reich, Wilhelm (1925). *Der triebhafte Charakter: Eine psychoanalytische Studie zur Pathologie des Ich*. Vienna: Internationaler Psychoanalytischer Verlag.

Reich, Wilhelm (1933). *Charakteranalyse: Technik und Grundlagen für Stu-*

dierende und Praktizierende Analytiker. Vienna: Im Selbstverlage des Verfassers.

Reith, Marian (1975). Perseverance Brings Good Fortune: It Furthers One to Cross the Great Waters. In Judy Rosenberg (Ed.), *Memories and Perspectives on the Centennial of C.G. Jung's Birth*, pp. 41–43. New York: Analytical Psychology Club of New York.

Ries, Paul (1995). Popularise and/or Be Damned: Psychoanalysis and Film at the Crossroads in 1925. *International Journal of Psycho-Analysis*, 76, 759–791.

Roazen, Paul (1993). *Meeting Freud's Family*. Amherst, Massachusetts: University of Massachusetts Press.

Roazen, Paul (1995). *How Freud Worked: First-Hand Accounts of Patients*. Northvale, New Jersey: Jason Aronson.

Roazen, Paul (2000). *Oedipus in Britain: Edward Glover and the Struggle Over Klein*. New York: Other Press.

Romm, Sharon (1983). *The Unwelcome Intruder: Freud's Struggle with Cancer*. New York: Praeger Publishers/CBS Educational and Professional Publishing, Division of CBS/Praeger Special Studies/Praeger Scientific.

Rudnytsky, Peter L. (1987). *Freud and Oedipus*. New York: Columbia University Press.

Rudnytsky, Peter L. (1989). Winnicott and Freud. *Psychoanalytic Study of the Child*, 44, 331–350. New Haven, Connecticut: Yale University Press.

Rudnytsky, Peter L. (1991). *The Psychoanalytic Vocation: Rank, Winnicott, and the Legacy of Freud*. New Haven, Connecticut: Yale University Press.

Rudnytsky, Peter L. (Ed.). (1993a). *Transitional Objects and Potential Spaces: Literary Uses of D.W. Winnicott*. New York: Columbia University Press.

Rudnytsky, Peter L. (1993b). Introduction. In Peter L. Rudnytsky (Ed.), *Transitional Objects and Potential Spaces: Literary Uses of D.W. Winnicott*, pp. xi–xxii. New York: Columbia University Press.

Rudnytsky, Peter L. (Ed.). (2000). *Psychoanalytic Conversations: Interviews with Clinicians, Commentators, and Critics*. Hillsdale, New Jersey: Analytic Press.

Sachs, Hanns (1939). [Editorial]. *American Imago, 1*, 2.

Sachs, Hanns (1944). *Freud: Master and Friend*. Cambridge, Massachusetts: Harvard University Press.

Schäfer, Ingo; Ross, Colin A.; and Read, John (2008). Childhood Trauma in Psychotic and Dissociative Disorders. In Andrew Moskowitz, Ingo

Schäfer, and Martin J. Dorahy (Eds.), *Psychosis, Trauma and Dissociation: Emerging Perspectives on Severe Psychopathology*, pp. 137–150. Chichester, West Sussex: Wiley-Blackwell/John Wiley and Sons.

Schreiber, Flora Rheta (1956). *Your Child's Speech: A Practical Guide for Parents for the First Five Years*. New York: G.P. Putnam's Sons.

Schreiber, Flora Rheta (1970). *A Job with a Future in Law Enforcement and Related Fields*. New York: Grosset and Dunlap/National General Company.

Schreiber, Flora Rheta (1973). *Sybil*. Chicago, Illinois: Henry Regnery Company.

Schreiber, Flora Rheta (1983). *The Shoemaker: The Anatomy of a Psychotic*. New York: Simon and Schuster.

Schur, Max (1972). *Freud: Living and Dying*. New York: International Universities Press.

Sinason, Valerie (2002a). Introduction. In Valerie Sinason (Ed.), *Attachment, Trauma and Multiplicity: Working with Dissociative Identity Disorder*, pp. 3–20. Hove, East Sussex: Brunner-Routledge/Taylor and Francis Group.

Sinason, Valerie (2002b). The Shoemaker and the Elves: Working with Multiplicity. In Valerie Sinason (Ed.), *Attachment, Trauma and Multiplicity: Working with Dissociative Identity Disorder*, pp. 125–138. Hove, East Sussex: Brunner-Routledge/Taylor and Francis Group.

Sinason, Valerie (2002c). Legal Issues Around Dissociative Identity Disorder. In Valerie Sinason (Ed.), *Attachment, Trauma and Multiplicity: Working with Dissociative Identity Disorder*, pp. 206–207. Hove, East Sussex: Brunner-Routledge/Taylor and Francis Group.

Sinason, Valerie (2006). *No Touch Please*—We're British Psychodynamic Practitioners. In Graeme Galton (Ed.), *Touch Papers: Dialogues on Touch in the Psychoanalytic Space*, pp. 49–60. London: Karnac Books.

Sinason, Valerie (2011a). Introduction. In Valerie Sinason (Ed.), *Attachment, Trauma and Multiplicity: Second Edition. Working with Dissociative Identity Disorder*, pp. 3–18. London: Routledge/Taylor and Francis Group; Hove, East Sussex: Routledge/Taylor and Francis Group.

Sinason, Valerie (2011b). The Shoemaker and the Elves. In Valerie Sinason (Ed.), *Attachment, Trauma and Multiplicity: Second Edition. Working with Dissociative Identity Disorder*, pp. 127–138. London: Routledge/Taylor and Francis Group; Hove, East Sussex: Routledge/Taylor and Francis Group.

Sinason, Valerie (2011c). Interview with Detective Chief Inspector Clive Driscoll. In Valerie Sinason (Ed.), *Attachment, Trauma and Multiplicity: Second Edition. Working with Dissociative Identity Disorder*, pp. 195–203.

London: Routledge/Taylor and Francis Group; Hove, East Sussex: Routledge/Taylor and Francis Group.

Smirnoff, Victor (1966). *La Psychanalyse de l'enfant*. Paris: Presses Universitaires de France.

Smith, Betty (1963). *Joy in the Morning*. New York: Harper and Row, Publishers.

Smith, Edward W.L., Clance, Pauline Rose, and Imes, Suzanne (Eds.), (1998). *Touch in Psychotherapy: Theory, Research, and Practice*. New York: Guilford Press.

Spiegel, David (1990). Hypnosis, Dissociation, and Trauma: Hidden and Overt Observers. In Jerome L. Singer (Ed.), *Repression and Dissociation: Implications for Personality Theory, Psychopathology, and Health*, pp. 121–142. Chicago, Illinois: University of Chicago Press.

Staggs, Sam (2012). *Inventing Elsa Maxwell: How an Irrepressible Nobody Conquered High Society, Hollywood, the Press, and the World*. New York: St. Martin's Press.

Sterba, Richard F. (1982). *Reminiscences of a Viennese Psychoanalyst*. Detroit, Michigan: Wayne State University Press.

Stevens, Richard (1983a). *Freud and Psychoanalysis: An Exposition and Appraisal*. Stony Stratford, Milton Keynes, Buckinghamshire: Open University Press/Open University Educational Enterprises.

Stevens, Richard (1983b). *Erik Erikson: An Introduction*. Stony Stratford, Milton Keynes, Buckinghamshire: Open University Press/Open University Educational Enterprises.

Stoller, Robert J. (1975). *Perversion: The Erotic Form of Hatred*. New York: Pantheon Books.

Stoller, Robert J. (1979a). *Sexual Excitement: Dynamics of Erotic Life*. New York: Pantheon Books.

Stoller, Robert J. (1979b). Centerfold: An Essay on Excitement. *Archives of General Psychiatry*, *36*, 1019–1024.

Stoller, Robert J. (1985). *Observing the Erotic Imagination*. New Haven, Connecticut: Yale University Press.

Storr, Anthony (1960). *The Integrity of the Personality*. London: William Heinemann Medical Books.

Storr, Anthony (1964). *Sexual Deviation*. Harmondsworth, Middlesex: Penguin Books.

Storr, Anthony (1968a). *Human Aggression*. London: Allen Lane/Penguin Press.

Storr, Anthony (1968b). On Aggression. *New Society*. 28 March, p. 466.

Storr, Anthony (1969). Misunderstanding Psycho-analysis. *Encounter*, *33*, Number 5, 88–89.

Storr, Anthony (1972a). *Human Destructiveness*. London: Chatto/Heinemann/Sussex University Press/Heinemann Educational Books.

Storr, Anthony (1972b). *The Dynamics of Creation*. London: Martin Secker and Warburg.

Storr, Anthony (1974). The Loved Ones. In Anthony Curtis (Ed.), *The Rise and Fall of the Matinée Idol: Past Deities of Stage and Screen, Their Roles, Their Magic, and Their Worshippers*, pp. 188–195. London: George Weidenfeld and Nicolson.

Storr, Anthony (1983). Introduction. In Carl Gustav Jung, *Jung: Selected Writings*, Anthony Storr (Ed.), pp. 13–27. London: Fontana Paperbacks.

Storr, Anthony (1985a). Psychoanalysis and Creativity. In Peregrine Hordern (Ed.), *Freud and the Humanities*, pp. 38–57. London: Duckworth/Gerald Duckworth and Company.

Storr, Anthony (1985b). Kafka's Sense of Identity. In Joseph P. Stern and John J. White (Eds.), *Paths and Labyrinths: Nine Papers Read at the Franz Kafka Symposium Held at the Institute of Germanic Studies on 20 and 21 October 1983*, pp. 1–24. London: Institute of Germanic Studies, University of London.

Storr, Anthony (1985c). Postscript. In Brian Masters, *Killing for Company: The Case of Dennis Nilsen*, pp. 317–325. London: Jonathan Cape.

Storr, Anthony (1985d). Isaac Newton. *British Medical Journal*, 21 December–28 December, pp. 1779–1784.

Storr, Anthony (1988). *The School of Genius*. London: André Deutsch.

Storr, Anthony (1989a). *Churchill's Black Dog and Other Phenomena of the Human Mind*. London: Collins/William Collins and Sons.

Storr, Anthony (1989b). *Freud*. Oxford: Oxford University Press.

Storr, Anthony (1991). *Human Destructiveness*. New York: Grove Weidenfeld/Grove Press.

Storr, Anthony (1992). *Music and the Mind*. Hammersmith, London: HarperCollins Publishers.

Storr, Anthony (1996). *Feet of Clay: A Study of Gurus*. Hammersmith, London: HarperCollins Publishers.

Sunderland, Margot (2006). *The Science of Parenting: Practical Guidance on Sleep, Crying, Play and Building Emotional Wellbeing for Life*. London: Dorling Kindersley.

Suraci, Patrick (2011). *Sybil: In Her Own Words. The Untold Story of Shirley Mason, Her Multiple Personalities and Paintings*. n.p.: n.p.

Temperley, Jane (1984). Settings for Psychotherapy. *British Journal of Psychotherapy*, 1, 101–111.

Thackeray, William Makepeace (1848). *Vanity Fair: A Novel without a Hero*. London: Bradbury and Evans.

Tierney, Kevin (1979). *Darrow: A Biography*. New York: Thomas Y. Crowell, Publishers.

Walker, Evelyn, and Young, Perry Deane (1986). *A Killing Cure*. New York: Henry Holt and Company.

Wechsberg, Joseph (1979). *The Vienna I Knew: Memories of a European Childhood*. Garden City, New York: Doubleday and Company.

Weinberg, Arthur, and Weinberg, Lila (1980). *Clarence Darrow: A Sentimental Rebel*. New York: G.P. Putnam's Sons.

Winnicott, Clare (1978). D.W.W.: A Reflection. In Simon A. Grolnick, Leonard Barkin, and Werner Muensterberger (Eds.), *Between Reality and Fantasy: Transitional Objects and Phenomena*, pp. 17–33. New York: Jason Aronson.

Winnicott, Donald W. (1945a). *Getting to Know Your Baby*. London: William Heinemann (Medical Books).

Winnicott, Donald W. (1945b). Primitive Emotional Development. *International Journal of Psycho-Analysis, 26*, 137–143.

Winnicott, Donald W. (1949). *The Ordinary Devoted Mother and Her Baby: Nine Broadcast Talks. (Autumn 1949)*. London: C.A. Brock and Company.

Winnicott, Donald W. (1955). Metapsychological and Clinical Aspects of Regression within the Psycho-Analytical Set-Up. *International Journal of Psycho-Analysis, 36*, 16–26.

Winnicott, Donald W. (1956). The Antisocial Tendency. In Donald W. Winnicott (1958). *Collected Papers: Through Paediatrics to Psycho-Analysis*, pp. 306–315. London: Tavistock Publications.

Winnicott, Donald W. (1957a). *The Child and the Family: First Relationships*, Janet Hardenberg (Ed.). London: Tavistock Publications.

Winnicott, Donald W. (1957b). *The Child and the Outside World: Studies in Developing Relationships*, Janet Hardenberg (Ed.). London: Tavistock Publications.

Winnicott, Donald W. (1963). Communicating and Not Communicating Leading to a Study of Certain Opposites. In Donald W. Winnicott, *The Maturational Processes and the Facilitating Environment: Studies in the Theory of Emotional Development*, pp. 179–192. London: Hogarth Press and the Institute of Psycho-Analysis, 1965.

Winnicott, Donald W. (1987). *Babies and Their Mothers*, Clare Winnicott, Ray Shepherd, and Madeleine Davis (Eds.). Reading, Massachusetts: Addison-Wesley Publishing Company.

Winnicott, Donald W. (1993). *Talking to Parents*, Clare Winnicott, Christopher Bollas, Madeleine Davis, and Ray Shepherd (Eds.). Reading, Massachusetts: Addison-Wesley Publishing Company.

Wolff, Larry (1988). *Postcards from the End of the World: Child Abuse in Freud's Vienna*. New York: Atheneum/Macmillan Publishing Company.

Wortis, Joseph (1934). Diary Entry. 11 October. In Joseph Wortis, *Fragments of an Analysis with Freud*, pp. 25–26. New York: Simon and Schuster, 1954.

Wright, Thomas (1601). *The Passions of the Minde*. London: V.S. for B.W.

INDEX